Nazi Germany

WILEY SHORT HISTORIES
General Editor: Catherine Epstein

This series provides concise, lively introductions to key topics in history. Designed to encourage critical thinking and an engagement in debate, the books demonstrate the dynamic process through which history is constructed, in both popular imagination and scholarship. The volumes are written in an accessible style, offering the ideal entry point to the field.

Published
Nazi Germany: Confronting the Myths
Catherine Epstein

Forthcoming
Postwar Europe: A Short History
Pertti Ahonen

Genocide in the Modern World: A Short History
Cathie Carmichael and Kate Ferguson

Human Rights: A Short History
Gerard Daniel Cohen

World War I: A Short History
Tammy M. Proctor

*To My Students
at Amherst College*

Contents

Illustrations

Maps

Figures

Preface

Nazi Germany shocks us. Adolf Hitler was a brutal dictator. He unleashed a world war that claimed the lives of some 55 million people. His regime carried out the murder of almost six million Jews. The Nazis starved or otherwise killed three million Soviet prisoners of war. They sterilized, incarcerated, and even murdered other "undesirable" persons, including the disabled, alcoholics, homosexuals, Afro-Germans, and Roma (Gypsies).

Nazi Germany was evil, no doubt about it. But we cannot just condemn the Third Reich. We need to explain it, along with its seeming paradoxes. Despite the Nazis' criminality, for example, most Germans viewed the Third Reich as a legitimate government. They supported Nazi policies. Millions of German soldiers even fought for the Nazis. In another seeming paradox, Hitler rarely made decisions. Yet, even though he had little interest in day-to-day governance, the Nazi regime carried out many of his wishes. Then, too, while many view Nazi Germany as a totalitarian regime, it is striking how much agency Germans had in the Third Reich. The Nazis, for example, were initially eager to have "Aryan" women stay at home to raise children. Yet, when they insisted that women work, many "Aryan" women simply evaded Nazi labor regulations. Not least, this was because Nazi Germany was under-policed, not over-policed.

This book examines the many sides of the Nazi regime. It addresses many questions that you likely have about Hitler and the Third Reich. How could Hitler come to power? How could the Nazis carry out so many crimes? Why did the Third Reich lose World War II? But the book also answers questions that you may never have thought to ask. How did Nazi ideology seep into every sphere of activity in the Third Reich? Why was the Nazi regime relatively popular? Why wasn't the German military the war machine of *Blitzkrieg* lore? Why did the Nazis plan to starve much of the Eastern European population?

In my view, history is not just "one damned thing after another." Put otherwise, it is not just a narrative of events. History makes sense only when it is framed in terms of questions and arguments. Every chapter in this book takes on myths or stereotypes about the Third Reich. By presenting material in the form of arguments against preconceived notions, I offer a set of conceptual tools through which to organize and understand the history of Nazi Germany. Busting myths, however, complicates the story of Nazi Germany. This is not a black-and-white story. Instead, the Third Reich offers many ambiguities and complexities that challenge simple, pat answers. Finally, throughout these pages, you will learn about scholars' different and often controversial interpretations of Nazi Germany. The history of the Third Reich is not a closed book. It remains resolutely open. It demands discussion and reflection.

Why yet another book about the Third Reich? Historians and others have published reams of work on Nazi Germany. Most of us, though, don't have the time or inclination to delve into all of them. We seek short, concise surveys of Hitler and Nazi Germany. It is true that some such works already exist. But, after many years of teaching about Nazi Germany, I am dissatisfied with current offerings. Some surveys of Nazi Germany are too expensive. Some are geared toward academics, not students. Some focus too much, others too little, on the period before 1933. Many are now somewhat dated.

In the past two decades, the study of Nazi Germany has undergone a sea change. In the past, historians wanted to know why democracy collapsed in 1933. They thus focused on how and why the Nazis came to power and consolidated their regime. Now, however, historians are more focused on race: how and why the Holocaust and other crimes unfolded in Nazi-occupied Europe. They look more to the years 1939–1945. This book reflects these changing foci. It certainly explores the Nazi rise to power in 1933 and the consolidation of the regime in the 1930s. But the longest chapters cover Nazi racial policies and the war years. They focus on the Holocaust and associated racial crimes, the Nazi occupation of Eastern Europe, and how and why Germany lost World War II.

I – and perhaps you – have a fascination with Hitler and the Third Reich. This history is hair-raisingly tragic. It raises profound ethical questions. Yet it also poses intriguing intellectual challenges. How can we understand this regime? What made it tick? As you read these pages, I hope that you will grapple with the arguments I present. I hope that you will confront preconceived views of the Nazi regime. Most of all, I hope that you will find the study of Nazi Germany both more disturbing and more engaging than you ever thought possible.

Citations for Quotations

Page *Source*

xi "one damned thing…" Arnold Toynbee, arguing against historians who believe this. History News Network, http://hnn.us/article/1328 (accessed January 31, 2014).

1

Germany before 1933

On January 30, 1933, Adolf Hitler was appointed chancellor of Germany. That evening, the Nazis celebrated their coming to power with a raucous torchlight parade in Berlin. They passed government buildings, their bright torches lighting up swastika banners. They paused before the Chancellory. There, Hitler and the man who had made him chancellor, President Paul von Hindenburg, greeted the jubilant crowds. While some Germans shared the Nazi euphoria at Hitler's appointment, others feared this latest turn in German politics. Few, however, could possibly have imagined the day's true outcome. In just a few short years, Hitler would unleash World War II. Before it was all over, some 55 million individuals would lose their lives, including almost six million Jews. The war would dramatically transform Germany, Europe, and the world.

The day after Hitler's appointment, his propaganda chief, Joseph Goebbels, noted in his diary, "Hitler is Reich Chancellor. Just like a fairy-tale." Many observers then and since have wondered just how the "fairy-tale" could have happened. Misperceptions on the matter abound. These include the notions that Hitler was the logical culmination of all German history; that the Nazi rise to power was a result of Germany following a "special path" to modernity; and that the Treaty of Versailles, imposed by the Allies on defeated Germany after World War I, brought the Nazis to power.

In fact, Hitler's appointment as chancellor was the immediate result of a series of intrigues surrounding the eighty-five-year-old President Hindenburg (see Chapter 2). There was nothing inevitable in Hitler's coming to power. As this chapter shows, though, there were long-term developments in German history that favored the rise of Nazism. World War I and its aftermath also helped to make Hitler's assumption of power possible, if hardly certain.

Nazi Germany: Confronting the Myths, First Edition. Catherine Epstein.
© 2015 John Wiley & Sons, Ltd. Published 2015 by John Wiley & Sons, Ltd.

Germany before World War I

Germany could have taken many different paths in the twentieth century. Nazism was only one, and hardly the most likely, German trajectory. Some observers, however, such as Robert Vansittart, a British diplomat before and during World War II, and the historian A.J.P.Taylor, have argued that Nazism was the logical conclusion to all of German history.They believed that Germany was by nature aggressive and militaristic, and given to authoritarian leadership. This national character trait (or flaw) allegedly explained why Germans supported the Protestant reformer Martin Luther and the Prussian King Frederick the Great in earlier centuries, and Chancellor Otto von Bismarck and Adolf Hitler in modern times. But one should be wary of any argument that claims that a nation (or a race) has some essential attributes – reasoning in essentialist categories comes perilously close to Nazi thinking. Instead, one should look to political, economic, or ideological reasons for why German history unfolded as it did.

A case in point involves the unification of Germany in the nineteenth century. Before 1870, there were many German-speaking lands but there existed no united Germany. Between 1864 and 1870, Chancellor Otto von Bismarck, on behalf of the Prussian king, William I, initiated three wars so as to achieve German unification under Prussian aegis. In January 1871, shortly after the Franco-Prussian War, Germany annexed Alsace-Lorraine and proclaimed the second German Reich (empire) in the Hall of Mirrors at the Palace of Versailles (the first German Reich, or Holy Roman Empire, lasted from 962 to 1806). German unification was very popular among German elites. German liberals, in particular, were willing to sacrifice civic freedoms so as to advance national unification. Not least, unification promised them economic benefit. Their support of Bismarck had nothing to do with an alleged German penchant for authority.

The "special path" thesis

Following German unification, the Iron Chancellor, as Bismarck was dubbed, created political and constitutional arrangements for the new empire. These gave rise to another interpretation of why the Nazis came to power, the "special path" (*Sonderweg*) thesis.According to this argument, Germany never had a bourgeois (middle-class) revolution – such as the French Revolution – to send it down the path toward liberal democracy. In alleged contrast to Britain and France, Germany thus failed to develop either democratic institutions or a liberal political culture.

For the new German Empire, Bismarck created a set of constitutional arrangements.The Reichstag (parliament) was elected by universal male suffrage, but it had very little real power. The chancellor was responsible not to the Reichstag but to the emperor. The emperor controlled military and foreign affairs. In addition, the Reichstag had little budgetary power since provincial states (such as Prussia) controlled most government monies.

Sonderweg proponents claimed that German leaders pursued aggressive policies because there was a mismatch between Germany's rapid industrialization and its backward political and social order. Bismarck sought ways to unite Germany's divided elites – agrarian estate owners, known as *Junkers*, had very different interests from industrialists – in support of the monarchy. Among other strategies, he pitted Germany's ruling classes against alleged "enemies" who threatened elite interests. He initiated a nasty campaign against Catholics, including against the minority Polish Catholic population. He also hounded the Social Democratic Party (SPD), the nascent socialist party, which supported political liberalization and the more equitable distribution of economic goods. The Iron Chancellor bequeathed a legacy of intolerant polarization to German politics.

In 1888, William II came to power and, soon thereafter, dismissed Bismarck. William ruled a society undergoing rapid industrialization. Germans poured into urban areas in search of factory or mining work. Conservatives decried the social ills – disease, poverty, immorality, urban crowding, and personal alienation – that accompanied modernization. Workers, in turn, were eager to better their lot; they voted for the SPD in the hope of securing a share of political power. William faced a dilemma. In an era of mass politics, he wished to legitimize his rule. But he was unwilling to limit his autocratic powers by democratizing the political system. Instead, he fastened on an aggressive foreign policy to win popularity from both German elites and workers. As we shall see, this proved disastrous.

Today, the *Sonderweg* thesis has been largely discredited. As its most prominent critics, David Blackbourn and Geoff Eley, argue, the western path from which Germany supposedly departed was only a perceived norm, not reality. Britain and France were less democratic polities than *Sonderweg* enthusiasts claimed. The German middle classes also asserted their political influence in arenas other than Reichstag politics. The *Sonderweg* thesis nonetheless retains some value. William II *did* pursue an aggressive foreign policy, rather than constitutional reform, to legitimize his monarchy. This led to World War I and, indirectly, to Hitler. And Germans *did* have little experience with democracy – a deficit that would have pernicious consequences.

Nationalism

Nineteenth-century Europe saw the rise of nationalism, scientific racism, and antisemitism. Germany was hardly unique in this regard. Take nationalism. Many liberals and conservatives across Europe came to share a set of beliefs about the "nation." They argued that one's supreme loyalty should be to the nation (rather than to town, region, class, or religion). To them, the nation was an organic entity with its own unique characteristics. At the same time, nationalists believed that a nation's members should be united in a nation–state, that nations needed overseas colonies to prosper, and that nations were locked in a zero-sum struggle in which one nation's gain was another's loss.

German nationalists drew on romantic myths of past German heroism and sacrifice. They harked back to the saga of Frederick Barbarossa, the crusading medieval Holy Roman Emperor who united warring Germanic factions and established peace in the German lands. Barbarossa was said to be sleeping in a mountain awaiting the rebirth of German glory. German nationalists also linked Germanness to the notion of *Volk* (variously translated as "nation," "people," or "race"). They championed a "blood-and-soil" (*Blut und Boden*) ideology: the notion that peasants ("blood") who farmed the countryside ("soil") were the true repository of traditional German values and authentic folk culture. In addition, some nationalists claimed a superior German "essence" that was rooted in the cosmic nature of the German forest landscape. Dark, mysterious, and profound, the forest was the alleged wellspring of German creativity, depth of feeling, and unity with other members of the *Volk*. German nationalists also believed that the German people cultivated profound inner values such as spirituality, idealism, and heroism. (The French, by contrast, supposedly fostered superficial values such as materialism and civilization.)

German nationalism had a mystical tone, but its many advocates worked to achieve concrete goals. Initially, they urged a nation–state. After unification, they demanded overseas colonies. But Germany entered the colonial race only late, in 1884, after other powers had laid claim to much of the globe. Still, Germany soon controlled some Pacific islands, Jiaozhou Bay in China, and the Cameroons, Togoland, German South West Africa (now Namibia), and German East Africa (now Tanzania) in Africa. In the 1890s, dissatisfied with what they saw as their puny empire, many Germans joined ultranationalist pressure groups that clamored for Germany to seek "its place in the sun." These groups included the Colonial League, the Navy League, the Pan-German League, and the Eastern Marches Society (aimed at expunging Polish influence in Germany's eastern provinces).

In response to this ultranationalist pressure, William pursued an ill-conceived *Weltpolitik* (world policy). This aggressive foreign policy had three major aims: parity with Britain as a world power, greater German influence in Eastern Europe, and additional overseas colonies. From 1897 onward, Germany spent enormous sums to build a "deterrent fleet" that would challenge British hegemony on the world's seas. But this only led Britain to seek new alliances with France and Russia. Meanwhile, attempts to enhance German influence in Eastern Europe alienated two sometime allies, the Russian and Austro-Hungarian Empires. Additional overseas colonies were only possible at other powers' expense. Germany's aggressive policies made the other great powers wary.

German imperial practice abroad generally differed little from that of the other great powers. Everywhere, colonial rule was cruel and unjust. Native uprisings were common. Between 1904 and 1907, however, the German military engaged in an unprecedented act of European colonial repression. To suppress a native uprising by the Herero in South West Africa, the German military commander, General Lothar von Trotha, unleashed genocide. Roughly 66–75% of the Herero people – some 40,000–60,000 individuals – perished. The historian Isabel Hull has argued that this genocide was another baleful consequence of German constitutional arrangements. Unlike more democratic countries such as Britain, there was no civilian oversight to check military excesses. Other historians, noting continuities in German racial views, military methods, and administrative personnel, explicitly link this genocide to the Holocaust forty years later.

Scientific racism

In the nineteenth century, racism joined nationalism as an integral element of European culture. In the 1850s, Arthur Comte de Gobineau published an *Essay on the Inequality of the Human Races*. According to Gobineau, "racial vitality" was the prime mover of history. That "racial vitality" was now found in an "Aryan" master race. "Aryan" referred to the ancient Indo-European culture from which European civilization had supposedly sprung. Gobineau believed that Europe's global hegemony resulted from the superior characteristics of the "Aryan" race. But he worried about "Aryans" engaging in miscegenation, or racial intermixing, which he saw as the demise of all great races.

Gobineau insisted that his racial history was a science. Nineteenth-century contemporaries hailed the power of science; they believed that science could explain and even perfect human nature and the social order. Today, we recognize that science (and pseudo-science) is all too often placed in the service of ideology. Scientific notions of racial superiority rationalized European rule over native populations. Science also underlay Social Darwinism. In 1859, Charles Darwin outlined his theory of evolution based on natural selection in his *On the Origin of Species*. Others took his ideas and applied them to the social world. Social Darwinism held that individuals, as well as nations or races, were engaged in an evolutionary struggle of the "survival of the fittest." For nations to survive, they needed virile populations, dynamic economies, and ever-growing territories.

Social Darwinism was closely linked to eugenics, or what the Germans called "racial hygiene." Eugenics aims to improve a nation's racial stock through selective breeding. In Germany, the rapid growth of the working classes generated fears that this population, living and working in squalid conditions, would sap the racial health of the nation. Advocates of racial hygiene argued that the strong should be encouraged to procreate and the weak prevented from doing so. Such notions were not confined to Germany. The US state of Indiana passed the first compulsory sterilization law in 1907. California and Washington followed two years later. While some Germans championed similar legislation, there was no sterilization law in Germany until the Nazis came to power.

Antisemitism

Besides nationalism and scientific racism, antisemitism was a third element of nineteenth-century thought that eventually flowed into Nazi ideology. In premodern times, Christian prejudice against Jews was rooted in religion. Many Christians blamed Jews for Christ's martyrdom. Many also believed that Jews murdered Christian children for ritual purposes. Christians long subjected Jews to discrimination. They also carried out pogroms against them. Yet this Christian hatred of Jews was directed at Jews as non-Christians. If Jews stopped being Jews — that is, if they were baptized, converted, or assimilated — Christians left former Jews, or those of Jewish origin, alone.

In the late nineteenth century, antisemitism was transformed: it became racialized. Houston Stewart Chamberlain, for example, the son-in-law of Richard Wagner, the antisemitic composer, insisted that Jews were a separate and identifiable race. He and others asserted that the "Jew" was the very antithesis of the "German." Germans, they insisted, were spiritual, idealistic, heroic, and productive, while Jews were materialistic, immoral, selfish, and cunning. Chamberlain claimed that Germans and Jews were locked in a mortal struggle in which Jews aimed to undermine the German race. For racial antisemites, Jews were always Jews; they could never escape their Jewish origins.

In the 1870s, a German, Wilhelm Marr, coined the term "anti-Semitism." (Today, when writing about antisemitism, many historians avoid the hyphenated term since its use suggests that "Semitism" existed and was opposed by antisemites. No one, however, ever used the term "Semitism" to suggest anything but hatred of Jews. In effect, using the hyphenated term adopts the language of antisemites.)

There is little evidence that German antisemitism was more virulent or widespread than its variants elsewhere. In the 1890s, France was rocked by the Dreyfus Affair when a Jewish officer, Dreyfus, was wrongly convicted of traitorous activity on behalf of Germany. In Austria, the antisemitic demagogue Karl Lueger was the popularly elected mayor of Vienna (at the time when Hitler moved to that city). In Russia, tsarist officials blamed a small but violent revolutionary movement on the Jews. Moreover, after the 1905 Revolution, that country saw a wave of antisemitic pogroms. Everywhere, antisemites saw Jews — whether as plutocrats or revolutionaries — as the evil force lurking behind modernity and its attendant upheavals.

In Germany, antisemitism and *völkisch* nationalism merged. Antisemitic *völkisch* nationalists believed that both liberalism and socialism were divisive Jewish ideologies that were tearing the nation apart. They crusaded against liberalism – laissez-faire capitalism, parliamentary democracy, and civic equality – and the individualism it spawned. They violently opposed socialism, linking it to equality, pacifism, and internationalism. To counter these ills, they posited a brave new world in which pure Germans would subordinate their personal strivings to a united *Volksgemeinschaft* (people's community) that embodied true German values. Before World War I, however, antisemitic *völkisch* nationalism was a marginal affair. Only war and the trauma of defeat allowed its enthusiasts to secure more widespread support.

World War I

Germany enters the war

In 1914, Germany was a strong country. Its population had surpassed that of Britain, growing from 41 to 67.7 million between 1871 and 1914. Germany's merchant marine was the second largest (after Britain's) in the world. Germany was Europe's leading industrial power. It outpaced Britain in iron and steel production and was only slightly behind in coal production. Germany had advanced electrical, chemical, and pharmaceutical industries. The label "Made in Germany" symbolized product quality and reliability. Germany's universities were the envy of the world. The country was home to many leading scientists and inventors. Art and culture flourished. To those who desired a more democratic system, German politics seemed to have some evolutionary potential: Catholics and workers maintained a strong oppositionalist press and were well represented in the Reichstag. Indeed, by 1912 the SPD was the largest parliamentary faction, representing roughly one-third of the electorate.

Germans had every reason to feel confident about their nation's future. But they didn't. Many Germans were frustrated by their country's inability to assert itself on the world stage. William's *Weltpolitik* had brought little success but much foreign enmity. After Germany unsuccessfully tried to assert its interests in Morocco in 1905 and 1911, and in the Balkans in 1912–1913, it was isolated diplomatically. Only Austria-Hungary, an empire crumbling under the weight of nationalist tensions, was a clear ally. Many Germans believed that they were encircled by enemies. A defensive war, they thought, would allow them to break out of their continental isolation.

On June 28, 1914, a Serb nationalist assassinated the heir to the Austro-Hungarian throne, Archduke Franz Ferdinand, and his wife, during a royal visit to Sarajevo. The Austrians (wrongly) believed that the Serbian government was involved in the assassination. Sounding out Berlin, they received William's famous "blank check" – that Germany would support Austria-Hungary whatever its choice of action. Several weeks later, Austria issued a set of demands to Serbia. Since fulfilling all of the demands would have violated its sovereignty, Serbia refused to accept the Austrian ultimatum. Three days later, on July 28, Austria declared war on Serbia. At that point, a series of alliance commitments sprang into action. Russia mobilized its troops to aid Serbia, and France, following Franco-Russian treaty obligations, followed suit. On August 1, Germany declared war on Russia and began a speedy mobilization to attack France. Three days later, German troops, en route to France, invaded neutral Belgium. Britain, in defense of Belgium, declared war on Germany. Germany and Austria, the Central Powers, were now ranged against Britain, France, and Russia, the Entente Powers.

The course of the war

Initially, Europeans welcomed war. War signaled release. Many Europeans were eager for a break from routine. In what became known as the "spirit of 1914," the European peoples rallied to their countries' colors. In Germany, William II announced a *Burgfrieden* (social peace) – a call for national unity and an end to all domestic conflict. The vast majority of Germans, convinced that their country was fighting a just, defensive war, supported the emperor. Even Social Democrats voted for government-requested war credits. They hoped that the emperor would reward their patriotism with democratic reforms. But the course of the war shattered these illusions. All too soon, the "spirit of 1914" gave way to disenchantment, the *Burgfrieden* to partisan division.

The German war plan, the Schlieffen Plan, was to prevent Germany from having to fight a two-front war. It presumed that Germany could hurriedly defeat France and then rush its troops eastwards to meet oncoming Russian armies. But the plan was flawed. Already in September 1914, the Germans, unable to defeat the French, were bogged down along the Marne river. On the western front, trench warfare – and military stalemate – ensued. A breakthrough proved elusive. Military commanders sent millions of soldiers to their deaths in battles that achieved no gains. In 1916, for example, the Germans attempted an all-out offensive against the French fortress system at Verdun. Despite casualties of more than 800,000 men (on both sides), the Germans were unable to break through the French lines. Verdun symbolized the tragedy of World War I. Soldiers were exposed to new and deadly weaponry such as barbed wire, poison gas, and mounted machine guns. Men died like flies – for no meaningful purpose.

While the ghastly experience of the western front has received much popular attention, the war on the eastern front deserves more. In August 1914, the Germans won an important victory when Generals Paul von Hindenburg and his chief of staff, Erich Ludendorff, halted Russian invasion forces in the Battle of Tannenberg. Hindenburg and Ludendorff became instant German heroes.

After dramatic advances in 1915, the Germans occupied lands that today encompass Belarus, Latvia, Lithuania, Poland, and Ukraine. To German occupiers, the east initially represented limitless possibilities of expansion and domination. Ludendorff, for example, established *Ober Ost*, a brutal military occupation regime determined to bring order and culture to northeastern areas that the Germans deemed chaotic, diseased, and barbarian. Difficulties during the war and defeat in 1918, however, dashed German hopes in the east. The Nazis would later build on negative German views of eastern populations that arose, in part, out of this wartime experience.

World War I was a "total war." All of the belligerents' resources, civilian and military, were mobilized for the war effort. In 1916, Hindenburg and Ludendorff took over the German High Command. They soon instituted a virtual military dictatorship. Among other measures, they introduced the Hindenburg Program, a plan to increase armament output. This demanded great efforts from the civilian population. Many women now took paid jobs in war industries or worked in or ran welfare-service agencies previously led by men. Meanwhile, many war veterans, maimed or otherwise traumatized, could not fulfill their role as family providers. "Total war" involved a transformation in gender relations.

As the war dragged on, many Germans resented what they saw as the unequal shouldering of wartime burdens. They believed that industrialists (in their imaginations, often Jews) earned soaring war profits while soldiers sacrificed their lives and ordinary civilians endured cold, hunger, and the loss of loved ones. Morale soon deteriorated. In opposition to SPD and union leaders, more radical socialists organized strikes intended to undermine the German war effort. (These wartime divisions soon led to a split between the SPD and what became the communists – a rift that proved significant in the Nazi rise to power.) By 1917, however, even moderate German politicians were advocating an immediate end to the war. Yet more strident German nationalists wished to continue. To them, only territorial acquisitions could justify German sacrifices and, not least, avert political and social revolution.

German defeat

Because the Central Powers controlled smaller quantities of the world's resources, they were at a distinct disadvantage in what became a war of attrition. Britain also imposed a naval blockade that prevented Germany from importing many goods. In response, the Germans initiated unrestricted submarine warfare. This, however, led the United States to declare war on the Central Powers in 1917. The Entente Powers, with America's vast resources of men and matériel now on their side, had the decisive edge. Still, the Germans remained optimistic. Russia, rocked by the 1917 Bolshevik Revolution, withdrew from the war. In March 1918, the Central Powers imposed a punitive peace, the Treaty of Brest-Litovsk, on Russia. The Bolsheviks were forced to cede 600,000 square miles – home to 50 million people and much of Russia's industrial potential and supply of natural resources.

Given this triumph in the east, the German population had little inkling that their own defeat was imminent. That same month, Germany began its final offensive. Initially successful, it soon stalled for lack of war matériel and reserve troops. By summer, the Allies had begun to pierce the German lines and, by early fall, the German military situation was hopeless. On September 29, recognizing the inevitable, Hindenburg and Ludendorff advised William to begin armistice negotiations.

Revolution

Hindenburg and Ludendorff believed that a more democratic government would bring more favorable armistice terms from the Allies – and especially from American President Woodrow Wilson (who detested the authoritarianism and militarism of imperial Germany). In October 1918, William thus acquiesced to making Germany a constitutional monarchy. The new chancellor, Prince Max von Baden, was responsible to the Reichstag, not to the emperor. Meanwhile, though, Hindenburg and Ludendorff refused culpability for military defeat. They insisted that the leaders of the reformist parties in the Reichstag conduct armistice negotiations. By taking responsibility for the negotiations, civilian leaders would take responsibility for Germany's defeat. By linking Reichstag leaders with national defeat, the German High Command delegitimized parliamentary rule right from the start.

Armistice negotiations proved slow going. In early November, German naval troops stationed in the Baltic mutinied. Simultaneously, imminent defeat led to antigovernment protests in the streets of many German cities. Soon, only William's abdication would satisfy many Germans and, most important, Wilson. On November 9, the chancellor and other advisors convinced William to relinquish his throne. Social Democrats, joined by other moderate politicians, proclaimed a revolution. They declared Germany a republic, a parliamentary democracy. Two days later, Matthias Erzberger, a Center politician, signed the armistice agreement on behalf of the new republic. Because of unfavorable armistice terms, the Nazis would soon vilify the new republic's leaders as "November criminals." For them, November 9 marked a day of infamy to be avenged (see Chapter 2 and Chapter 4).

The armistice presaged the harsh terms of the Treaty of Versailles (see below). Since Germany had become a republic, many citizens assumed that the Allies would not impose tough conditions. They were wrong. At the same time, most Germans did not realize the extent of German military defeat. After all, not a battle of the war was fought on an inch of German soil. Germany had just triumphed on the eastern front. Many Germans still thought of their country as a strong power. The shock of defeat gave rise to a powerful "Stab-in-the-Back" legend. Assiduously propagated by Ludendorff, it held that the German army had not been conquered in the field but rather "stabbed in the back" by the treachery of Jews and socialists at home.

The Stab-in-the-Back legend both reflected and gave rise to growing anti-semitism. During the war, many Germans sought a scapegoat to explain their difficulties. Antisemitic rumors circulated that Jews were war profiteers at home and soldiers shirking combat assignments at the front. In 1916, the German High Command, submitting to antisemitic pressure, carried out a census of all Jewish soldiers. This census refuted the rumors, but military leaders refused to publish the results. At the same time, at war's end, a number of prominent revo-lutionaries were Jews, fueling antisemitic charges that Jews, as communists and socialists, were bent on destroying the nation. Still, while a low-grade antisemi-tism was ubiquitous, it was hardly *the* dominant or defining social value. Germans were much more exercised by the loss of national prestige, symbolized by the Treaty of Versailles.

The Treaty of Versailles

On June 28, 1919, Germany signed the humiliating Treaty of Versailles. This peace was dictated. The Germans were not party to the treaty negotiations. Germany lost 13% of its territory and 10% of its population. It gave up all of its overseas colonies. Alsace-Lorraine was returned to France. Germany ceded many of its eastern areas to the new Polish state. Poland demanded access to the Baltic Sea, forcing Germany to give up a "Corridor," a large strip of territory that separated East Prussia from the rest of Germany. The German port city of Danzig (today Gdańsk) was placed under permanent League of Nations man-date. The Saar area, an industrial region bordering on France, was subject to League mandate for fifteen years. Germany and Austria were not permitted to join together in union.

The treaty made it impossible for Germany to attack or defend itself from stronger neighbors. The army was reduced to just 100,000 men, with 4,000 officers. Germany lost much of its navy and was not permitted submarines, tanks, or airplanes. The west bank of the Rhine, and a strip of territory approxi-mately thirty miles to the east, was demilitarized. On the left bank of the Rhine, the Allies were allowed occupation troops for fifteen years, with Germany pay-ing the costs of occupation. Adding insult to injury, the French used black troops mustered from their colonies as occupation soldiers. Some 14,000–25,000 black soldiers (out of roughly 200,000) were deployed. Many Germans believed that the French, by placing blacks in positions of authority, were threatening European civilization. In addition, to the horror of their compatriots, some

Map 1.1 Germany after World War I.

German women had relationships with black soldiers. The resulting offspring, known as the "Rhineland bastards," suffered a cruel fate under the Nazis (see Chapter 4).

The Treaty of Versailles was intended to hamper Germany's economic recovery. Many Germans believed that it amounted to economic enslavement. Article 231, the famous "war-guilt clause," held Germany and its allies legally responsible for the material damages caused by the war. These damages, the Allies argued, included not only the physical ruin of French infrastructure but also pensions paid by Allied governments to their disabled soldiers and war widows. In 1921, an Inter-Allied Reparations Committee determined the reparations bill: 132 billion gold marks ($442 billion in 2011 US dollars).

Ever since 1914, historians have passionately debated the "war-guilt" issue. There is little doubt that William II was eager for a victory abroad so as to shore up his monarchy at home. Rather than diffusing the crisis, he issued the "blank check," thereby escalating the conflict. Still, Germany alone was not responsible for the outbreak of war. All of the European powers bear some measure of blame; none tried to halt the seemingly inexorable push to war. Historians today generally concur that the treaty was unjustly punitive, especially since Germany was not the lone aggressor.

At the same time, many observers have argued that the Treaty of Versailles led directly to the Nazi assumption of power. Germans, they argue, turned to Hitler to restore their national honor and to rescue their economy, burdened with crushing reparations payments. In this reading of history, the Allies bear responsibility for Hitler and World War II. This is wrong, however. Had the Great Depression not intervened, Germans most likely would have lived down the treaty. Already in the 1920s, Germany was finding ways to mitigate the treaty's burdens. The military, for example, embedded former air-unit officers into the new officer corps so as to maintain expertise in aerial warfare. Germany also negotiated security guarantees with its western neighbors and the withdrawal of most occupation troops (see below). Moreover, the reparations payments were not beyond what Germany could reasonably pay. *Not* the Treaty of Versailles, but rather the Great Depression, led directly to the Nazi assumption of power. Still, Germans bitterly resented the Versailles peace, and Hitler *did* exploit anti-treaty feeling to win electoral support.

The legacy of war and defeat

Absent World War I, it is hard to imagine Hitler's ascendance. Most important, since parliamentary rule was associated with the Versailles peace, defeat soured many Germans on democracy. Subsequent events, described below, only confirmed many Germans' disdain for democracy. War and defeat bred political attitudes and moral sensibilities that later resonated with Nazism. These included the growth of state intervention, the polarization of society, the glorification of militarism and violence, and the cheapening of life.

To an unprecedented degree, the state intervened in the lives of its citizens during and after World War I. It conscripted soldiers, enlisted factory workers, and deported undesirable persons. It categorized the population so as to distribute ration cards, issue passports, and determine war-related pensions. The growth of state expertise in the classification of individuals later aided Nazi projects that depended on the cataloging of whole populations – including Jews, Roma (Gypsies), Poles, and homosexuals, along with those "unfit" to reproduce or "unworthy of living" (see Chapter 4, Chapter 6, and Chapter 7).

Veterans often had enormous difficulties reintegrating into civilian life. What was then called "shell shock," now posttraumatic stress disorder, afflicted millions of soldiers. Alienated from mainstream society, former soldiers sought community with fellow veterans. While some joined together to champion pacifism, most turned to right-wing groups. Some hardened veterans reveled in vigilante groups, known as the Free Corps (see below and Chapter 2). Many former soldiers flocked to right-wing veterans' associations, especially the five-million-strong Stahlhelm (Steel Helmet).

Despite defeat, militarism remained a much-prized value. Indeed, even politics became militarized. A "friend–foe" mentality predominated. Every major political party had a paramilitary force. Uniformed political combatants battled for control of street corners or neighborhood pubs. Assassination was quite common. This militarization of politics, however, undermined the democratic order Compromise and tolerance, so at odds with military culture, are essential for the smooth functioning of democracy.

The war fostered a cult of violence. Violence was seen as transformative; war allegedly created a New Man. Born in struggle, nurtured in masculine comradeship, and steeled in grizzly battle, the New Man could solve the challenges of the modern age. Violence, it was thought, would clear the way for a better future. The war had already swept away hitherto presumed certainties such as empire, political order, and gender relations. In the quest for a utopian society, many believed, all else could be upended, too.

Almost two million German soldiers died in World War I. Many Germans became callous to the loss of human life. In turn, the cheapening of life allowed perverse notions to gain currency. Some Germans, and not least future Nazis, came to believe that murder could improve society. By killing off undesirable groups, so this thinking went, the German people would be strengthened.

The spread of these and related values was hardly unique to Germany. Many were important elements of fascism, a movement closely associated with the Italian leader, Benito Mussolini. Fascism took its name from the ancient Roman *fasces*, a bundle of wooden rods that symbolized the magistrate's power, as well as strength in unity. The fascist movement emphasized devotion to a supreme, heroic leader; national unity; an activist state; and collective rejuvenation through political violence, militarism, and imperialism. Fascism was also defined by what it opposed: it was anti-individual, antiliberal, and anticommunist. (Fascism and Nazism shared many parallels, but racism and antisemitism were much more central to Nazism than Italian fascism.) Mussolini and his fascist movement came to power in Italy in 1922. Meanwhile, Germany underwent an experiment in democracy, the Weimar Republic.

The Weimar Republic

In the new republic, the first elections – to a National Assembly – took place in January 1919. They resulted in a decisive victory for parties committed to republicanism. Some 76% of the electorate voted for the SPD, the Catholic Center

Party, or the left-liberal German Democratic Party (DDP). To avoid the revolutionary chaos of Berlin, the elected National Assembly met in the city of Weimar – thus giving the republic its unofficial but ubiquitous name. In July, the assembly adopted a constitution. The Weimar Constitution foresaw a president as head of state, a chancellor as head of government, and a democratically elected Reichstag. While the president appointed the chancellor, the chancellor had to have the support of a Reichstag majority. Although the constitution was widely praised for its democratic attributes, some of its features eventually facilitated the Nazi rise to power (see Chapter 2).

Despite this auspicious beginning, many historians have argued that the new republic was doomed to fail. Too many political and economic forces, so this argument goes, were arrayed against it. In fact, however, the new regime's fate was open ended. The history of the Weimar Republic is generally divided into three parts. The first years, 1918–1923, were years of inflation and political upheaval. The middle period, 1924–1929, saw a degree of political and economic stability. The last stage of the republic, 1929–1933, was characterized by depression and presidential dictatorship. This was when Hitler and the Nazi movement enjoyed tremendous successes, and is described in Chapter 2.

Weimar politics, 1918–1923

Many Germans were soon dissatisfied with the Weimar Republic. In November 1918, for example, German employers had feared the revolutionary potential of eight million veterans and other disgruntled citizens. They had thus concluded an agreement with trade unionists, the Stinnes–Legien Agreement. This pact prevented the nationalization of industry and protected private property. But it also granted labor an eight-hour work day and worker participation in some management decisions. Employers soon rued these concessions and blamed the republic for an industrial order that favored workers.

Similarly, in November 1918 the cochairman of the provisional government, the Social Democrat Friedrich Ebert, had feared further revolutionary upheaval. He now made a pact with General Wilhelm Groener, second-in-command of the army: the army would aid the republic in maintaining law and order, but the government would respect the military's autonomy. The Ebert–Groener and Stinnes–Legien agreements protected two pillars of the old imperial elite, industrialists and officers, in the new republic. At the same time, the new government refused to purge personnel in other leading institutions of society, such as the bureaucracies, the universities, or the churches. As a result, antidemocratic Wilhelmine elites maintained their positions of power and, as we shall see, used them to undermine the new republic.

The Ebert–Groener Pact was soon tested. In January 1919, the Spartacist Uprising, a communist revolt in Berlin, was suppressed by the Reichswehr (as the army was now called). In addition, members of a Free Corps unit, one of many vigilante armed groups supported by the regular army, brutally murdered Rosa Luxemburg and Karl Liebknecht, the two most important communist leaders. The fact that Social Democrats – fellow socialists – had repressed a communist uprising seemed a betrayal to the radical left. The government, along with the army, went on to suppress further leftist uprisings in May 1919, March 1920, March 1921, and October 1923. While the SPD supported the Weimar Republic, communists – soon organized into the Communist Party of Germany (KPD) – took inspiration from the Bolshevik Revolution in the Soviet Union and hoped to institute a communist regime in Germany. The KPD viewed the Weimar Republic as part and parcel of the capitalist system of oppression. These divisions eventually prevented the left from joining together to counter the Nazi threat.

While the army enthusiastically suppressed left-wing revolts, it was reluctant to put down right-wing coup attempts. In March 1920, Walther von Lüttwitz, the commander of the Berlin army district, and Wolfgang Kapp, a right-wing politician, staged a coup. Free Corps units seized control of Berlin. Hans von Seeckt, commander in chief of the Reichswehr, refused to allow army troops to suppress the insurgency. The republic was saved only because workers called a general strike to thwart the coup. The Kapp Putsch threw into relief the army's limited loyalty to the republic. Army officers begrudged support for a regime that had implemented the Versailles Treaty's restrictions on troop numbers, equipment, and operations.

At the beginning of 1923, the German government failed to deliver reparations in the form of wood and coal to the Allies. The policy of nonfulfillment was intended to show that Germany could not pay reparations and thus should be excused from future payments. Unpersuaded, France and Belgium occupied the industrial Ruhr area. In turn, the German government urged a policy of "passive resistance." It encouraged civil servants to go on strike but continued to pay them. To finance this, the government simply printed money. Neither gold reserves nor anything else backed the currency. Galloping hyperinflation ensued. One US dollar was soon worth an incredible 4.2 trillion – 4,200,000,000,000,000 – German marks. Since wages depreciated on an hourly basis, employees were paid two or three times a day. Germans carted around wheelbarrows of paper money to buy a bottle of milk or a loaf of bread.

The Great Inflation had its origins in the financing of World War I. At that time, the emperor's government had been reluctant to raise taxes to pay for the war. Instead, it issued war bonds. After the war, moderate inflation benefited the Weimar government. It lowered the costs of repaying war bonds. It also financed a measure of social stability. Employers passed on their higher labor costs by increasing the price of goods. Workers could keep up because they earned higher wages. Inflation also helped individuals paying off mortgages or other debts. The Great Inflation, however, was another matter. It was an economic catastrophe. Civil servants and other individuals living on fixed incomes were unable to pay their daily expenses. Those with savings lost all of their monetary assets, often a lifetime of work. Hyperinflation undermined all certainties. Fairness and equity seemed out of reach.

In 1923, the Weimar Republic was on the brink of collapse. Many Germans questioned democracy, and rightly so. Democracy seemed to breed instability; there were ten different cabinets between January 1919 and May 1924. With so many uprisings and attempted coups, the republic seemed unable to uphold law and order. In addition, democracy had brought only humiliation and loss to many Germans   from right-wing nationalists to left-wing radicals. Now, however, the republic got a reprieve. In August 1923, Gustav Stresemann, a pragmatic politician, became chancellor. On November 15, he ended the Great Inflation by introducing a new currency, soon called the *Reichsmark*, which was linked to the gold standard in 1924.

Weimar culture

To the dismay of many future Nazis, the Weimar Republic saw a many-sided cultural ferment. The dizzying crisis atmosphere spawned an efflorescent creativity. Most famously, there was an outpouring of "Weimar culture," modernist experimentation in the arts. Some avant-garde artists espoused Dada, an "anti-art" movement that questioned traditional aesthetics. Expressionist artists reveled in depicting subjective experience, often psychological or other anguish. German film directors made some of the world's greatest silent movies, including *Metropolis* and *The Cabinet of Dr. Caligari*. German architects founded the Bauhaus, a movement emphasizing streamlined functionality that remains influential even today.

Yet, while some Germans were drawn to the avant-garde, many more enjoyed mass commercial entertainment. Germans, and especially urban Germans, enjoyed new, modern pleasures. They attended lowbrow theater productions, feel-good films, and raucous cabaret and variety shows. They cheered sports teams in large, new stadiums. Eschewing traditional notions of modesty, they went sunbathing at nearby lakes or seashores. They flocked to dance halls and penny arcades, and shopped in big, bright department stores. They filled their apartments with mass-produced goods. They read cheap paperbacks and illustrated magazines, and listened to broadcasts on a new media, radio.

Weimar Germany also saw a sexual revolution. Social workers insisted on the importance of satisfying sex lives. A vibrant gay scene emerged, even though homosexual acts remained a criminal offense. Birth control became more accessible. The Weimar Republic was also famous for the "New Woman." She was slender and athletic, single and employed. She bobbed her hair, wore seductive clothing, and brandished a cigarette holder. By testing the limits, she seemed Weimar incarnate. Despite her media dominance, however, the "New Woman" was a statistical rarity.

For many liberal and leftist Germans, these cultural trends pointed to the liberating potential of the Weimar Republic. For cultural conservatives, however, these developments rankled. The new modernist artworks exposed the sordid rather than celebrated the beautiful. The new sexuality was morally repugnant. Mass production threatened artisanal crafts. Mass entertainment played to base human instincts. To conservative critics, these trends symbolized all that was wrong with the new republic. As we shall see, the Nazis picked up and echoed many of these criticisms.

Weimar politics, 1924–1929

After the stabilization of the economy in late 1923, the Weimar Republic enjoyed a measure of prosperity. Industry financed expansion through short-term American loans. Still, even though economic conditions were much better than during the Great Inflation, economic performance remained sluggish. Germans blamed reparations for poor economic performance, but historians today argue that the Weimar economy suffered from structural weaknesses. Labor costs skyrocketed, but worker productivity barely grew. This was partly because the economy was organized in cartels that fixed prices, marketing, and production and thus undermined free enterprise. In the absence of competition, there was little incentive for German companies to innovate. From 1926 onward, there was also a worldwide agrarian depression that hurt German farmers.

In the mid-1920s, foreign relations allowed some optimism about Germany's situation. Stresemann, now Germany's foreign minister, fulfilled German treaty obligations in the hope that this would bring about revision of the Versailles Treaty. Proving his strategy, France soon withdrew many troops from the Ruhr. The 1924 Dawes Plan aimed to resolve the reparations issue by scaling back the annual level of payments. In 1925, Germany and the Allies signed the Treaty of Locarno. All parties agreed to recognize and guarantee Germany's current western borders (but not its eastern borders). Germany shed its status as a pariah nation. In 1926, it joined the League of Nations, and was even awarded a permanent seat on its Council of Ten. In 1928, it participated in the Olympics for the first time since the outbreak of war.

During these middle years of the republic, many Germans came to be *Vernunftrepublikaner* (pragmatic republicans) – that is, they made their peace with democracy. They could point to some Weimar successes. Local governments improved municipal services, built ambitious housing projects, and funded clinics and other welfare services. Many other Germans, however, remained die-hard opponents of parliamentary rule. To them democracy was a dirty word, imposed on Germany by the SPD and foreign powers. Right-wing parties were relentless in their agitation for authoritarian government and overturning the Versailles Treaty.

Could the republic have survived? The jury remains out. As more Germans lived democracy, they might have come to see its benefits (as happened in West Germany after World War II). But the odds were against this. In the interwar years, democracy seemed unable to solve the great problems of the day. While Britain, France, and Czechoslovakia remained democracies, many other European countries turned to fascism or other forms of authoritarianism. Still, absent the Great Depression, it is possible to imagine a stable Weimar democracy. After the onset of the 1929 Depression (see Chapter 2), this becomes impossible. The republic could draw on only limited reserves of legitimacy.

But even then, Hitler and the Nazis were not inevitable. Developments discussed in this chapter – *völkisch* nationalism, the democratic deficit, the trauma of war and defeat, and the upheaval of the Weimar years – did not necessarily lead to Nazism. They were, however, its indispensable preconditions. Just how, then, did Hitler and the Nazis actually come to power in Germany?

Citations for Quotations

Page   Source

1   "Hitler is Reich Chancellor..." Quoted in Ian Kershaw, *Hitler 1889–1936: Hubris* (New York: W.W. Norton, 1998), 423.

4   "its place in the sun." Quoted in Richard J. Evans, *The Coming of the Third Reich* (London: Penguin, 2003), 18.

Bibliography

Bartov, Omer. *Mirrors of Destruction: War, Genocide, and Modern Identity.* Oxford: Oxford University Press, 2000.

Blackbourn, David and Geoff Eley. *The Peculiarities of German History: Bourgeois Society and Politics in Nineteenth-Century Germany.* Oxford: Oxford University Press, 1984.

Campt, Tina. *Other Germans: Black Germans and the Politics of Race, Gender, and Memory in the Third Reich.* Ann Arbor: University of Michigan Press, 2005.

Chickering, Roger. *We Men Who Feel Most German: A Cultural Study of the Pan-German League, 1886–1914.* Boston: Allen & Unwin, 1984.

Craig, Gordon. *The Politics of the Prussian Army, 1640–1945.* New York: Oxford, 1955.

Eley, Geoff. *Reshaping the German Right: Radical Nationalism and Political Change after Bismarck.* New Haven: Yale University Press, 1980.

Evans, Richard J. *The Coming of the Third Reich.* London: Penguin, 2003.

Ferguson, Niall. *The Pity of War: Explaining World War I.* New York: Basic Books, 1999.

Grady, Tim. *The German–Jewish Soldiers of the First World War in History and Memory.* Liverpool: Liverpool University Press, 2011.

Hull, Isabel V. *Absolute Destruction: Military Culture and the Practices of War in Imperial Germany*. Ithaca: Cornell University Press, 2005.

Kershaw, Ian. *Hitler 1889–1936: Hubris*. New York: W.W. Norton, 1998.

Liulevicius, Vejas G. *War Land on the Eastern Front: Culture, National Identity, and German Occupation during World War I*. Cambridge: Cambridge University Press, 2000.

McElligott, Anthony, ed. *Weimar Germany*. Oxford: Oxford University Press, 2009.

Mosse, George L. *The Crisis of German Ideology: Intellectual Origins of the Third Reich*. New York: Grosset & Dunlap, 1964.

Mosse, George L. *The Nationalization of the Masses: Political Symbolism and Mass Movements in Germany from the Napoleonic Wars through the Third Reich*. New York: H. Fertig, 1975.

Stern, Fritz. *The Politics of Cultural Despair: A Study in the Rise of Germanic Ideology*. Berkeley: University of California Press, 1961.

2

Hitler and the Nazi Movement

At the end of World War I, an unknown soldier, Adolf Hitler, lay in a military hospital in Pasewalk, supposedly blinded by a mustard gas attack. Here, he later wrote, he heard the shocking news of Germany's defeat and revolution. In the tormented days and nights that followed, he mulled over the situation. Hitler then claimed that he had an epiphany: "I, for my part, decided to go into politics." This story and much else in his 1925 autobiography, *Mein Kampf* (My Struggle), was untrue, simplified, or embellished. Still, after World War I, Hitler *did* become a politician. In the following years, his political fortunes waxed and waned. But, in January 1933, President Paul von Hindenburg appointed Hitler – a failed art student, lowly private, and convicted traitor – Germany's chancellor.

It is a common myth that Hitler seized power in a coup. In fact, he came to power legally. In Weimar Germany the chancellor was not elected by the people but appointed by the president. Hindenburg, however, named Hitler chancellor because the Nazi leader commanded the votes of millions of Germans. Indeed, more than one in three Germans voted for Hitler in free elections. But, just as important, almost two-thirds of the electorate did not.

Some historians have made class-based arguments about the rise of Nazism. Marxist historians suggest that big business supported the Nazis, and that Nazism was simply a tool to perpetuate monopoly capitalism. Others claimed that Nazism was a movement of lower-middle-class peasants and small businessmen who opposed both free-market liberalism and socialism. Yet others contend that Nazism represented a "revolt of the masses," a rebellion of the common man against his lowly place in society. We now know, though, that Nazi voters ranged

Nazi Germany: Confronting the Myths, First Edition. Catherine Epstein.
© 2015 John Wiley & Sons, Ltd. Published 2015 by John Wiley & Sons, Ltd.

across German society. Almost one in three Nazi voters was a worker. Class-based analyses do not explain Hitler's rise to power.

Hitler's assumption of power was neither necessary nor inevitable. Rather, it is best explained through immediate causes that arose during the Great Depression: a failing political system, Nazi electoral tactics, and the intrigues of conservative politicians. This chapter describes Hitler's early life and rise to political prominence. It then charts the development of the NSDAP, the National Socialist German Workers' Party (the official name of the Nazi Party). Finally, it ties the story of German history (Chapter 1) to that of the Nazi movement to show just how Hitler assumed power.

Hitler's Early Life

Hitler's early life has been the source of various misperceptions, including some that he himself put into circulation in *Mein Kampf*. Hitler was born into a comfortable lower-middle-class family in Braunau, in the Austro-Hungarian Empire, on April 20, 1889. His father, Alois, was a minor customs official. Although illegitimate (the identity of Alois' father remains unclear), it is virtually certain that Alois was not of Jewish origins – a rumor long circulated by Hitler's enemies. Alois was an ill-tempered disciplinarian, and father and son had ongoing conflict. Hitler, however, adored his mother, Klara, a submissive wife and doting mother. After Alois' death in 1903, Klara moved the family to Linz, where Hitler, a poor student, finished school in 1905. Klara then supported her son in an idle life of drawing, daydreaming of artistic greatness, and attending performances of Wagner operas. The combination of a stern father and weak mother may have had psychological consequences for the future dictator. It is impossible, though, to firmly link Hitler's early relationships to his later crimes.

In late 1907, Klara Hitler succumbed to breast cancer. During her illness, she was treated by a Jewish doctor, Eduard Bloch. In gratitude, Hitler not only gave Bloch some of his artwork but years later ensured his safe passage out of Nazi-occupied Europe. While some have argued otherwise, Hitler's antisemitism was not rooted in the fact that his beloved mother died under a Jewish physician's care.

Hitler hoped to become an artist. Shortly before his mother's death, he moved to Vienna to seek admission to the Academy of Fine Arts. He failed the entrance exam. This was a crushing disappointment for an adolescent who imagined himself a creative genius. The following year, he was not even permitted to sit for the exam. Hitler's rejection from art school likely resulted in his bitter resentment of the conventional, bourgeois establishment. Living in an egocentric fantasy world, he now imagined that he would become a famous architect. But his wild bursts of creative energy always dissipated into unfinished projects.

Hitler led the life of a loner. Although he made a few friends, these relationships inevitably soured. He also appears to have had a highly repressed sex life (even though rumors that he had only one testicle are untrue). Hitler hit rock bottom in 1909 and was homeless for a time. The following year, he moved into a men's home. He now earned small sums by selling his hand-painted pictures of Viennese landmarks. He also engaged in haphazard reading of nationalist, racist, and antisemitic tracts, although precisely what he read remains unknown.

In *Mein Kampf*, Hitler claimed that his worldview became fixed during his Vienna years: "In addition to what I then created, I have had to learn little; and I have had to alter nothing." With this sentence, Hitler was eager to underscore the self-evident truth of his political views. In fact, though, his ideology developed gradually. In Linz, Hitler imbibed the Pan-Germanism of Georg Ritter von Schönerer – a hodgepodge of antisemitic, antiliberal, antisocialist, anti-Catholic, and anti-Habsburg ideas. He also developed a passion for the romantic nationalism of Wagner's operas. In Vienna, he cemented his hatred of the multinational Austro-Hungarian Empire. The advance of Slavic and other minorities, he believed, was sapping the vitality of the empire and its German leadership. He also learned the power of propaganda through the example of Karl Lueger, the antisemitic rabble-rouser mayor. Although Hitler likely harbored a rough antisemitism, he had good relations with Jewish acquaintances who helped him peddle his pictures.

In May 1913, Hitler fled Vienna for Munich, the capital of Bavaria, in Germany. He had long admired imperial Germany. Yet the timing of his departure was significant. He waited until after his twenty-fourth birthday (April 20), when he would receive his share of his father's inheritance. Just then, however, Austrian officials were hot on his heels for draft evasion; Hitler did not wish to serve the military of the multinational Austro-Hungarian Empire. Soon after his arrival in Munich, he was arrested for draft-dodging and forced to return briefly to Austria. Austro-Hungarian military authorities now determined that he was too weak for military service. It is no small irony that the dictator who extolled military virtues was himself a draft-dodger and deemed unfit to be a soldier. Hitler returned to Munich, where he continued his desultory existence.

Hitler's First World War

But for World War I, this lazy ne'er-do-well would likely have lived his life in total oblivion. The war proved a godsend for him. At first it offered Hitler purpose and later it permitted his political ascendance. Shortly after Germany declared war, Hitler volunteered to serve in the Bavarian military. He was assigned to a unit known as the List Regiment (named after its first commander) and became a dispatch runner. This work was dangerous but safer than frontline combat duty. For his military exploits, Hitler was awarded both the Iron Cross First and Second Class. For reasons unknown, however, he was not promoted and he remained a private throughout the war. Although his fellow dispatch runners viewed him as a reclusive oddball, Hitler developed good relations with some of them. His dearest companion, though, was a stray dog, Foxl.

While we know little about Hitler's political views during the war, he seems to have been preoccupied with German racial and ethnic purity. In February 1915, he wrote a Munich acquaintance that when veterans returned to the "fatherland" he hoped that they "will find it a purer place, less riddled with foreign influences." In October 1916, he was wounded in his left thigh. After his convalescence, he went to Munich on home leave. There, he claimed in *Mein Kampf*, he was disgusted by civilians' defeatism and Jews' shirking of combat duty: "Nearly every clerk was a Jew and nearly every Jew was a clerk." We don't know, though, whether Hitler really felt this way in wartime Germany – or only some years later, when writing *Mein Kampf*.

As for Pasewalk in fall 1918, Hitler was not hospitalized for temporary blindness but rather for "war hysteria" in the psychiatric unit. Historians have rightly questioned his alleged Pasewalk epiphany. As the following section suggests, not Pasewalk but subsequent events in Munich pushed him toward a political career.

Revolutionary Munich

In *Mein Kampf*, Hitler devoted few words to his actions between November 1918 and May 1919. For good reason. His actions at this time were hardly those one might expect of the future Nazi leader. In November, radical leftists, led by a Jewish revolutionary, Kurt Eisner, came to power in Bavaria. After Eisner was assassinated by a right-wing fanatic in February, his supporters insisted on maintaining an illegitimate Bolshevik-style government. In May, regular army and Free Corps units converged on Munich to battle this socialist regime. In the short civil war that ensued, the right emerged victorious, but not before radical socialists had shot ten hostages in a schoolyard. In response, Free Corps units unleashed massacres that left hundreds of leftists dead. In traditionally conservative Bavaria, anti-Bolshevism proved a potent rallying cry, and Munich soon became a refuge for right-wing extremists. It is no accident that National Socialism was born in the Bavarian capital.

But where was Hitler in all of this? After leaving Pasewalk, he rejoined his regiment in Munich. He now worked for an army propaganda unit that served the *socialist* government in power. There is even film footage of Hitler walking in the funeral cortege for Eisner. That spring, Hitler also did not join any of the

Free Corps units that battled the socialists. Why not? It seems that he was at a loss as to how to make his way in the postwar world. Most of all, he wished to avoid demobilization; besides the military, he had no other home or purpose. Still, it is unlikely that Hitler actually supported the socialists during spring 1919. Once the right gained control of the military, he was appointed to a commission that examined soldiers' political activities during the "Red Republic." His distaste for the revolutionary republic must have been known. In June 1919 he was delegated to a military course that gave soldiers right-wing political instruction. He proved such a good student that by August he was an instructor himself. Hitler now discovered his true gift. In his words, "I could 'speak.'"

Antisemitism was now Hitler's defining animus. We don't know how or why he became such a fanatical antisemite. In September 1919, however, his superior, Captain Karl Mayr, asked him to respond to an inquiry about the "Jewish Question." This reply was Hitler's first known antisemitic harangue. The ultimate aim of antisemitism, he insisted, "must unshakably be the removal of the Jews altogether." The historian Saul Friedländer has coined the phrase "redemptive anti-Semitism" to describe Hitler's brand of antisemitism. For Hitler, "the Jew" was the principal evil in western history; "the Jew" aimed to destroy all of humanity. If not eliminated, Hitler believed, "the Jew" would ruin the Aryan race and the German *Volk*. Hitler came to see his purpose as redeeming the world through the elimination of Jews. He would harbor a pathological antisemitism until his dying day.

The Early NSDAP

On September 12, 1919, on behalf of the army, Hitler went to inspect a fledgling political party, the German Workers' Party (DAP). The DAP was one of many tiny right-wing extremist groupings in Munich. It had been founded the previous January by Anton Drexler, a locksmith, and Karl Harrer, a journalist. In *Mein Kampf*, Hitler wrote that he was singularly unimpressed by what he saw. He had already heard the lecture by the speaker Gottfried Feder at a different right-wing gathering. Feder was an antisemitic economist who raged on about the alleged role of Jews in "finance capitalism." Although Hitler liked the lecture (Feder was soon an important advisor), he found the DAP "a dull organization." Afterward, though, he read a pamphlet by Drexler that sparked his interest. About a week later, he learned that he had been accepted as a party member (he had never applied). Shortly thereafter, possibly on Mayr's orders, he joined the DAP. Although on the army payroll until March 31, 1920, Hitler soon devoted all of his energy to the party.

Hitler had an immediate impact on the DAP. His message resonated with the established *völkisch* nationalist scene that thrived in Bavaria's capital. A number of early DAP members, for example, were associated with the Thule Society, a ritzy *völkisch* club founded in Munich in 1917–1918. But, in the feverish atmosphere of postwar Munich, Hitler's message had appeal beyond convinced *völkisch* nationalists. Many Germans were looking for explanations for their own and their country's woes. Hitler blamed all of Germany's ills on the Jews. Eliminating "Jewry," he insisted, would relieve Germany's suffering and humiliation and restore its honor and strength.

There was nothing original about Hitler's views. They were typical of the *völkisch* nationalist milieu that espoused antisemitism, chauvinistic nationalism, and German racial superiority. Hitler's success lay not in his message but in its remarkable delivery. He was a sensational speaker. Initially, he spoke quietly to garner his listeners' rapt attention. Soon, though, he thundered his points in loud crescendos. Punctuating his words with practiced gestures, Hitler worked his audience up into a frenzy of fever-pitched emotion.

In late February 1920, the DAP held its first mass meeting. Two thousand people attended. In the midst of a lively speech, interrupted by repeated applause (and some heckles from opponents in the hall), Hitler announced the Manifesto of Twenty-Five Points, the party program. Most of the points were typical right-wing fare. They included the "union of all Germans" in a "Great Germany," the

Figure 2.1 Hitler practices his gestures for a speech (1925). The photo was taken by Heinrich Hoffmann, Hitler's personal photographer. *Source*: Getty Images.

abolition of the Versailles Peace Treaty, the demand for colonies, the removal of Jews' citizenship rights, and the prevention of non-German immigration. The manifesto also called for socialist measures (although the word "socialist" itself never appeared). These included "the abolition of incomes unearned by work," the confiscation of all war profits, and the "nationalization of all businesses." Finally, the manifesto advocated racial hygiene measures. It argued that the "state must see to raising the standard of health in the nation," not least by "increasing bodily efficiency by obligatory gymnastics and sports laid down by law." Soon after, the party began to call itself the National Socialist German Workers' Party (NSDAP).

Besides Hitler, a number of men – and they were *all* men – played an important role in the party's early history. Drexler and Feder were part of the party's inner circle. Dietrich Eckart was an older *völkisch* poet and, for a time, a close friend of Hitler. Well connected, he introduced Hitler to Munich's high society. He also arranged for the acquisition of the *Völkischer Beobachter* (the *Völkisch Observer*), the official newspaper of the party. Max Amann, a former officer in the List Regiment, directed the party's publishing house. Alfred Rosenberg, a Baltic intellectual who had fled Soviet rule, influenced Hitler's extreme anti-Bolshevism. Rudolf Hess, a student of the geopolitician Karl Haushofer, introduced Hitler to the concept of *Lebensraum* (living space). Hans Frank became Hitler's personal lawyer. Ernst Röhm, a well-connected military officer, brought in recruits and built up a secret cache of weapons. Hermann Göring, a flamboyant veteran flying ace, introduced Hitler to wealthy patrons.

Hitler brought success but also dissension to the party. As the NSDAP attracted more supporters, there was talk of a merger with other right-wing extremist groups. This brought on a party crisis in July 1921. Drexler wanted the NSDAP to merge with a rival *völkisch* organization. But Hitler would have none of it. In a larger party, he feared, he would not be the dominant figure. As merger talks continued, Hitler impulsively resigned from the party. Without Hitler's magnetism, Drexler and others now worried, the NSDAP might not survive. Drexler sought Hitler's return, but the price was high. Hitler insisted on being chairman of the party "with dictatorial power." Party headquarters were to be in Munich. The party program could not be altered. And there were to be no more merger attempts. His demands met, Hitler was the uncontested leader of the party.

In September 1921, Hitler formed the paramilitary SA (Sturmabteilung) or storm troopers. The SA protected Nazi party meetings and broke up opponents' political meetings. The SA men were tough beer-hall thugs, many of whom had fought in Free Corps units. With their muscle and zeal, they terrorized adversaries. Beginning in 1924, storm troopers wore distinctive mustard-brown shirts.

Hitler now cajoled other extreme right-wing groups to join *his* party. In October 1922, for example, Julius Streicher, a rabid antisemite, brought his

Nuremberg branch of a rival political organization into the NSDAP. Streicher became editor of *Der Stürmer* (The Stormer), a pornographic antisemitic publication. As Germany lurched from crisis to crisis, the NSDAP enjoyed significant growth. From 2,000 members in January 1921, the NSDAP jumped to 6,000 in January 1922, to 20,000 in fall 1922, and to 50,000 in November 1923.

Propaganda

Hitler attached enormous importance to propaganda. Propaganda, he believed, should be cast in simple, one-sided, and absolute terms; nuance would kill any argument. The masses, he declared in *Mein Kampf*, were easily manipulated through emotion. Propaganda should elicit wild enthusiasm or intense hatred. There was no place for rational understanding. To convey its message, the NSDAP deployed all matter of propaganda techniques: press, posters, and speeches; staged uniformed demonstrations, mass rallies, and party rituals; and, later, new media such as film and radio.

In 1920, Hitler designed the party banner – a black swastika in a white circle on a red background. It was bold, simple, and suggestive. White was the color of German nationalism, red the color of socialism. Among ancient Hindu symbols, the swastika represented the sun. German *völkisch* nationalists had long popularized the swastika to mean "Unconquerable" or "the Strong One from Above." Hitler also borrowed the fascist salute from Mussolini. The outstretched right-arm salute became the "Heil Hitler" greeting.

While Hitler engaged in effective propaganda, he did not "brainwash" his followers. "Brainwashing" is the use of unethical, manipulative methods to induce an individual to act or believe in a particular way, often against his or her conscience. Hitler's speeches were manipulative in that they roused his listeners to nationalist ecstasy. Participants, however, were rarely forced to attend. Moreover, the Nazi movement and later regime did not use techniques of bodily torture to force individuals to believe in its tenets.

The Beer Hall Putsch

By fall 1923, Hitler hoped to seize power. The French occupation of the Ruhr and hyperinflation dominated headlines (see Chapter 1). Germany seemed ripe for the taking. A right-wing conspiracy, organized by leading Bavarian political and military authorities, hoped to topple the republic. Hitler, not least because the SA was seen as a potential auxiliary military force, was privy to these plans. Once Gustav Stresemann began to stabilize the republic, however, top Bavarian officials lost heart. Not Hitler. He and leaders of several other right-wing paramilitary organizations, loosely united in the Kampfbund (German Combat

League), remained bent on a military coup or "putsch." Their aim was to force leading Bavarian officials to join in a march on Berlin – emulating Mussolini's earlier (faked) March on Rome. This was to take place on November 9, the fifth anniversary of the November Revolution, which had ushered in the Weimar Republic.

On the evening of November 8, members of the SA surrounded the Munich Bürgerbräukeller, where a leading Bavarian official, Gustav Ritter von Kahr, was giving a speech. Hitler rushed into the hall, fired a shot into the air, and declared the Bavarian government deposed. He then took Kahr and two others into a side room. He had, he said, four bullets – one for each of them and the last one for himself. The men had little choice but to follow Hitler. Joined by General Erich von Ludendorff, who backed Hitler, they returned to the hall in a show of unity. Hitler soon left the hall. Now, poor preparation showed. Kampfbund insurgents had failed to secure the army barracks and the telephone exchange. Inexplicably, Ludendorff permitted the hostages to go free. Once released, Kahr and the others reversed the military orders issued by the putschists.

By early morning, the coup had failed. Hitler and Ludendorff nonetheless decided to stage a march on the Munich city center. The two men, along with 2,000 armed supporters, headed in the direction of the Ministry of War. Facing an armed cordon of police, the Nazis taunted their opponents. One or the other side fired the first shot – and a hail of bullets followed. In short order, fourteen Nazis and four policemen lay dead. One of the fallen Nazis, Max Erwin von Scheubner-Richter, had been walking arm in arm with Hitler. Had the bullet that struck Scheubner-Richter landed a foot or so to the right, Hitler might have been killed. As it was, he merely dislocated his shoulder. Two days later, he was arrested.

As the Beer Hall Putsch showed, the Weimar Republic still retained legitimacy. Hitler had failed to persuade right-wing officials, the military, and the police to join his coup. Bavarian officials now banned the NSDAP and jailed its leader. Hitler's political career seemed at an end. In early 1924, however, the putschists stood trial. Hitler quickly turned the proceedings to his advantage. He glorified his attempt to overthrow those who had committed "the crime of November 1918." The sympathetic court found Hitler guilty of high treason but sentenced him to just five years' imprisonment – with the prospect of early release.

The NSDAP, 1924–1928

The years 1924–1928 are often referred to as Hitler's time in the "wilderness." Hitler was a fringe political leader, the NSDAP a marginal extremist party. Still, these were the years when Hitler laid the groundwork for the NSDAP's eventual assumption of power. He consolidated his worldview, developed a cult of the Führer (leader), and made the NSDAP a more effective organization.

Hitler spent 1924 jailed in a comfortable room in Landsberg Fortress. He was permitted visitors and was surrounded by loyal devotees also serving prison time. Hitler enjoyed *völkisch* adulation as the martyr who had initiated a coup, mounted a stirring defense against the republic, and was now imprisoned for his actions. These months proved just how important Hitler was to the NSDAP and the *völkisch* movement more generally. Without him, the party and movement fractured into countless competing splinter groups. No leader emerged to rival Hitler. Hitler's biographer, Ian Kershaw, argues that all this led Hitler to believe that he – and he alone – was destined to be Germany's savior. Only he had the messianic qualities necessary to lead his adopted country to national salvation.

In Landsberg, Hitler dictated *Mein Kampf*, part autobiography and part rambling exposition of the few crude ideas that animated his worldview. He insisted that the "Germanic" race was biologically superior. Racial purity, he insisted, was the basis for national health and survival; the intermixing of races brought social decay. He raged on about Jews, claiming that Bolshevism was a Jewish strategy for world domination. He also linked anti-Bolshevism to the notion of *Lebensraum*. By destroying Soviet Russia, he argued, Germany would eradicate world Jewry and acquire additional territory, thus securing the future of the "Germanic" race. Given Hitler's hostility toward Marxism, one may well wonder what was socialist or proworker about the NSDAP – even if its official name was the National *Socialist* German *Workers*' Party. For Hitler, however, the "social idea" was not based on a conventional understanding of socialism as government control of industry and advancing workers' rights. Instead, it meant forging a "national community" (*Volksgemeinschaft*), based on racial purity, that would overcome class and other divisions in society.

Against the wishes of the Bavarian state prosecutor, Hitler was released from prison in December 1924. He now changed political tactics. He would seek power not through a coup (like the Beer Hall Putsch) but through legal means. He soon managed to have the NSDAP legalized. He then set about using democratic freedoms, including the ballot box, to destroy the republic.

In February 1925, Hitler refounded what had become a badly factionalized party. A north German wing, under Gregor Strasser and Joseph Goebbels, was eager to challenge the dominance of the corrupt Munich wing. It was also more committed to a conventional understanding of socialism. Hitler worked to unite the warring factions. At the 1926 Bamberg party conference, he won over Strasser and Goebbels. Once again, he secured personal mastery over the party. The "Heil Hitler" greeting, made compulsory within the party that same year, symbolized the growing Führer cult. As many scholars have noted, Hitler had become the party's sole program and organizational focal point. His charismatic leadership was *the* integrative force of the party. No loyal party member questioned Hitler's leadership or program. Dissenters soon found themselves outside the National Socialist fold.

Gregor Strasser played a key role in developing the party's organization and tactics. He turned the NSDAP into a nationwide party organization, with party cells in every part of the country. Party membership tripled – to 150,000 – between the Beer Hall Putsch and the eve of the Great Depression. Strasser also developed Nazi associations that catered to diverse groups in society. Among others, he built up the Hitler Youth, the NS-Frauenschaft (a women's organization), and the National Socialist German Students' League – Nazi society in embryo. At the same time, the party experimented with new tactics. Between 1926 and 1928, it followed an urban plan of trying to win over German workers. Workers, however, refused to abandon their loyalties to the Social Democratic Party (SPD) and the Communist Party of Germany (KPD). In summer 1928, the NSDAP changed tactics, now adopting a nationalist-rural plan. It trumpeted a chauvinistic nationalism to middle-class Germans while appealing to farmers angry with the ongoing agrarian depression. The Nazis had found a recipe for success.

Early followers

Virtually all of the leading men in the Third Reich joined the NSDAP in the 1920s. Besides those already mentioned, these included Heinrich Himmler – later head of the Schutzstaffel (Protection Squad), better known as the SS – and Martin Bormann, later head of the Party Chancellory and Hitler's private secretary. Many second-tier Nazis, including most of the regional party leaders, known as *Gauleiters*, also joined in the 1920s. So, too, did many others who later became Nazi functionaries. Perhaps more than anything else, Hitler prized loyalty in his followers. Those who joined the party before he came to power were even known as "Old Fighters" – an official title that carried perquisites.

But who were the early followers? What distinguished them? Historians long believed that early Nazi devotees were disillusioned war veterans – often Free Corps volunteers – who failed to reintegrate into society after World War I. Unable to give up the life of combative adventure, so this argument went, these men were attracted to the violent extremism of the NSDAP. While some early Nazis fit this description, most were not war veterans at all.

Many early Nazis were too young to have fought in World War I. They spent the war years playing war games and listening to patriotic speeches. Brought up on war propaganda, they were shocked by Germany's defeat and the ensuing Treaty of Versailles. They felt cheated in that the war was over before they could prove their manhood in battle. The French occupation of the Rhineland and Ruhr heightened their rabid nationalism. Hyperinflation was another shock. As the youngest in a glut of workers, they were often unable to secure jobs. University-trained professionals faced similarly uncertain job prospects. Young

German adults thus made up a "superfluous" generation. For them, only radical solutions held promise. They flocked to the Nazis.

In 1934, a sociologist at Columbia University, Theodore Abel, ran an essay contest among pre-1933 NSDAP members for the "Best Personal Life History of an Adherent of the Hitler Movement." These autobiographies suggest the appeal of Nazism to early devotees, whether war veterans or the younger generation. The promise of a "true" national community distinguished Nazism from other right-wing movements. One author, for example, insisted on the NSDAP's "uncompromising will to stamp out the class struggle, snobberies of caste, and party hatreds." Members were drawn into the movement by Nazi discipline, energy, and violence. As an early follower wrote, "I always felt happy to see the… brown-clad soldiers march through the city with rhythmic strides and straightforward mien." Perhaps most important, Hitler's charismatic leadership – and especially his extraordinary speaking abilities – won over countless passionate followers. "As the Fuehrer addressed us," one early party member remembered, "his eyes became like hands that gripped men never to let go again." Unlike the established political parties, the NSDAP bespoke missionary zeal, fanatical devotion, and passionate engagement. "The joy of fighting for Hitler's principle gave my life a new meaning," an early NSDAP activist declared. To early Nazi adherents, Hitler and his movement portended both their own and Germany's salvation.

The Nazi Rise to Power, 1929–1933

Even before the Great Depression set in at the end of 1929, the NSDAP was gaining traction. While the party won just 2.6% of votes – and twelve seats – in the Reichstag elections in May 1928, it gained in local and state elections in 1929. In June 1929, the NSDAP even won a municipal election in Coburg, which became the first town subject to Nazi rule. Hitler also received an unexpected boost from the newspaper magnate Alfred Hugenberg, the leader of the right-wing German National People's Party (DNVP). In fall 1929, Hugenberg invited Hitler to join his campaign against the Young Plan, an international agreement to reduce and reschedule reparations that involved Germany making payments until 1988. Although the campaign against the Young Plan was a resounding failure, the Hugenberg press gave Hitler much free publicity. Hitler's verve struck an appealing contrast to the stuffy elitism of Hugenberg and other right-wing politicians.

In late October 1929, the New York Stock Exchange crashed after the bubble burst on millions of investors who had borrowed money to invest in a speculative stock market. Lenders now called in not only American debt but also short-term loans that they had made to German businesses. Many German companies, short of capital, collapsed. Already by the end of 1929, 1.9 million Germans had no work. In the next years, German industrial production dropped by 42%. The German stock index fell by two-thirds. By summer 1932, roughly one-third of the workforce, 6.2 million Germans, was unemployed. German city streets, crowded with vagrants, panhandlers, and urchins, became scenes of unalleviated misery. The Depression sealed the fate of the Weimar Republic – and opened the door to Nazi triumph.

The demise of the Weimar Republic

The demise of the Weimar Republic and Hitler's assumption of power are two separate stories. Hitler did not destroy the republic. Conservative elites did that. In this, they were aided by the Weimar Constitution. Most important, the constitution gave the president considerable powers. The president had the right to dissolve parliament and call new elections (Article 25). He had the right to appoint and dismiss a chancellor and cabinet ministers (Article 53). He had the power to issue decrees in emergency situations (Article 48). And he had the right to remove an elected (provincial) state government if the security of the Reich was threatened (also Article 48). In the 1930s, Field Marshal Paul von Hindenburg, the hero of World War I, was president. Elected in 1925, Hindenburg had sworn an oath to uphold the Weimar Constitution. At heart, though, he preferred authoritarian government. At the same time, he was an octogenarian, no longer at the height of his physical and mental powers. He was easily manipulated by a small coterie of sycophantic advisors.

The president's strong executive power contrasted with the weakness of the parliament. The Weimar Constitution foresaw proportional representation. Even fringe parties received Reichstag seats corresponding to their percentage of the popular vote. The proliferation of parties meant that all governments were coalition governments. But coalition government is inherently unstable; it is always hostage to the whims of its partners. In its fourteen-year history, the Weimar Republic saw fifteen different chancellors and twenty-one different cabinets.

In March 1930, a coalition government, involving both the SPD and the pro-business German People's Party (DVP), could not agree on how to fund the unemployment insurance program (which faced deficits resulting from the unemployment crisis). That government fell, and Heinrich Brüning, a right-wing politician who belonged to the Catholic Center Party, became the new chancellor. Brüning did not engage in work creation or other government spending to counter the effects of the Depression. Instead, he and other conservatives believed that it was necessary to slash state spending so as to preserve a stable currency. The hyperinflation of 1923 thus came back to haunt German politics. Fear of inflation locked German decision makers into a set of policies that only deepened economic misery; indeed, Brüning's uncaring policies earned him the epithet "Hunger Chancellor." The chancellor's policies were also rooted in other motives. Brüning wished to use the economic downturn to break the influence of the SPD, weaken the role of the Reichstag, and prove that Germany was unable to make reparations payments.

Unable to secure a stable majority in the Reichstag, Brüning initiated "presidential" government: bypassing parliament, he relied on presidential powers to issue laws. This began in July 1930 when the Reichstag rejected Brüning's proposed budget bill. In turn, the chancellor used Article 48 to issue the budget by emergency decree. The Reichstag, as was its right, then rescinded the budget. Next, Brüning had Hindenburg dissolve the parliament. By law, elections had to take place within sixty days. In the interim, Brüning reissued his economic measures via emergency decree. Since the new parliament was not yet in existence, no parliamentary authority could challenge him. The chancellor thus began the process of subverting Weimar democracy – and paving the way for the Nazi assumption of power.

Brüning hoped that the new Reichstag election would return a working majority for him. But the outcome of the September 1930 elections proved a shock to everyone. Voters abandoned the moderate and liberal parties that supported the Weimar Republic to give the Nazis an astonishing victory. The Nazi vote rocketed from 2.6% to 18.3% of the electorate. With 107 seats, the NSDAP became the second-largest party in the Reichstag.

As Table 2.1 suggests, by 1930, German politics had become so polarized that no viable coalition was possible. The SPD, Center, and liberal parties could not agree on a response to the Depression; the SPD and the KPD had been allergic to each other since the 1919 Spartacist Uprising; the Center and the NSDAP, committed to very different politics, could not work together; and the Nazis and the KPD collaborated only to create parliamentary chaos. As election results show, there was no plausible working majority in the early 1930s. (In 1932, two parties intent on destroying the republic, the NSDAP and KPD, even held a majority of Reichstag votes.)

Nazi tactics

By summer 1930, the NSDAP had developed a well-oiled electoral machine. The Nazis engaged in frenetic saturation campaigning. Nazi leaders gave passionate speeches at campaign rallies. Nazi supporters went door to door explaining their message. They tirelessly distributed their political literature. They plastered cities, towns, and villages with their posters. The SA displayed the strength of its uniformed ranks in countless marches. Everywhere, Germans saw energetic Nazis on the go, working for the cause, eager for change. As one housewife later wrote, "There was a feeling of restless energy about the Nazis.

Table 2.1 Election results of major parties, Reichstag elections 1928–1933.

Party	May 20, 1928		September 14, 1930		July 31, 1932		November 6, 1932		March 5, 1933	
	% of vote	No. deputies	% of vote	No. deputies	% of vote	No. deputies	% of vote	No. deputies	% of vote	No. deputies
Center	12.1	62	11.8	68	12.5	75	11.9	70	11.7	74
DDP	4.9	25	3.8	20	1.0	4	1.0	2	0.8	5
DNVP	14.2	73	7.0	41	5.9	37	8.8	52	8.0	52
DVP	8.7	45	4.5	30	1.2	7	1.9	11	1.1	2
KPD	10.6	54	13.1	77	14.6	89	16.9	100	12.3	81
NSDAP	2.6	12	18.3	107	37.4	230	33.1	196	43.9	288
SPD	29.8	153	24.5	143	21.6	133	20.4	121	18.3	120
Total		491		577		608		584		647

Due to votes for minor parties, the percentages do not add up to 100%. Similarly, the numbers of deputies do not add up to the total number of deputies in any given Reichstag.

Source: Roderick Stackelberg, *Hitler's Germany: Origins, Interpretations, Legacies*, Second Edition (London: Routledge, 2009), pp. 104–105.

You constantly saw the swastika painted on the sidewalks… I was drawn by the feeling of strength about the party." Such zealous activity contrasted sharply with the sleepy campaigns of the other parties.

Hitler remained the party's most valuable asset. In mass rallies, he downplayed his antisemitism, knowing it had limited appeal to most Germans. A true politician, he tailored his message to his audience. To farmers, he promised high tariffs to eliminate foreign competition. To small retailers, he denounced department stores. To big-business leaders, he emphasized the sanctity of private property. Mostly, though, he railed on about the divisiveness of parliamentary politics, the self-interest of political leaders, and the national humiliation imposed by the Versailles Treaty. In the republic's stead, he promised a vague vision of a strong Germany. Nazism would overcome class divisions, Germans would work together as a racial community, and the Nazis would rebuild the economy. Germany would win back its rightful place on the world stage.

Nazi violence seemed to help, rather than hurt, the movement. Many Germans (wrongly) believed that Social Democrats and communists were on the verge of insurrection. Some welcomed Nazi violence against leftists – whether street battles, disruption of socialist rallies, or the beating up of individual oppositional politicians. Other Germans, though, found the general violence distasteful. Indeed, SA storm troopers fomented violence so that the Nazis could fulminate against the republic's inability to maintain law and order. At the same time, many early Nazis believed that the police and the judiciary favored leftists in the Weimar Republic. They later recalled this period as a "time of struggle" (*Kampfzeit*), when all the forces of the establishment were allegedly arrayed against them. More often than not, though, the police looked away when SA thugs attacked leftists.

The Nazis deployed a host of unethical practices in their electoral campaigns. They threatened to boycott farmers or small businessmen who did not join or otherwise support the party. Nazi employers discriminated against non-Nazi workers; during the Depression, some workers faced the stark choice of being fired or showing support for the Nazis. The Nazis also disrupted other parties' campaign events. They heckled others' rallies or scheduled counter-marches to demonstrate their strength vis-à-vis other paramilitary groupings. On occasion, they continuously rented out choice venues, making it impossible for others to use those locations for *their* political events. These sorts of practices complicate the notion that the Nazis came to power "legally." While the Nazis assumed power by the letter of the law, at every turn they violated the spirit of the Weimar Constitution.

Nazi voters

Who voted for the Nazis? While Hitler's party made the greatest inroads among voters in the Protestant towns and rural areas of northern Germany, the Nazis attracted German voters of all stripes: northern and southern, urban and rural, old and young, men and women, rich and poor, educated and uneducated, reputable and ignoble. Just two groups proved resistant to the Nazis. Catholics stuck to their Center Party, and most urban workers continued to support the SPD or the more militant KPD.

Many historians suggest that Nazi voters were primarily protest voters. Fed up with the republic, they voted for the Nazis to protest a system they despised. The historian Peter Fritzsche, however, argues that the Nazis offered a new kind of politics that many Germans found appealing. These Germans fondly recalled the "spirit of 1914," when the country had pulled together for the war effort. They now sought a politics that transcended the polarizing interest-group politics that characterized the Weimar political system. They were drawn to a dynamic movement that seemed to promote both nationalism and social justice. Hitler's message of German unity, strength, and renewal resonated with them.

Political stalemate

Although Hitler achieved a stunning victory in September 1930, he was a long way from power. Only the president could appoint him chancellor, but Hindenburg was reluctant to do so. Furthermore, conservative elites faced a quandary: how to alter Germany's political system without an outright violation of the constitution. Since only parliament could approve constitutional changes, they needed Reichstag, and thus Nazi, support. Hitler, though, proved an elusive partner.

Throughout 1931, German politics remained in a stalemate. Brüning headed a minority government tolerated by Social Democrats (who feared the advent of an even more rightist government). The chancellor frequently resorted to emergency decrees. In March 1931, for example, he curbed press freedom, particularly where it concerned criticism of the government. His actions anticipated Nazi press laws. Meanwhile, the German economy continued to sour. This, however, allowed Brüning to make headway on the reparations issue. In the face of Germany's catastrophic economic situation, he secured a one-year moratorium on reparations payments in June 1931. The following year, he laid the groundwork for negotiations that ended reparations payments altogether.

Despite their electoral success, Hitler and the NSDAP faced a series of crises. The SA, now led by Ernst Röhm, was difficult to control. Many storm troopers were impatient with Hitler's insistence that he achieve power through legal means. Too often, the SA unleashed violence at inopportune moments. Hitler was also implicated in scandal. He seems to have been romantically involved with his niece, Geli Raubal. In September 1931, using Hitler's pistol, Raubal committed suicide. While Hitler was initially inconsolable, his life revolved around politics. While German tabloids fed on Raubal's suicide, Hitler threw himself into his quest for power.

1932: The year of elections

In 1932, most Germans voted in five major elections: two rounds of presidential elections in March and April, state elections in late April, and Reichstag elections in July and November. In March, Hitler challenged the aging Hindenburg for the presidency. The Nazis pulled out all their electoral stops. Hitler won 30% of the vote. Since Hindenburg failed to secure the absolute majority needed (other candidates split the remaining votes), a second round followed in April. In a first for German politics, Hitler chartered an airplane for his electoral campaign. Under the slogan "the Führer over Germany," he flew from city to city, dropped in on mass rallies, and fired up his listeners. The Nazis also swamped Germany with posters, leaflets, meetings, and marches. While Hindenburg won – with the support of the SPD and liberal parties – Hitler captured 37% of the vote. Shortly thereafter, in state elections, the Nazis won 36.3% of the votes in the largest state, Prussia. But, as Goebbels noted, "We must come to power in the foreseeable future. Otherwise we'll win ourselves to death in elections."

In May 1932, Hindenburg was displeased with Brüning's inability to stabilize the political situation, and the chancellor resigned. Advisors to the president, including the maverick General Kurt von Schleicher, suggested Franz von Papen, a nominal member of the Center Party with little political experience, as the next chancellor. Since Schleicher and Papen were old friends, the general expected Papen to follow his orders. As of June 1932, Papen headed a so-called "cabinet of barons" – men with weak party affiliations who claimed to rule in Germany's national interest. Papen, too, hoped to create a more authoritarian order. In search of Reichstag support, he turned to Hitler. The Führer promised vague cooperation, provided that a recent ban on the SA was rescinded and that new elections take place. Papen duly had the Reichstag dissolved. New elections were set for July 31.

A summer of political violence ensued. The SA battled leftists in nasty street incidents all across Germany. On July 20, Papen's cynical response was to depose the Prussian government, run by the SPD, for its alleged inability to uphold law and order. Using Article 48, Papen became Reich commissar in Prussia. In one blow, he weakened the SPD, undermined German federalism, and centralized state power. The SPD lodged a legal protest. But it could do little else. Calling a general strike was out of the question – too many unemployed workers would take over strikers' jobs. In spring 1933, the Nazis would imitate Papen's tactics in taking over other provincial states.

The July 1932 elections were another milestone for the Nazis. Using their tried and tested methods, the Nazis won the support of 37.4% of the electorate – the high-water mark of Nazi ballot success. With the votes of 13.7 million Germans, the NSDAP had 230 seats in the Reichstag and was by far the largest parliamentary faction. Hitler now aimed for the chancellorship, even though he, too, did not command a Reichstag majority. But he received a rebuff. Hindenburg refused to appoint the "Bohemian corporal," as he contemptuously called Hitler, chancellor. The president insisted that he could not hand over governmental power to a single party known for its intolerance. He offered Hitler the vice-chancellorship. Hitler, however, resorted to brinkmanship, a hallmark of his career. He insisted that he would be named chancellor or not participate in government at all.

Hitler's strategy carried enormous risks. The Nazis had enjoyed extraordinary electoral successes. But, as Goebbels rightly feared, if the Nazis could not show results – that is, come to power – their support would ebb. By later summer 1932 the party was desperately short on cash, raised largely through membership fees and local party groups' fundraising activities. Now, however, morale in the movement was flagging. The 400,000 SA men were restless. Many Nazi voters were unhappy with Hitler's refusal to enter government.

In its very first act, the Reichstag elected in July passed a vote of no confidence in Papen's government. New elections were called for November 6. These elections confirmed the Nazi disarray. The NSDAP polled 33.1% of the vote, a loss of some two million votes and thirty-four Reichstag seats. In a December 1932 election in Thuringia, Nazi electoral support plunged by 40% from its July high. The Nazi movement had seemingly crested.

Papen's intrigues

Just when the Nazi threat seemed to have diminished, intrigue revived Hitler's fortunes. Following the November elections, Papen had little support in the Reichstag. He hoped, though, to use Article 48 to revise the constitution in favor of a stronger executive, a weakened parliament, and perhaps a ban on extremist political parties. Schleicher and other conservatives, however, feared that Papen's proposed actions might provoke leftists to begin a civil war that the army could not suppress. Schleicher thus engineered Papen's fall. In turn, he became chancellor in early December. Papen was furious with his erstwhile friend, and he had Hindenburg's ear. As events soon showed, the old president was annoyed with Schleicher for having ousted Papen. Although seemingly trivial, these personal antipathies played a major role in bringing Hitler to power – underscoring just how much Hitler's appointment as chancellor was due to chance.

Schleicher aimed to create an authoritarian regime that relied on Nazi popular support. He thus made overtures to Gregor Strasser, the Nazi leader who took the party's commitment to socialism most seriously. This precipitated further crisis in the NSDAP. Hitler feared that Strasser might join Schleicher, potentially splitting his movement. But, while Strasser bitterly opposed Hitler's all-or-nothing strategy, he had no intention of challenging Hitler. Instead, the popular Nazi resigned from the party. Shortly thereafter, the Nazis faced another electoral campaign: the tiny state of Lippe, overwhelmingly rural and Protestant, was to hold elections on January 15, 1933. Pouring everything they had into the campaign, the Nazis secured 39.5% of that vote. They could thus claim a resounding electoral victory.

By then, a series of meetings had taken place that would culminate in Hitler's appointment as chancellor. Papen was desperate to topple Schleicher and wanted to use Hitler to accomplish his aims. In mid-December, he had a chance meeting with a Cologne banker, Kurt von Schroeder. Schroeder, a Nazi sympathizer, offered to host a secret meeting between Papen and Hitler. The January 4 meeting proved inconclusive. Both Hitler and Papen insisted on being chancellor in any joint cabinet. Still, the door was open to further negotiations. In the next weeks, Papen had several further meetings with Hitler and other top Nazis. He also sounded out politicians in other parties about serving in a cabinet with Hitler. Finally, he apprised the president's closest advisors of his plans. Most important, Papen recognized that he would have to accede to Hitler's demand to be chancellor. He believed, though, that he would be able to "tame" Hitler.

Papen's efforts went into high gear after Hindenburg refused Schleicher's request to dissolve the Reichstag. The chancellor, having lost the president's support, resigned on January 28. Papen now even misled Hindenburg. Hitler, like his predecessors, expected to use presidential powers to rule. Papen, however, told Hindenburg that the planned government, headed by Hitler and with representatives from other parties, would command a majority in the Reichstag. In turn, Hindenburg was convinced by his close advisors that a government headed by Hitler would break the political impasse. Reluctantly, he assented to Papen's urging that he name Hitler as chancellor.

On January 30, 1933, Hindenburg swore in Hitler as chancellor. Hitler thus attained power through legal means. His new government included just three Nazis (see Chapter 3). "Within two months," Papen told a skeptical conservative acquaintance, "we will have pushed Hitler so far into a corner that he'll squeak." Papen, the new vice-chancellor, and other conservatives had underestimated Hitler. They believed that they could control him. But they, not Hitler, would soon squeak.

Contingency and history

There was nothing inevitable about the Nazi assumption of power. By January 1933, the NSDAP had suffered significant electoral losses. It was deep in debt. Members were leaving in droves. Erstwhile supporters cancelled subscriptions to the party press. In student union elections, Nazi support dropped from 48% in 1932 to 43% in early 1933. Moreover, the worst of the Depression was over. The value of stocks and bonds traded on the Frankfurt Stock Exchange had risen by 30% since spring 1932.

Long-term historical trends created the context in which Hitler's coming to power was possible. In the nineteenth century, chauvinistic nationalism, scientific racism, and antisemitism had shaped a strong right-wing milieu in Germany. At the same time, divisive Bismarckian politics and Wilhelmine militarism had left Germans ill prepared for future democracy. After World War I, the Treaty of Versailles, hyperinflation, and the Great Depression caused Germans to question democracy. Many Germans thus sought an alternative to the liberal Weimar Republic. At the same time, bitter hostility between Social Democrats and communists prevented leftist unity against the Nazi threat.

Hitler's assumption of power is best explained through short-term developments. From 1919 onward, Hitler proved his political finesse. He turned the NSDAP from a debate club into a disciplined party. He developed himself into a spellbinding, charismatic leader. He brilliantly exploited the fallout of the Beer Hall Putsch. He organized the party into an electoral juggernaut. Hitler also benefited from the blunders, miscalculations, and intrigues of others. Bavarian authorities could have kept him in prison; at the time of his release in 1924, he had served only a small portion of a light sentence for high treason. In addition, the chancellors who preceded Hitler bear responsibility for his rise to power. They could have focused on halting him, rather than destroying democracy. Brüning could have taken steps to alleviate mass misery, thus eliminating the economic discontent that fed Nazi success at the polls. Papen could have curbed the SA, not weakened the SPD. He could have checked his desire for revenge against Schleicher. Schleicher might have used various parliamentary tactics to delay convening the Reichstag; in the interim, the economy might have improved and the Nazi movement fallen further into disarray. Finally, President Hindenburg, who alone had the power to appoint the chancellor, could have ignored his small-minded confidantes' advice and continued to block Hitler's path to the chancellorship.

Hitler's rise illustrates the power of contingency in history. While many Germans disliked Weimar democracy, this did not ensure a Nazi dictatorship. In the early 1930s, other scenarios – such as military dictatorship or continued presidential government – might have resolved the republic's crisis. It is true, of course, that Hitler's political skills made him a viable candidate for chancellor. Still, he did not command a working majority in the Reichstag. Hindenburg did not have to appoint him chancellor. In fact, Hitler came to power just when his electoral fortunes were waning. A small group of unaccountable politicians, eager to smash democracy in Germany, handed Hitler the chancellorship. In no small measure, Hitler's success rested on luck and chance.

Citations for Quotations

Page	Source

Page   *Source*

21   "I, for my part, …" Adolf Hitler, *Mein Kampf* (Boston: Houghton Mifflin, 1943), 206.

21   "revolt of the masses." From title of José Ortega y Gasset, *The Revolt of the Masses* (New York: Norton, 1932).

23   "In addition to…" Hitler, *Mein Kampf*, 22.

24   "fatherland," and "will find…" Quoted in Thomas Weber, *Hitler's First War: Adolf Hitler, the Men of the List Regiment, and the First World War* (Oxford: Oxford University Press, 2010), 70.

24   "Nearly every clerk…" Hitler, *Mein Kampf*, 193.

24   "war hysteria." Quoted in Weber, *Hitler's First War*, 221.

25   "I could 'speak.'" Hitler, *Mein Kampf*, 215–216.

25   "must unshakably be…" Quoted in Ian Kershaw, *Hitler 1889–1936: Hubris* (New York: W.W. Norton, 1998), 125.

25   "redemptive anti-Semitism." Saul Friedländer, *Nazi Germany and the Jews: The Years of Persecution, 1933–1939* (New York: HarperCollins, 1997), 73–112.

25   "a dull organization." Hitler, *Mein Kampf*, 219.

26   "union of all Germans…" Quoted in Louis L. Snyder, ed., *Hitler's Third Reich* (Chicago: Nelson-Hall, 1981), 23–25.

27   "with dictatorial power." Quoted in Kershaw, *Hitler 1889–1936*, 164.

42   "Unconquerable" and "the Strong One…" Quoted in Kershaw, *Hitler 1889–1936*, 50.

29   "the crime of November 1918." Quoted in Kershaw, *Hitler 1889–1936*, 214.

29   "wilderness." Quoted in Kershaw, *Hitler 1889–1936*, 299.

32   "superfluous." Detlev J.K. Peukert, *The Weimar Republic: The Crisis of Classical Modernity* (New York: Hill and Wang, 1992), 89.

32   "uncompromising will to…" Quoted in Theodore Abel, *Why Hitler Came into Power: An Answer Based on the Original Life Stories of Six Hundred of His Followers* (New York: Prentice-Hall, 1938), 143.

32   "I always felt…" Quoted in Abel, *Why Hitler Came into Power*, 176.

32   "As the Fuehrer…" and "his eyes became…" Quoted in Abel, *Why Hitler Came into Power*, 153.

32   "The joy of fighting…" Quoted in Abel, *Why Hitler Came into Power*, 146.

34   "Hunger Chancellor." Quoted in Richard J. Evans, *The Coming of the Third Reich* (London: Penguin, 2003), 254.

34   "There was a feeling…" Quoted in William Sheridan Allen, *The Nazi Seizure of Power: The Experience of a Single German Town 1922–1945*, Revised Edition (New York: Franklin Watts, 1985), 32.

38   "the Führer over Germany." Quoted in Kershaw, *Hitler 1889–1936*, 363.

38   "We must come to power…" Quoted in Kershaw, Hitler 1889–1936, 364.

38   "cabinet of barons." Quoted in Henry Ashby Turner Jr., Hitler's Thirty Days to Power: January 1933 (Reading, MA: Addison-Wesley, 1996), 8.

39   "Bohemian corporal." Quoted in Kershaw, Hitler 1889–1936, 371.

40   "Within two months" and "we will have…" Quoted in Evans, The Coming of the Third Reich, 308.

Bibliography

Abel, Theodore. *Why Hitler Came into Power: An Answer Based on the Original Life Stories of Six Hundred of His Followers.* New York: Prentice-Hall, 1938.

Allen, William Sheridan. *The Nazi Seizure of Power: The Experience of a Single German Town 1922–1945.* Revised Edition. New York: Franklin Watts, 1985.

Bessel, Richard. *Political Violence and the Rise of Nazism: The Storm Troopers in Eastern Germany, 1925–1931.* New Haven: Yale University Press, 1984.

Bullock, Alan. *Hitler: A Study in Tyranny.* New York: Harper, 1952.

Campbell, Bruce. *The SA Generals and the Rise of Nazism.* Lexington: University Press of Kentucky, 1998.

Donson, Andrew. *Youth in the Fatherless Land: War Pedagogy, Nationalism, and Authority in Germany, 1914–1918.* Cambridge, MA: Harvard University Press, 2010.

Evans, Richard J. *The Coming of the Third Reich.* London: Penguin, 2003.

Fest, Joachim C. *Hitler.* New York: Harcourt, Brace, Jovanovich, 1974.

Fritzsche, Peter. *Germans into Nazis.* Cambridge, MA: Harvard University Press, 1998.

Gordon, Harold J. *Hitler and the Beer Hall Putsch.* Princeton: Princeton University Press, 1972.

Hitler, Adolf. *Mein Kampf.* Boston: Houghton Mifflin, 1943.

Kershaw, Ian. *Hitler 1889–1936: Hubris.* New York: W.W. Norton, 1998.

Merkl, Peter H. *Political Violence under the Swastika: 581 Early Nazis.* Princeton: Princeton University Press, 1975.

Orlow, Dietrich. *The History of the Nazi Party: 1919–1933.* Pittsburgh: University of Pittsburgh Press, 1969.

Peukert, Detlev J.K. *The Weimar Republic: The Crisis of Classical Modernity.* New York: Hill and Wang, 1992.

Turner, Henry Ashby, Jr. *Hitler's Thirty Days to Power: January 1933.* Reading, MA: Addison-Wesley, 1996.

Waite, Robert G.L. *Vanguard of Nazism: The Free Corps Movement in Postwar Germany 1918–1923.* Cambridge, MA: Harvard University Press, 1952.

Weber, Thomas. *Hitler's First War: Adolf Hitler, the Men of the List Regiment, and the First World War.* Oxford: Oxford University Press, 2010.

3

The Nazi Party-State

"If we do one day achieve power," Adolf Hitler told a crowd on October 17, 1932, "we will hold on to it, so help us God. We will not allow them to take it away from us again." Hitler held true to his words. After he came to power, he established a dictatorial regime. He eliminated the last vestiges of the parliamentary order. Brooking no challenge to his rule, he destroyed the political opposition. It would take World War II, and the combined might of the Allies, to dislodge Hitler from power.

There is a myth that the Third Reich terrorized all Germans into fearful submission. While terror and coercion *did* accompany the regime's consolidation, the reality of Nazi dictatorship was more complex. There is also a myth that the Nazi dictatorship was an efficient, streamlined operation. Once installed, however, the Nazi regime was chaotic. Hitler rarely made decisions, leaving officials to discern his wishes. Party and state offices duplicated each other. The regime fragmented into the personal fiefdoms of top Nazis.

This chapter outlines how Hitler achieved total control of Germany. It details the imposition of one-party rule. It explores the process of *Gleichschaltung* (coordination) – that is, how the Nazis came to control German society. It then turns to how Hitler destroyed the paramilitary Sturmabteilung (SA) and its leader, Ernst Röhm. Next, it describes the coercive apparatus of the Third Reich, especially the all-important fusion of the police and the Schutzstaffel (SS), the Nazi Party's "Protection Squad." Finally, it raises intriguing questions about the nature of Nazi dictatorship. How did the dualism of party-state rule play out? What role did Hitler play in the Third Reich? Was he a "strong" or "weak" dictator?

Nazi Germany: Confronting the Myths, First Edition. Catherine Epstein.
© 2015 John Wiley & Sons, Ltd. Published 2015 by John Wiley & Sons, Ltd.

The Death of Democracy

Once appointed chancellor on January 30, 1933, Hitler headed a cabinet in which he was one of just three Nazis. Besides Hitler, Wilhelm Frick was interior minister and Hermann Göring minister without portfolio. Otherwise, Franz von Papen was vice-chancellor. Alfred Hugenberg, leader of the conservative German National People's Party (DNVP), was economics minister. Franz Seldte, head of the Stahlhelm, the paramilitary veterans' organization, was minister of labor. President Paul von Hindenburg had personally chosen the minister of defense, General Werner von Blomberg. Other ministers were holdovers from the Brüning, Papen, and Schleicher governments. With so many non-Nazi ministers, it seemed that Hitler would have little leeway to determine developments.

Events soon proved otherwise. As a condition for assuming the chancellorship, Hitler insisted on new elections. He was eager to secure a two-thirds Reichstag majority so that he could make changes to the constitution. Elections were set for March 5. The government's campaign slogan was "Attack on Marxism." As in earlier elections, the Nazis blanketed the country with electoral propaganda. But, this time around, they had plenty of funds. At a meeting with leading businessmen, Hitler and Göring bullied industrialists into making financial sacrifices so as to defeat the threat of Marxism; the meeting ended with industrialists pledging some three million Reichsmarks to Nazi campaign coffers.

The Nazis also deployed the resources of the state to their electoral advantage. Just like the preceding three chancellors, Hitler made use of presidential emergency powers. As early as February 4, the government issued a Decree for the Protection of the German People. This allowed the government to impose more press restrictions. It also permitted "protective custody." For up to three months and without due process, the government could imprison individuals who had committed acts of armed violence. This provision was not, of course, used against Nazis – those who committed the brunt of such violence. Instead, the government banned leftist newspapers and arrested members of the Communist Party of Germany (KPD) and the Social Democratic Party (SPD).

In addition, the Nazis used the police to their benefit. While Göring had no portfolio in the federal government, he was acting Prussian minister of the interior. On February 22, he made some 50,000 SA, SS, and Stahlhelm members auxiliary police in Prussia. This gave license to bands of marauding Nazi thugs to attack Jews, KPD and SPD activists, and other political opponents. Moreover, the SA set up makeshift jails and improvised concentration camps; there were 100 such camps in the Berlin area alone. SA men tortured prisoners with iron bars, whips, and rubber truncheons.

On the evening of February 27, the Reichstag went up in flames. A Dutchman, Marinus van der Lubbe, allegedly set the fire so as to draw attention to the misery of the working class. Because the fire played so well into Nazi strategy, however, observers have long wondered whether the National Socialist German Workers' Party (NSDAP) was somehow involved. Recent publications have renewed but not resolved this controversy. Regardless, Hitler, Göring, and Joseph Goebbels rushed to the scene. With no evidence at all, Hitler insisted that the fire signaled the start of a communist insurrection. The regime immediately set about arresting thousands of communists.

The next morning, February 28, Hitler presented the cabinet with another emergency decree, "For the Protection of People and State." This decree suspended – with no end date – personal liberties guaranteed by the Weimar Constitution. It abrogated freedoms of speech, association, and the press. The government could hold individuals indefinitely in "protective custody." The decree also permitted the Reich cabinet (not the president) to override the autonomy of the federal states so as to restore order. Coming just a week before elections, the decree stymied the KPD's campaign. KPD leader Ernst Thälmann and many other communists were arrested. Government officials ransacked KPD offices, broke up meetings, and banned party newspapers. The Nazis also targeted SPD and trade-union activists. Many Germans, fearful of a leftist uprising, welcomed these draconian measures.

Elections took place on March 5. Despite their advantages, the Nazis improved their share of the vote to just 43.9%. Their coalition partners, the conservatives, won 8%. The KPD managed to win 12.3% and the SPD 18.3% of the vote (see Table 2.1). More than half of the electorate still favored other parties over the NSDAP, and almost a third backed leftist parties. Hitler was disappointed. He was determined to secure an Enabling Act that would allow him to issue legislation without Reichstag consent for a period of four years. He would also no longer have to rely on Hindenburg to issue emergency presidential decrees. But, to pass an Enabling Act – to change the constitution – the Nazis needed not only a two-thirds majority but also a set quorum, two-thirds of parliamentary representatives present. Together with their conservative partners, they held just 340 of the 647 seats in the new Reichstag.

The Nazis now finagled a Reichstag vote in their favor. As presiding officer of the Reichstag, Göring decided that the KPD delegation simply didn't count. This high-handed measure reduced the necessary quorum. (In fact, every one of the eighty-one elected communist deputies was arrested, living underground, or had fled the country.) To ensure a quorum of remaining Reichstag members, Göring carried out another sleight of hand. Representatives absent without excuse would be counted as present. Still, the Nazis needed thirty-eight additional "yes" votes. By harassing Catholic civil servants and promising religious autonomy, they bullied Catholic Center Party deputies into capitulation. At the Reichstag meeting on March 23, the SPD leader, Otto Wels, spoke courageously against the proposed legislation. But it made no difference. By a vote of 441 to 94 (the entire SPD delegation present voted no), the Enabling Act passed. The Reichstag stripped itself of its powers – a supreme act of democratic self-abnegation. Hitler could now rule Germany free of parliamentary control. Just like his appointment as chancellor, he achieved the Enabling Act by formally legal (if dubious) means. The Reichstag renewed the Enabling Act in 1937 and 1939. In 1943, it was made permanent.

In March 1933, the Nazis took over many provincial state governments. In a scenario repeated in a number of states, SA thugs created violent disturbances. Local Nazis then turned to Frick, minister of the interior, seeking Reich intervention. Under the pretense of restoring order (following the emergency decree of February 28), Frick appointed a Nazi Reich commissar. This commissar, in turn, ensured that the state police were brought under Nazi control, thus allowing the Nazis to attack their enemies with impunity. These or similar events took place in a majority of Germany's sixteen provincial states.

The destruction of the workers' movement

The Nazis, along with their conservative supporters, claimed that workers had enjoyed too much political influence in Weimar Germany. They were eager to curb the labor movement for both political *and* economic reasons. For the Nazis, a strong workers' movement raised the specter of socialist revolution. It also permitted the high wages and welfare spending that they believed – however wrongly – had brought on the Depression.

In spring 1933, Hitler destroyed the leftist parties. Already by mid-March, the KPD, never formally outlawed, existed only in clandestine remnants. The Nazis also terrorized the SPD. Some SPD activists went underground, while others, fearing for their lives, fled the country. On June 22 Hitler banned the venerable party on the pretext that SPD leaders abroad were engaged in treasonous activity.

The Nazis used both the carrot and the stick vis-à-vis workers. May 1, the traditional day to pay homage to workers, became a paid holiday, a long-standing demand of the working-class movement. For May 1, 1933, the Nazis proclaimed a "Day of National Labor" and staged huge rallies in honor of workers. Yet, as the slogan suggested, the Nazis turned a holiday intended to celebrate worker solidarity into a demonstration of loyalty to the nation. Moreover, the very next day, police broke into SPD-oriented trade-union offices, ransacked files and furniture, shut down union newspapers, and arrested union officials. Within days, all independent trade unions had disbanded. The Nazis thus crushed a once-assertive labor movement, thereby protecting the economic interests of Germany's elites.

The end of independent political parties

In spring and summer 1933, Hitler forced the dissolution of all political parties other than the NSDAP. The Nazis browbeat the liberal German Democratic Party (DDP) and the German People's Party (DVP) into dissolving themselves. Next, the Stahlhelm was effectively disbanded in April; Seldte joined the NSDAP and Hitler took over the organization's leadership. In June, the Stahlhelm was swallowed into the SA. Meanwhile, Hugenberg, the DNVP minister of economics, was increasingly isolated in Hitler's cabinet. Hitler dismissed him on June 26. The next day, the DNVP disbanded itself. In part, the dissolution of political parties and associations occurred because these groups' leaders were open to the Nazi "national revolution." Having failed to win over the electorate themselves, many liberals and conservatives were willing to give the Nazis a chance. In the name of national unity and renewal, they welcomed authoritarian rule and its suppression of the workers' movement.

The last party to disband, the Center Party, ceased on July 5. This was related to ongoing negotiations between the Vatican and Nazi Germany (see Chapter 5). Like so many other Germans, Catholics were eager to participate in the new national community. They also wished to ensure church autonomy in the Third Reich. The Catholic hierarchy thus renounced political activity in return for promises of religious freedom – promises that the Nazis soon broke.

Within six months of coming to power, Hitler had established a one-party state. On July 14, he decreed the NSDAP the only legal political party in Germany. July 14 is Bastille Day, the French national holiday celebrating the French Revolution. By choosing that date, Hitler showed his contempt for liberty and democracy. He soon declared of the party system that "one would never have thought so miserable a collapse possible." But it was Nazi coercion and terror that forced the "collapse." SA thugs taunted and often physically abused anti-Nazi activists. Tens of thousands of political opponents were arrested. In Prussia alone, some 25,000 individuals had been taken into "protective custody" by April. Throughout Germany, as many as 200,000 citizens were temporarily detained in 1933. Those jailed had little recourse to the legal system. Neither the police nor the judiciary protected them from Nazi abuse. Those still free sensed the frightening conditions of Nazi captivity. Since opposition hardly seemed worth the terrible costs involved, many Germans turned away from politics.

Meanwhile, SA terror continued unabated. By June, SA thugs had murdered 500–600 individuals, including at least forty-three Jews. Increasingly, though, Germans were dismayed by SA violence. Many Germans disliked the fact that gangs of SA men were roaming the streets, intimidating the public. They were disgusted by SA bullies vandalizing Jewish businesses. Negative stories about Nazi violence also began to appear in the foreign press. In July, Hitler decided to end SA rampages. As he put it, "The revolution is not a permanent condition... It is necessary to divert the river of revolution... into the secure bed of evolution."

To Hitler, further "revolution" – read violence – would only hurt the Nazi regime. Göring soon took away the SA's role as auxiliary police in Prussia. No longer permitted to unleash violence, the SA was now in search of a mission.

Gleichschaltung (Coordination)

The Nazis took over not only the political system but also society as a whole. In what became known as *Gleichschaltung*, they "coordinated" or "synchronized" virtually all areas of life in Germany. The metaphor *Gleichschaltung* came from the workings of electricity. It suggested that all of society was on one circuit. A single master-switch could activate or shut down the whole system.

On April 7, 1933, the Nazis "coordinated" the civil service. A Law for the Restoration of the Professional Civil Service purged most Jews and leftists from government bureaucracies. At Hindenburg's insistence, however, individuals who had fought at the front or who had lost fathers or sons in World War I were not subject to dismissal (this exemption was lifted in 1935). On the basis of this law, the government fired roughly 1–2% of Germany's public employees, some 15,000 to 30,000 individuals. The law disproportionately affected higher-ranking civil servants, including university professors. By 1934, the regime had dismissed some 1,600 out of 5,000 faculty members at German universities. Some of those fired – such as Albert Einstein – were world-famous scientists.

The sixteen provincial states were also subject to *Gleichschaltung*. In January 1934, the Nazis issued the Law for the Reconstruction of the Reich. It destroyed German federalism by transferring the sovereignty of the states to the Reich. As Frick declared, Germany was now "converted from a federal to a unitary state." German states no longer had residual rights (such as control of the police). State parliaments, already eviscerated, ceased to exist. State governors were now responsible to the minister of the interior and could no longer put up resistance to the Reich government.

Independent associational life also came to an end. The Nazis disbanded youth groups, religious organizations, professional associations, and even local clubs dedicated to innocuous activities such as bowling, singing, or gardening. In their place, the NSDAP founded or expanded numerous affiliated organizations intended to marshal support from particular groups of Germans. The Hitler Youth organized male youths; the League of German Girls, female youths; the German Labor Front, workers; the National Socialist Womanhood (NS-Frauenschaft) and the German Women's Enterprise (Deutsches Frauenwerk), women; the National Socialist Physicians' League, doctors; and the National Socialist Teachers' League, school teachers. The list could go on and on. These affiliated organizations served as NSDAP "transmission belts." Although often focused on seemingly nonpolitical matters, they carried out their activities in line with Nazi goals and ideology. They also followed the Nazi leadership principle. Each had a national command structure that stretched downward from a Führer at the helm to the local organization at the bottom.

Gleichschaltung took place in the cultural realm, too. In March 1933, Goebbels was named head of the new Reich Propaganda Ministry. He soon established a Reich Chamber of Culture that included Reich Chambers for Film, Fine Arts, Music, Press, Radio, and Theater. All individuals employed in the arts had to register with a Reich Chamber. Jewish and leftist artists, however, were not admitted and saw their employment prospects dwindle. Some 2,000 artists fled Nazi Germany in 1933. The list of their names reads as a "who's who" of Weimar culture: Walter Gropius in architecture; Otto Dix and Paul Klee in art; Arnold Schoenberg and Kurt Weill in music; Bertolt Brecht and Thomas Mann in literature; and Fritz Lang and Billy Wilder in film. Meanwhile, conformist intellectuals, provincial artists, and mediocre performers peopled the Nazi cultural scene.

Book burnings marked the apogee of the *Gleichschaltung* of culture. University students – no less – made lists of "un-German" authors and ransacked libraries for their works. On May 10, 1933, students in nineteen university towns burned some 20,000 books in an "Action against the Ungerman Spirit." As Heinrich Heine, a famed nineteenth-century author, wrote of book burnings in an earlier era, "Where books are burned, in the end people will be burned too."

Propaganda was essential to the process of *Gleichschaltung*. In Goebbels' view, the goal of the press (and propaganda more generally) was that people should "think uniformly, react uniformly, and place themselves body and soul at the disposal of the government." The Nazis quickly shut down most non-Nazi periodicals, including 200 SPD and thirty-five communist newspapers. They took over the physical plant of these papers, thereby expanding their own press capacity. While the Catholic and liberal press lingered on, editors were careful not to provoke the government into banning or otherwise curtailing their publications. In addition, the Nazis took over many publishing houses, including illustrious Jewish ones.

The Propaganda Ministry also controlled radio broadcasting. To encourage radio listening, the Nazis produced a cheap radio, the VE 301 (People's Receiver 301). The very radio set celebrated the regime: 301 stood for January 30, the day and month that Hitler had come to power. By 1939, some 3.5 million radio sets had been manufactured, and 70% of German households enjoyed radio transmission. (And, not to be ignored, the sale of radio licenses covered 90% of the Ministry of Propaganda's operating expenses.) For those unable to acquire a radio, the Nazis trumpeted their message through 6,000 loudspeakers set up in factories and public spaces throughout Germany. When Hitler gave a major address, the nation reverberated with his words. Germans were inundated with the Nazi message.

There was little opposition to *Gleichschaltung*. Fearing Nazi pressure, most independent groups disbanded themselves. Their former members retreated into private life or joined Nazi groups. At the same time, civil servants voiced little dismay about the dismissal of their Jewish or leftist colleagues. Few artists or intellectuals defended their silenced or exiled colleagues. Most Germans did not regret the demise of federalism. Indeed, rather than resisting *Gleichschaltung*, many Germans embraced it. They engaged in "self-coordination," rushing to join the Nazi party. When Hitler came to power, there were 849,000 NSDAP members. Three months later, the party had swollen to 2.5 million members. Fearing that new members were just opportunists, the NSDAP closed its membership rolls on May 1, 1933. It did not admit new members again until 1937.

Hitler Assumes Total Power

The Night of Long Knives

In spring 1934, many Germans were disillusioned with Hitler. While the economy had improved, recovery was still slow. Several million Germans remained unemployed. At the same time, the sinister features of the Nazi regime dismayed some Germans. Hitler now believed that he had to shore up his power so as to ensure continued Nazi rule. He faced two important centers of resistance: the presidency and the Reichswehr (military forces, renamed the Wehrmacht in 1935). The two were actually linked: the president, as head of state, was supreme commander of the armed forces.

Hitler knew that President von Hindenburg's days were numbered. On his death, Hitler hoped to assume the powers of head of state. Military leaders, however, would have to recognize him as supreme commander. Hitler had the support of Minister of Defense Blomberg and of Blomberg's chief aide, Colonel Walther von Reichenau. But other top military leaders, including the new army commander in chief, Werner von Fritsch, were wary of Hitler and his movement. Not least, Reichswehr leaders felt threatened by the military pretensions of Ernst Röhm, the SA leader.

Historians have long debated Röhm's intentions. Did Röhm wish to bring the army under SA control, as military leaders thought? Or did he intend for the SA to function as a mere militia alongside the regular army? Some historians also believe that Röhm was eager for a "second revolution," a populist and anticapitalist radicalization of the Nazi regime. In addition, many SA men were disappointed with the Third Reich. They had expected jobs and sinecures from the new Nazi state. Moreover, since crushing the left in spring and summer 1933, they had no clear mission.

Regardless of his true aims, Röhm and his 4.5 million storm troopers posed a dilemma for Hitler. While Röhm was a longtime ally, Hitler was determined to have the military's support. Even though the SA had been indispensable to Hitler, many Germans were now displeased with it. Röhm also posed something of a public relations problem. The Nazis abhorred homosexuality (see Chapter 4), but the SA leader and many of his top associates were known to be homosexuals.

Adding to Hitler's concerns, conservatives hoped to curb him by restoring a monarchy after Hindenburg's death. On June 17, 1934, Papen publicly warned the Nazis against carrying out any "second revolution." He criticized the Nazi regime for its "selfishness, lack of character, insincerity, lack of chivalry, and arrogance." He also suggested that he might offer his resignation to Hindenburg. This would have ended the coalition government still formally in power. Hitler worried that Hindenburg might dismiss him. He also feared that conservatives, in league with the army, might thwart his ambition to take over the powers of head of state. By suppressing the SA, Hitler could allay military leaders' fears, thereby taking away their impetus to forge a military–conservative alliance.

Heinrich Himmler, head of the SS (see below), fed Hitler rumors of a pending SA insurrection. Himmler was eager to suppress the SA so as to enhance the influence of his SS. Röhm, however, was hardly planning a putsch. In June, he went on sick leave. He issued orders for the entire SA to go on leave in July. Still, Hitler claimed to believe rumors of an imminent SA uprising.

During the night on June 30, Hitler began a rampage. He had earlier summoned SA leaders to a conference at Bad Wiessee. Brandishing a pistol, Hitler stormed up to Röhm's hotel room. He declared his erstwhile ally a traitor under arrest. Röhm vehemently denied the charges. He and members of his staff were arrested and transported to Stadelheim prison in Munich. Some were shot later that evening, but Hitler, ambivalent about killing a loyal ally, authorized Röhm's murder only on July 1.

Meanwhile, the regime went after a host of alleged enemies, mostly conservatives who had stood in Hitler's way at one time or another. The author of Papen's June 17 speech, Edgar Jung, was killed. Gregor Strasser was shot in a Gestapo cell. General Kurt von Schleicher and his wife were murdered in their own home. Gustav Ritter von Kahr, who had refused to go along with Hitler's 1923 Beer Hall Putsch, was killed. Altogether, there were eighty-five known victims. The Night of the Long Knives, as the purge was soon called, underscored the brutality of Hitler's regime.

The purge of the SA was a key moment in Hitler's assumption of total power. Ironically, it brought a resurgence of Nazi popularity; many Germans welcomed the suppression of the SA and its violence. The storm troopers, although not disbanded, never again played an important role in the Nazi movement. The purge also proved to army leaders that Hitler supported the traditional military (even though Schleicher and another general were murdered). It also allowed Hitler to squash past and present inner-party opposition, a lesson to would-be opponents. Finally, it marked the ascendancy of the SS, Himmler's extralegal police organization.

Hindenburg's death

On August 2, 1934, President Hindenburg passed away. The day before his death, Hitler had the cabinet sign a law stating that on the president's passing the office of Reich president would be joined to that of Reich chancellor. Rather than assume the title of president, Hitler chose to be known as "Führer and Reich Chancellor" (shortened to just "Führer" in 1939).

The army aided Hitler's assumption of presidential functions. Independently, army leaders Blomberg and Reichenau decided that every officer and soldier would swear an oath of unconditional loyalty to the person of Hitler as Führer. This was a departure from Weimar practice. Reichswehr personnel had earlier sworn an oath to uphold the constitution, not a pledge of loyalty to the person of the president. Army leaders hoped that this oath would bind Hitler more closely to the armed forces. In fact, the opposite occurred. The Reichswehr bound itself to Hitler. Army leaders relinquished their autonomy. Among other baleful consequences, military personnel later claimed that their oaths prevented them from engaging in resistance against Hitler.

On August 19, the Nazis held a referendum to affirm Hitler's new position as Führer. In a democratic age, plebiscites give authoritarian regimes the veneer of popular legitimacy. Even though citizens vote, plebiscite questions usually give voters no real choice. Moreover, election procedures such as open voting (rather than a secret ballot) are common. The very act of voting, however, makes citizens complicit in the regime. The Nazis pressured all German citizens to vote – and to thus show consent for the regime. In the August 19 plebiscite, roughly 95% of the German population voted. If official figures are to be believed, 89.9% of voters affirmed Hitler's unlimited powers. The Führer could claim that he had the overwhelming support of the public. (For more on Nazi plebiscites, see Chapter 5.)

Hitler now held total power: he was head of state, head of government, leader of the party, and supreme commander of the military. *Triumph of the Will*, Leni Riefenstahl's famous propaganda film, celebrated this moment in Hitler's career. It documented the Nuremberg Party Congress that took place a few weeks later, in September 1934. Reflecting recent events, the film paid respects to the military; it also honored the now impotent SA and its new leader, Viktor Lutze. Mostly, though, it glorified Hitler. The film opens with Hitler descending from the clouds, a godlike figure to save Germany. In the streets of Nuremberg, he is greeted by wildly cheering crowds. Many scenes proclaim the Führer as the embodiment of the people and Reich. The film resounds with the message of "One People, One Reich, One Leader." *Triumph of the Will* is a masterly visual document of Hitler as undisputed leader of Germany.

SS–Police Terror

To achieve his goals, Hitler employed all the resources of the state *and* the NSDAP. This was especially effective as concerned the police. Heinrich Himmler fused the SS, a paramilitary party institution, with traditional state police bodies; this allowed German police to operate outside the law. In addition, Himmler advocated *preventative* policing – that is, the ferreting out of ideological and other enemies *before* they actually posed a demonstrated threat. This was very different from traditional *reactive* policing – when a criminal is apprehended *after* a crime is committed. The amalgamation of the SS and the police, along with preventative policing, proved very powerful coercive practices.

The son of a strict Roman Catholic schoolmaster in Bavaria, Himmler studied agriculture after World War I and tried his hand at chicken farming. Drawn to *völkisch* nationalist circles in Munich, he was a standard bearer at the side of Ernst Röhm during the Beer Hall Putsch. In the mid-1920s, he was secretary to Gregor Strasser. (During the Röhm purge, Himmler was involved in the murders of both former mentors.) In January 1929, Hitler appointed Himmler head of the SS, the Führer's personal bodyguard.

Himmler was a convinced racist and antisemite. He was obsessed with the occult and the ancient Germanic race (see Chapter 4). He also despised Christianity. To him, Christian values such as compassion, humility, and love for one's neighbors were a lame humanitarianism that would only weaken the German nation. Himmler proved a ruthless organizer and administrator. In just a few years, he developed a veritable SS–police empire that spanned the party's paramilitary institutions, all state police formations, and a network of concentration camps.

The SS

In 1929, when Himmler took over, the SS had 280 members and was charged with protecting Hitler and with other special tasks. Himmler worked hard to differentiate his SS from the much larger SA, to which it was subordinate. Among other innovations, he devised an SS uniform: all black with the death's head insignia. In contrast to the hooliganism of the SA, the SS developed a reputation of disciplined professionalism. By January 1933, the SS had 52,000 men.

For Himmler, the cardinal virtue of an SS man was loyalty to Hitler. The SS motto was "Your honor means loyalty."

Himmler dreamed of molding the SS into an elite Nordic tribe – a modern-day Order of Teutonic Knights – that would lead the way to a greater Germanic Reich. He insisted on SS men's racial purity. SS members had to document pure "Aryan" lineage, sometimes back to 1750. They also had to prove the absence of hereditary and mental diseases. In 1931, Himmler issued an "Engagement and Marriage Order." Prior to marriage, SS men and their future brides had to undergo "hereditary health" examinations to ensure the genetic health of their offspring.

Shortly after the Röhm Putsch, Hitler declared the SS independent of the SA. As SS leader, Himmler was now subordinate only to Hitler as Führer. By December 1934, the SS had grown to roughly 200,000 men. Himmler divided SS men into three sections. The first made up the Armed SS (SS-Verfügungstruppe), the predecessor of the Waffen-SS. It included the armed security detail that protected Hitler (Leibstandarte SS Adolf Hitler). The second included SS concentration-camp guards, the Death's Head formations (see below). The third was the General SS, roughly 95% of all SS members.

The SD

In 1931, Himmler initiated an SS intelligence unit, the SD (Sicherheitsdienst, or security service). He chose Reinhard Heydrich, a former naval officer, to organize the SD. Tall, athletic, and imposing – sometimes called the "Blond Beast" – Heydrich embodied the Aryan ideal. The son of the founder of the Halle Conservatory, Heydrich was an accomplished violinist. Yet, despite his musical bent, Heydrich lived a disciplined SS ethic. In his logic of cold, rational "sobriety," violence could create a racially cleansed, regenerated Germany. Heydrich attracted like-minded fellows to the SD. A generation of young, educated, and ideologically motivated individuals – Germany's "best and brightest" – formed the nucleus of the SS security apparatus.

Initially, the SD rooted out spies in the Nazi movement. Due to electoral successes in the early 1930s, many new members had joined the NSDAP. The Nazis, however, suspected "enemy" infiltrators among the new recruits. After 1933, the SD focused on KPD and SPD networks. By 1935, it had broken the leftist opposition. Still, Himmler and Heydrich tirelessly preached their security message: at all times, nefarious enemies lurked, waiting to be discovered. To successfully battle opponents, they believed, the regime had to engage in comprehensive preventative policing. In their view, the work of the police should not be fettered by old-fashioned niceties such as due process or other checks on police power. Only uncompromising ruthlessness, they insisted, could accomplish the Nazis' security goals.

Figure 3.1 SS-Chief Heinrich Himmler (left) and SD-Chief Reinhard Heydrich view preparations for the funeral of President Paul von Hindenburg (August 1934). *Source*: Scherl / Süddeutsche Zeitung Photo.

The Gestapo

Soon after the Nazis came to power, Himmler began his quest to take over all police institutions in Germany. In March 1933 he was named Munich police president. Meanwhile, Hermann Göring, as Acting Interior Minister in Prussia, created the Gestapo – an abbreviation taken from the term *Geheimes Staatspolizei*, meaning secret state police. Shortly thereafter, Himmler was named head of the Gestapo equivalent in Bavaria. He now used SS or SD men to infiltrate political police units in individual German states. In turn, he engineered to have himself – as SS leader – named head of those political police units. Since many Nazi police chiefs believed they needed the SS to combat the unruly SA, Himmler was successful. In April 1934, for example, Göring, fearful of the undisciplined SA, ceded Himmler operational leadership of the Prussian Gestapo.

Chief of German police

In the next two years, Himmler unleashed police terror on Nazi political opponents. He also aimed to establish a centralized police organization (policing was in the purview of individual German states). Both irked Frick and his Interior Ministry officials, who wished to control all police activity. Himmler and other Nazi officials, however, felt that Frick's ministry was too legalistic to accomplish the necessary terror. After considerable infighting between Frick and Himmler,

Hitler named Himmler chief of German police in June 1936, creating Germany's first centralized police force. It was, however, no ordinary police force. The SS and the SD were now active in German state policing operations. But, as party institutions, they were not subject to legal checks.

As chief of German police, Himmler created two main offices. Heydrich headed the main office, the "Sipo and SD." An intelligence agency, the SD was charged with broad issues of security. It *identified* "enemies." By contrast, the Sipo (*Sicherheitspolizei*, or security police) *detained* "enemies." It merged the Gestapo, criminal police (*Kriminalpolizei* or Kripo), and border police. The other main office was the Order Police, headed by Kurt Daluege. It included the uniformed police in cities (Schutzpolizei), the uniformed police in rural districts (Gendarmerie), the local police (Gemeindepolizei), the traffic police, and smaller administrative police units. In 1938, the Order Police had some 100,000 officers – far more than the much smaller numbers of employees in the Sipo and SD (roughly 9,000 and 7,000 in 1937).

SS men were placed in all police units. This meant that the entire German police was made up of a hybrid of state and party security officials. At any time, police officials who were SS members could claim to be working under SS orders. They could thus act with impunity, terrorizing alleged Nazi opponents at will. Although all police branches were technically subordinate to Frick's Ministry of the Interior, Himmler functioned largely independent of the ministry. He also based police operations on the Reichstag Fire Decree, which suspended all basic citizen protections. The Third Reich was under a permanent state of emergency.

The concentration camps

The SS maintained a system of concentration camps separate from the regular judicial prison system. In spring 1933 Himmler established the first concentration camp in a former munitions factory in Dachau, outside Munich. Theodor Eicke, a fanatical Nazi, headed the camp in 1933–1934. There he developed the "Dachau model." The camp was sealed off from the outside world. Inmates were assigned to work details. Eicke organized Death's Head units, a corps of professional SS camp guards who deployed systematic arbitrary violence. Despite ubiquitous rules, capricious terror reigned supreme. As Eicke told his guards, "tolerance means weakness." After his stint at Dachau, Eicke headed the so-called Inspection of the Concentration Camps, the office in charge of all SS concentration camps.

In 1936, Himmler opened Sachsenhausen, located outside Berlin. It was purpose-built as a concentration camp, with rows of barracks for prisoners, workshops for prison laborers, and separate housing for SS personnel. Command posts and guard towers allowed omnipresent surveillance. All subsequent official concentration camps (those run by the SS) were built along the lines of Sachsenhausen. Although in plain sight of the German population, the camps were a world apart. Police officials, often working outside the law, delivered prisoners to the camp gates. Inside the camps, inmates were at the whim of the Death's Head units. They had no recourse to courts, media, or other potential intervening authorities.

Before World War II – except for a brief period in 1938 – concentration-camp prisoners were rarely Jews. Instead, the inmate population consisted of leftists, clergymen, and those groups (not Jews) deemed racially inferior (see Chapter 4). In 1937, Himmler claimed that camp prisoners "are the dregs of criminality, of people who have taken the wrong path… There are people there with hydrocephalus, people who squint, people with deformities, half-Jews, a mass of racially inferior material." In 1939, there were six official concentration camps, including a camp for women, Ravensbrück; these camps housed some 21,400 inmates.

Law and the judicial system

Law was another instrument of terror in the Third Reich. The Nazis believed that law should serve the interests of the national community. As Hitler once stated, "Not the individual but only the nation must be regarded as the center of legal concern." To the Nazis, the Weimar legal code focused too much on the protection of individual rights. In addition, the notion of equality before the law violated the Nazis' sense of racial hierarchy. In deciding cases, judges in Nazi Germany were to follow their "healthy" instincts as to what was best for the German people. The Nazis also favored judicial "elasticity" – judges' leeway to act as they saw fit.

While the Nazis maintained regular courts, they also instituted new courts aimed at political "enemies." In March 1933, special courts began to try those charged with all political crimes except high treason. The judges were fervent Nazis, not trained lawyers. These courts, for example, tried those accused of violating the Malicious Practices Act, a law that criminalized telling jokes or making other negative remarks about the regime. The Nazis also established the infamous People's Court. This court, made up of two trained judges and three Nazi officials, tried those accused of high treason. Many Germans arrested for resistance stood before this kangaroo court. Neither the special courts nor the People's Court permitted appeals.

Surprisingly, much of the Weimar legal code remained intact. In a modern, industrialized society, legal rules are essential for the smooth functioning of society. The Nazis thus upended only those parts of the law that contravened their ideological goals. They neither abrogated the Weimar Constitution nor promulgated a new constitution. Instead, they issued sweeping orders that superseded or simply coexisted with Weimar-era laws. This, too, was a hybrid system of Nazi and traditional German law. At the same time, lawyers and judges – whether due to pressure or conviction – Nazified their procedures. The very individuals who were to uphold the law were complicit in its subversion.

The Nazi Party-State

Popular stereotypes of the Nazi dictatorship suggest top-down rule. Hitler issued orders, orderlies clicked their heels, and the Führer's wishes were implemented. In fact, the Nazi party-state was anything but a well-run machine that translated orders into policy. Hitler was a desultory executive. Administrative chaos prevailed. Party and state authorities vied with each other. Jurisdictional overlap was the norm. Nazi potentates refused to cooperate, jealously guarding their fiefdoms. But this governmental fragmentation made Hitler the system's linchpin. Access to and support from the Führer became the key to power.

The NSDAP

Before 1933, the NSDAP was geared toward coming to power. Once in power, however, the party's role was unclear. Would the NSDAP take over the state bureaucracies? Would it oversee the state bureaucracies? In fact, the relationship between party and state was never resolved. The NSDAP did not have enough cadres with suitable qualifications to assume civil-service or other leading positions. To address these matters, Hitler established the office of the Führer's Deputy for Party Affairs, with Rudolf Hess as its head. Martin Bormann headed the staff of this office. (Eventually, this office became the Party Chancellory and Bormann became one of the most powerful men in the Third Reich.) Hess and Bormann ran the NSDAP's Political Organization (PO), an office that was supposed to be a party watchdog over the government bureaucracy. They hoped that it would control party officials, too.

Hess and Bormann faced stiff competition in their aim of controlling NSDAP personnel. There were a number of independent centers of power within the Nazi party. Robert Ley, for example, not only headed the German Labor Front (Deutsche Arbeitsfront, or DAF) but also held the title "Head of the Reich Organization." In the latter capacity, he was responsible for the organization and training of NSDAP cadres. Over a long period of conflict, however, Ley lost control of lower-ranking personnel to the deputy Führer's office. While the PO came to assert control over the NSDAP rank and file, this was not the case with many ranking Nazis – thanks to Hitler.

Hitler insisted that many leading Nazis were responsible only to him. This was especially true of the *Gauleiters*, the men who led the thirty-two (later forty-three) regional districts (*Gau*) in the Third Reich. Hitler trusted the *Gauleiters*, many of whom had been among his earliest followers. He repeatedly stated that the *Gauleiters* answered only to him. Similarly, Hitler created sixteen Reich leaders (*Reichsleiter*), heads of various NSDAP departments (such as the treasury), who were also responsible only to him. Other leaders of the party's affiliated organizations – such as the DAF and the Hitler Youth – also evaded PO control. As a result, the NSDAP remained an unwieldy, balkanized institution, unable to unify the regime and thus mobilize the population toward a particular goal.

The state bureaucracy

The Nazis strengthened central state power against that of local governments. The abolition of federalism, for example, enhanced the central state bureaucracy in the Third Reich. Local state offices became nothing more than branch offices of Berlin ministries. At the same time, however, Hitler repeatedly took away state powers (especially from the Ministry of the Interior) and gave it to hybrid party-state agencies. In large measure, this was because Hitler believed that all problems could be solved through inspiration and will power. To cut through alleged bureaucratic red tape, he appointed trusted individuals to address particular problems. These appointees, in turn, saw themselves as Hitler's personal agents, responsible only to him. To fulfill their Führer-given tasks, they created whole new agencies with new bureaucracies. Inevitably, these new agencies overlapped with existing government departments.

These hybrid agencies included the Todt Organization for public works programs under Fritz Todt, the Hitler Youth under Baldur von Schirach, and the vast Four-Year Plan organization under Göring (see Chapter 4 and Chapter 5). Hitler also appointed Albert Speer, his favorite architect, general building inspector of the Reich in 1937. Speer was to rebuild Berlin and other German cities according to Nazi aesthetic values (see Chapter 4). In the process, however, Speer ran roughshod over municipal authorities. Hitler's practice of creating new offices and agencies without detailing specific competencies created a bureaucratic jungle. As an Interior Ministry official, Wilhelm Stuckart, declared: "The excessive fragmentation of agencies leads… to inflation of offices, war between offices, duplicated work, empty work, unproductive work." The situation frustrated all rational government decision-making.

Just as the police was a dual party-state institution, so too was the entire party-state apparatus. While in some ways inefficient, the hybrid nature of the party-state also lent the regime dynamism. Many ranking party members held state positions. The *Gauleiters*, for example, were usually also regional governors. They could thus draw on both state and party authority – whichever proved most useful in the moment – to exercise enormous authority in their fiefdoms.

The same was true of many other officials throughout the Nazi regime. The dualism of the party-state allowed the Nazis to martial the unbounded resources of the state for party projects and vice versa.

Hitler's Leadership

The Führer's lifestyle

Hitler's lifestyle tells us much about his rule. He cultivated an image of solitary power and invulnerability. He had no family. While a devoted entourage surrounded him, he had few, if any, true intimates. He did have a longtime mistress, Eva Braun. She was a pretty brunette, twenty-three years his junior. Most Germans knew nothing of her existence. Hitler believed that his bachelor status enhanced his appeal to the German people. He did not want marriage to compromise his relationship with the public (who might have questioned either his priorities or choice of bride). He also did not want children; he did not want to produce heirs who would have the impossible task of succeeding him.

A wealthy man, Hitler lived a life of luxury. He made millions from royalties on *Mein Kampf* and the use of his image on postage stamps. Accordingly, he kept magnificent apartments in Berlin and Munich. He also had a massive mountain retreat on the Obersalzberg near Berchtesgaden in Bavaria. His favorite residence, this complex was known as the Berghof. The Berghof sported both the largest retractable window and the largest one-piece marble tabletop (eighteen feet long) in the world. Besides his homes, Hitler maintained a special train with sleeping compartments. A fleet of limousines and three airplanes stood ready for his use.

Hitler's daily routine usually began mid-morning, when he woke up. Around 10 a.m., he heard reports from the head of his Reich Chancellory, Hans-Heinrich Lammers. When he lunched around 1 p.m., his company included adjutants, chauffeurs, and his photographer, Heinrich Hoffmann; sometimes, top Nazis such as Göring, Goebbels, or Himmler also joined him for the meal. In the afternoon, Hitler held meetings with officials, foreign dignitaries, or those seeking audiences with him. While at the Berghof, he often spent afternoons strolling to a tea-house on the premises or walking down the mountain (where a car stood ready to bring him back uphill). Occasionally, he greeted the streams of ordinary Germans who came to gawk at him. His mealtime companions there included Eva Braun, Albert Speer, and Martin Bormann. In the evening, Hitler watched movies – perhaps the latest Hollywood film or a special favorite such as *King Kong*. Late at night, he held forth on his cherished topics, such as racial purity or his World War I exploits.

For his guests, tedium was the price of access to the Führer. Hitler usually went to bed in the early morning hours.

Hitler's governance

Hitler exercised charismatic leadership. As defined by the sociologist Max Weber, charismatic leaders enjoy legitimacy by virtue of their unique, exceptional qualities, often believed to be superhuman or divine. In Weber's understanding, it is not the leader's personality *per se* but rather followers' perception of the leader that grants charismatic authority. Put otherwise, Hitler would not have been Hitler if others had not made him such. His followers imbued him with heroism, greatness, and a world-historical mission to save Germany. These attributes fused into the Führer Myth, a cult of personality that surrounded Hitler. According to the myth, Hitler was the incarnation of Nazism, the personification of all that was best for Germany, and the embodiment of the will of the German people. As Hess declared at the 1934 Nuremberg Rally, "when you [Hitler] judge, the people [*Volk*] judge." In the Third Reich, Hitler *was* Germany.

Hitler's charismatic rule was enhanced by the quasi-religious tones of Nazism. Indeed, for many, Nazism was the new religion. The Führer was the messiah. Racism was dogma. Nazi rituals and symbolism inspired awe. The vanguard of SS and party members presaged destiny. The national community (*Volksgemeinschaft*) was a priesthood of all believers. The removal of enemies (see Chapter 4) promised a state of perfection. For many Germans, Nazism was a new religion that promised national salvation.

By definition, charismatic leaders do not feel bound by rules or conventions. As his lifestyle suggests, Hitler was a lazy administrator and seldom busied himself with paperwork. He had little interest in routine government; he did not want to be hemmed in by government administration. He also saw no advantage in coordinating state policy. In 1935, he held just twelve cabinet meetings, and after February 1938 he held none at all. Hitler was also a reluctant decision maker. In part, this was because he did not want to be associated with a "wrong" or "unpopular" decision. He thus rarely intervened in his subordinates' disputes. He usually let matters take their course, presuming the stronger man would (in his view, rightly) prevail.

When Hitler did make decisions, they became so-called Führer Orders, invested with the force of law. As a Nazi theorist opined, "the will of the Führer, in whatever form it is expressed, creates law and alters existing law." Nazi leaders vied for Führer Orders that would support their favored policy positions. Securing a Führer Order could involve Hitler expressing a view in the earshot of others. But a lunchtime nod could also be construed as a Führer order. Authority thus stemmed from access to Hitler. Could you secure the Führer's consent? That was the measure of power in Hitler's Third Reich.

Hitler's role: the debate

Historians have engaged in heated debate about Hitler's role in the Third Reich. Some historians, known as intentionalists, argue that Hitler dominated the Nazi regime, orchestrated all major developments, and translated his ideological obsessions into government policy. They also believe that Hitler had a set of goals (such as the removal of Jews from Germany) that he consistently pursued from the mid-1920s until 1945. When confronted with the organizational chaos of the Nazi regime, these historians insist that Hitler deployed a "divide and rule" strategy. Competition among his subordinates, they argue, enhanced Hitler's powers as dictator. He was the ultimate arbitrator.

Other historians, known as structuralists (or functionalists), emphasize the administrative chaos of the Third Reich. They note the dualism of party-state rule, the overlap in bureaucratic jurisdictions, and the vying for influence among various centers of power. In their view, government disorder made Hitler a "weak" leader. The Führer could not simply dictate his wishes and expect that they would be carried out. Hitler's powers were also circumscribed by public opinion. Since regime support rested in no small measure on Hitler's personal popularity, he could not afford to make too many unpopular decisions. At the same time, structuralist historians believe that the administrative chaos explains the radical nature of the Nazi regime. The pressures of jockeying for position led to a "cumulative radicalization" of policy. To win the support of Hitler or other top Nazi leaders, subordinates chose ever more extreme solutions to the problems they faced (such as the "Jewish Question").

Historians have critiqued both positions. They challenge the intentionalist position by noting that there were clear limits on Hitler's rule. In a complex, modern society, no single individual can determine all or even most developments. Hitler also needed public support. His actions were limited by what the public would tolerate. Moreover, critics suggest that the intentionalist position implies that Hitler alone was responsible for the crimes of the Third Reich. In the intentionalist interpretation, they argue, other Nazi leaders and the German population evade blame.

Critics of the structuralist position acknowledge the administrative chaos of the Nazi regime but question its significance. All modern democracies, they insist, are characterized by factional intrigues, personal rivalries, duplication of functions, and external pressures. Bureaucratic disorder alone cannot explain the destructiveness of the Nazi regime. Critics also suggest that the structuralist interpretation implies that very large numbers of individuals bear blame for Nazi crimes – making it impossible to determine just who was responsible. Alternatively, they argue that the emphasis on impersonal bureaucracies running amok means that no one was really responsible for Nazi crimes.

"Working towards the Führer"

Most historians now subscribe to a mix of the intentionalist and structuralist positions. No historian doubts the importance of Hitler and his ideological beliefs in determining Nazi policy. His ideological obsessions shaped the Third Reich. The Führer commanded adulation and universal respect. His authority was the glue that held together the Third Reich. Only Hitler could resolve conflicts and make binding decisions for all. No important decision made by Hitler was ever ignored. At the same time, though, Hitler was not omnipotent. He needed to uphold his personal popularity. Governmental disarray limited what he could achieve.

To a degree, the historian Ian Kershaw has synthesized the two positions by arguing that officials in Nazi Germany were "working towards the Führer." In Kershaw's view, Hitler provided a purpose – his will – around which the fragmented Nazi regime could coalesce. The Führer's will, however, was often ambiguous. Eager to secure favor, Nazi officials tried to divine Hitler's wishes and to act accordingly. As they anticipated Hitler's desires, however, they initiated policies that the Führer never explicitly articulated. This, in turn, created a radicalizing dynamic, likely welcomed by Hitler. The dynamic of "working towards the Führer" played an especially important role in the Holocaust (see Chapter 7).

While this chapter has emphasized the coercive elements of the Nazi regime, the next focuses on the most important way in which the Third Reich cemented support: the forging of a racial state. The Nazi focus on a racial national community resonated with many Germans. It helps to explain why so many Germans not only tolerated but truly appreciated Hitler's dictatorship.

Citations for Quotations

Page   Source
45   "If we do one day…" and "we will hold…" Quoted in Richard J. Evans, *The Coming of the Third Reich* (London: Penguin, 2003), 323.

46   "Attack on Marxism." Quoted in Ian Kershaw, *Hitler 1889–1936: Hubris* (New York: W.W. Norton, 1998), 439.

49   "one would never…" Quoted in Jackson J. Spielvogel and David Redles, *Hitler and Nazi Germany: A History*, Sixth Edition (Boston: Prentice-Hall, 2010), 76.

49   "The revolution is not…" Quoted in Kershaw, *Hitler 1889–1936*, 502.

50   "converted from a federal to a unitary state." Quoted in Albert Lepawsky, "The Nazis Reform the Reich," *American Political Science Review* 30, no. 2 (April 1936): 327.

51   "Action against the Ungerman Spirit." Quoted in Kershaw, *Hitler 1889–1936*, 483.

51   "Where books are burned, …" Quoted in Evans, *The Coming of the Third Reich*, 431.

51   "think uniformly, …" Quoted in Michael Burleigh, *The Third Reich: A New History* (New York: Hill and Wang, 2000), 209.

53   "selfishness, lack of character, …" Quoted in Richard J. Evans, *The Third Reich in Power* (London: Penguin, 2005), 29.

56   "Your honor means loyalty." Quoted in Peter Longerich, *Heinrich Himmler* (Oxford: Oxford University Press, 2012), 118.

56   "Blond Beast." Quoted in Robert Wistrich, *Who's Who in Nazi Germany* (New York: Macmillan, 1982), 135.

56   "sobriety." Quoted in Robert Gerwarth, *Hitler's Hangman: The Life of Heydrich* (New Haven: Yale University Press, 2011), 73.

58   "tolerance means weakness." Quoted in Nikolaus Wachsmann, "The Dynamics of Destruction: The Development of the Concentration Camps, 1933–1945," in Jane Caplan and Nikolaus Wachsmann, eds., *Concentration Camps in Nazi Germany: The New Histories* (London: Routledge, 2010), 21.

59   "are the dregs…" Quoted in Longerich, *Heinrich Himmler*, 243.

59   "Not the individual…" Quoted in Spielvogel and Redles, *Hitler and Nazi Germany*, 109.

61   "The excessive fragmentation…" Quoted in Jeremy Noakes, "Hitler and the Nazi State: Leadership, Hierarchy, and Power," in Jane Caplan, ed., *Nazi Germany* (Oxford: Oxford University Press, 2008), 76.

63   "when you [Hitler] judge, …" Quoted in *Triumph of the Will*, dir. Leni Riefenstahl, 1935.

63   "the will of the Führer, …" Quoted in Jeremy Noakes, "Hitler and the Nazi State," 74.

64   "cumulative radicalization." Hans Mommsen, "Cumulative Radicalisation and Progressive Self-Destruction as Structural Determinants of the Nazi Dictatorship," in Ian Kershaw and Moshe Lewin, eds., *Stalinism and Nazism: Dictatorships in Comparison* (Cambridge: Cambridge University Press, 1977), 75–87.

65   "working towards the Führer." Kershaw, *Hitler 1889–1936*, 529–530.

Bibliography

Browder, George C. *Foundations of the Nazi Police State: The Formation of Sipo and SD.* Lexington: University Press of Kentucky, 1990.

Burleigh, Michael. *The Third Reich: A New History.* New York: Hill and Wang, 2000.

Caplan, Jane, ed. *Nazi Germany.* Oxford: Oxford University Press, 2008.

Caplan, Jane and Nikolaus Wachsmann, eds. *Concentration Camps in Nazi Germany: The New Histories.* London: Routledge, 2010.

Evans, Richard J. *The Coming of the Third Reich.* London: Penguin, 2003.

Evans, Richard J. *The Third Reich in Power.* London: Penguin, 2005.

Gerwarth, Robert. *Hitler's Hangman: The Life of Heydrich.* New Haven: Yale University Press, 2011.

Hancock, Eleanor. *Ernst Röhm: Hitler's SA Chief of Staff.* New York: Palgrave Macmillan, 2008.

Hett, Benjamin Carter. *Burning the Reichstag: An Investigation into the Third Reich's Enduring Mystery.* New York: Oxford University Press, 2014.

Kershaw, Ian. *Hitler.* London: Longman, 1991.

Kershaw, Ian. *Hitler 1889–1936: Hubris*. New York: W.W. Norton, 1998.

Kogon, Eugen. *The Theory and Practice of Hell: The German Concentration Camps and the System behind Them*. New York: Farrar, Straus, 1950.

Longerich, Peter. *Heinrich Himmler*. Oxford: Oxford University Press, 2012.

Spielvogel, Jackson J. and David Redles. *Hitler and Nazi Germany: A History*. Sixth Edition. Boston: Prentice-Hall, 2010.

4

The Racial State

The Nazis aimed to create a pure "Aryan" race. They believed that a racially pure national community (*Volksgemeinschaft*) would restore Germany to greatness. Joined in pride and belonging, the national community would wage a war for *Lebensraum* (living space). Yet, while the *Volksgemeinschaft* touted unity, it was based on exclusion. To create a national community, the Nazis excised "community aliens," those deemed racially inferior. Such persons, the Nazis argued, sapped Germany of strength and morale – and were best ejected from the *Volksgemeinschaft*.

There is a presumption that Nazi racial policy primarily affected Jews. Nazi racial measures, however, targeted *everyone* inside Nazi Germany. The Nazis practiced racial hygiene, a popular interwar eugenics movement. Racial hygienists believed it possible to improve a nation's "fit" elements while removing "unfit" elements. The Nazis introduced a battery of measures to raise the birthrates and general health of the "Aryan" population. They also trained "Aryan" youth to carry out roles befitting a "master" race. At the same time, though, they oppressed "community aliens." Jews, of course, were a main target. But the Nazis also persecuted many others: the disabled, black Germans, "asocials," homosexuals, and the Roma (Gypsies).

Since the 1990s, the dominant framework for studying Nazi Germany has been that of the "racial state." As a measure of regime aims and practices, it accurately describes the Third Reich. Racial ideology shaped not only policies aimed at persons but also cultural production and even scientific inquiry. In Nazi Germany, racial ideology seeped into virtually *every* undertaking.

Nazi Germany: Confronting the Myths, First Edition. Catherine Epstein.
© 2015 John Wiley & Sons, Ltd. Published 2015 by John Wiley & Sons, Ltd.

Finally, policies associated with the racial state fostered loyalty to the Nazi regime; for many Germans, the racial state was a truly positive feature of the Third Reich.

Nazi Policies toward the "Aryan" Population

Nazi policy affected every "Aryan" man, woman, and child. Few Nazi policies, however, targeted men as *men* (unless they were homosexuals — see below). The history of Nazi Germany, however, *is* a history of men. Every top-ranking Nazi leader was a man. Most "Aryan" men benefited from and served the regime: "Aryan" men found or secured better employment, participated in Nazi rallies or rituals, joined the Sturmabteilung (SA) or Schutzstaffel (SS), or fought in the Wehrmacht. Moreover, the entire regime was organized around masculine ideals. Nazi posters, films, and other visuals pictured determined male party members, muscle-rippled workers, and warrior soldiers. The regime's self-professed values – order, manliness, heroism, domination in struggle – were all stereotypically male virtues. Still, while the following pages include sections on "Aryan" women and youth, they do not include a section on men. In large measure, this reflects the vast literature on the Third Reich; there are many books on women and youth in Nazi Germany but virtually none that examine men as men.

"Aryan" Women

At the 1934 Nuremberg Party Rally, Hitler famously declared his view of gender relations: "If it is said that the man's world is the state, that man's world is his struggle, and his readiness to serve his community, so we might perhaps say that woman's world is a smaller one. For her world is her husband, her family, her children, and her home." It would seem that Hitler accorded women little importance. In fact, however, he declared women vital to society: "Providence has entrusted to woman the care of this, her very own world, and only upon it can man's world be fashioned and constructed." To Hitler, women ensured the smooth functioning of society. Nazi success – in the large world of war and imperialism – depended on women's reproductive and other capacities.

The Nazis tirelessly propagated their ideal German woman. She was to bear many children and be a helpmate to her husband. She was to remain physically fit while cooking healthy, organic meals. She was to be a thrifty shopper and to recycle or repurpose used goods. She was to forego cosmetics and haute couture in favor of more natural fashion choices. Finally, she was to raise her children as good "Aryans," eager to serve and sacrifice for the national community.

Reproductive policies

In Nazi Germany, your body was not your own. It belonged to the national community. Reproductive policy was a matter of state. As SS Chief Heinrich Himmler put it in 1937, "all things which take place in the sexual sphere are not the private affair of the individual, but signify the life and death of the nation, signify world power or 'swissification.'" If a nation did not work to increase its population, so Himmler claimed, it condemned itself, like Switzerland, to small-power status or even neutrality.

The Nazis, eager for more "valuable" children, implemented numerous measures to encourage "Aryan" women to have children. In June 1933, they decreed the Law to Reduce Unemployment. If a future bride left the labor force, the couple was eligible for an interest-free loan of 1,000 RM, in the form of vouchers for furniture or other household goods. An additional decree stipulated that, with the birth of each child, one-quarter of the loan was reduced until, with the fourth child, it was completely forgiven. The Nazis also awarded small cash allowances to low-income families with many children. In 1938 they introduced the Honor Cross of the German Mother. Prolific mothers were awarded three grades of cross: bronze, for mothers of four or five children; silver, for six or seven; and gold, for eight or more children. As Hitler once declared, "The woman has her own battlefield. With every child she brings to the world, she fights her battle for the nation."

In 1938, the Nazis eased divorce conditions so that men and women could remarry and start new families. Individuals could seek divorce if they had lived apart for three years and their marriage had broken down (they did not have to document adultery or other egregious causes). They could also obtain divorces on the basis of "premature infertility" or "refusal to procreate." While the new laws seemed liberal, they reflected the Nazis' determination to raise birthrates.

Himmler was obsessed with raising the numbers of "valuable" children. In 1939 he even issued a "Procreation Order." SS officers were barred from promotion if they did not marry or, if married, they did not produce offspring. The SS also ran the Lebensborn (Well of Life) program. Popular myth has it that Lebensborn involved SS stud farms, in which strapping SS officers inseminated beautiful blondes. This is untrue. Lebensborn provided maternity homes for the wives of SS men and for racially "valuable" unmarried pregnant women. Single women could deliver their babies in a safe, comfortable environment, far from prying neighbors and relatives.

The Nazis also engaged in coercive practices to raise the number of "valuable" children. According to the 1935 Marriage Health Law, couples seeking to marry had to obtain a "Certificate of Suitability for Marriage." If the racial value of a couple was in doubt, the certificate could be denied. The Nazis also made it much more difficult to obtain birth control. In 1941, birth control was banned altogether (although the military won an exemption for condoms). Finally, the Nazis cracked down on abortion. They imposed severe prison sentences for women undergoing and doctors performing abortions. By 1943, carrying out an abortion on a racially "valuable" woman was punishable by death.

Did these measures work? In Nazi Germany, marriage rates initially rose. Most historians, however, believe that this was due to the end of the Depression (and ensuing economic stability) rather than the marriage-loan policy. Birth rates also rose. But here, too, the role of Nazi incentives remains questionable. At first, many couples likely had the children that they had delayed having during the Depression. Moreover, despite financial incentives, most couples who took out a marriage loan had only one child. Birthrates in the Third Reich remained stubbornly below those of the early Weimar Republic. On balance, the Nazi measures to increase the birthrate were ineffective: the financial incentives were too low, the honors too hollow.

Women in the workforce

In keeping with Hitler's views on gender, women played virtually no role in the "large" world of politics in the Third Reich. Not a single woman held a leading position in the Nazi Party or state. Even Gertrud Scholtz-Klink, who led the two Nazi women's organizations, the NS-Frauenschaft and Deutsches Frauenwerk, had no say beyond her own organizations. Some historians argue that the NS-Frauenschaft and Deutsches Frauenwerk offered women a space for professional autonomy and opportunity. If so, these women's influence was limited to a marginal arena of Nazi politics.

In Nazi Germany, various restrictions prevented women from pursuing professional careers. In 1933, the Nazis extended a Weimar-era law that dismissed married women from civil-service positions if their husbands were state employees. As of 1936, women lawyers could no longer serve as judges or argue court cases, although they could work in administrative posts and private practice. Women doctors continued to work, but they had difficulty securing plum jobs. The Nazis also officially restricted the number of women students to ten percent of university enrollment. While this quota was regularly ignored, the measure still curtailed many women's professional ambitions.

With regard to women and paid work, Nazi ideology soon collided with reality. Initially, the Nazis were eager to have women leave the workforce. They wanted women to stay at home to raise children. They also wanted to employ men who had lost jobs during the Depression. But, once the Nazis faced a labor shortage, they encouraged women to enter the workforce. The number of working women actually increased during the Third Reich.

During the war, roughly 14 million women were in the workforce. Yet, although the Nazis desperately needed more wartime workers, many women – especially middle-class women – refused to work. Hitler was reluctant to antagonize these women or their male relatives, many of whom were serving in the armed forces. Although a 1943 decree made all women (at first, just those aged seventeen to forty-five) subject to labor conscription, it had numerous loopholes and was never universally enforced.

"Aryan" women: victims or accomplices?

Nazi policies toward women have led some historians to engage in heated debate about whether women were "victims" of the Nazi regime. Gisela Bock argues that women in the Third Reich were forced into subordinate roles and became little more than reproductive machines. By contrast, Claudia Koonz suggests that women were more accomplices than victims of the regime. As she notes, "Aryan" women held Nazi beliefs; gave open or tacit support to many Nazi gender and other policies; and created comfortable homes for their husbands, including those carrying out Nazi crimes. In another take on this debate, Jill Stephenson emphasizes that women in Nazi Germany were encouraged, but not forced, to have more children. The continued low birthrate, she argues, attests to women's independent reproductive choices.

Historians have also argued that Nazi policies toward women were a setback from the Weimar period. This view, however, is based on an overly positive assessment of women's situation before 1933. Given the drudgery of most female labor, many women in the Third Reich were happy to retreat into their "small" worlds. They resisted Nazi calls to join the workforce. In practice, "Aryan" women in Nazi Germany had considerable leeway to determine their life choices. It is difficult to see women *per se* as victims of the Nazi regime.

"Aryan" Youth

In the Third Reich, young people enjoyed a special status: they were the future of the racial state. The Nazis were eager to forge a new kind of person: individuals who would become "masters" of a new world order. While boys were to be disciplined warriors, girls were to be fit mothers. To achieve these new persons, the Nazis created a system of total youth socialization. Young people belonged to the Nazi youth organization, the Hitler Youth. School curricula reinforced Nazi ideology. The Nazis also undermined parental and church authority so as to liberate youth from traditional morality.

The Hitler Youth

In June 1933, Hitler appointed Baldur von Schirach Youth Leader of the German Reich. Under Schirach's leadership, the Hitler Youth grew by leaps and bounds. "Coordination" fueled this growth. The Gestapo hounded non-Nazi youth

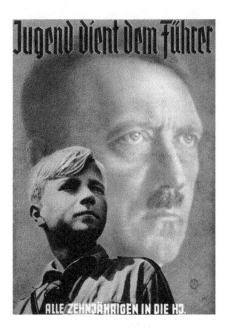

Figure 4.1 This Hitler Youth poster reads "Youth serves the Führer" and "All ten-year-olds join the Hitler Youth." *Source*: akg images.

groups out of existence. Peer pressure also did its part. Many children were eager to join in the fun of the Hitler Youth. Children who did not join – either because they did not want to or because their parents did not allow them to – were ostracized by their schoolmates.

In December 1936, the Hitler Youth was charged with coordinating the "the entire German youth." At the time, there were 5.4 million voluntary members. In March 1939, Hitler Youth membership became compulsory. All "Aryan" youths aged ten to eighteen had to enroll. To encourage uniformity and community, boys wore brown shorts, a brown shirt, a black kerchief, a leather belt, brown shoes, and a brown cap. Girls wore white blouses and dark-blue ankle-length skirts. Boys were to cut their hair to the length of matches. Girls were to wear their hair in long braids or rolls.

The Hitler Youth was organized according to age and sex. The Young People (Jungvolk) enrolled boys aged ten to fourteen years old, the Hitler Youth those fourteen to eighteen years old. The League of German Girls (Bund Deutscher Mädel, or BDM) was a separate organization within the Hitler Youth. The Young Girls (Jungmädel) enrolled girls aged ten to fourteen, the BDM young women aged fourteen to twenty-one. "Faith and Beauty" (Glaube und Schönheit), a BDM division for young women aged seventeen to twenty-one, was founded in 1938. Every year on the Führer's birthday (April 20), a new birth-year cohort was inducted into the Hitler Youth. These ritual gatherings – symbolizing a gift to Hitler – were a rite of passage in the Third Reich.

In preparation for their future role as warriors, the Hitler Youth strove to inculcate boys with military virtues such as discipline, obedience, honor, courage, and physical prowess. Hitler Youth groups went hiking and camping. They held boxing, swimming, and other sports competitions. They played war games, practicing strategy, reading maps, and spotting imaginary enemies. Even the youngest Hitler Youth enrollees used small-bore rifles and dummy hand grenades. Older boys did paramilitary training, including marching and drilling while shouldering army packs. Youth leaders tirelessly propagated undying patriotism, selfless devotion to Germany, and fervent loyalty to Hitler.

There is some debate about BDM aims. Most historians argue that the BDM focused on girls as future mothers. Dagmar Reese, however, questions the centrality of motherhood to the BDM's mission. She insists that the BDM aimed to raise girls' self-esteem so that they could contribute in myriad ways to the national community. While this may be true, there is no doubt that the BDM educated girls in many aspects of domestic life: childcare, nursing, hygiene, nutrition, handicrafts, and fashion. The BDM also stressed the importance of physical fitness. As a 1939 BDM slogan declared: "You have the duty to be healthy." To keep their bodies fit for future pregnancy, girls camped, hiked, and took part in other sports activities. In keeping with Nazi gender notions, girls'

Figure 4.2 Rhythmic gymnastics competition organized by Strength through Joy (June 1941). *Source*: Scherl / Süddeutsche Zeitung Photo.

sports emphasized teamwork over competition or individual achievement. Rhythmic gymnastics was the quintessential BDM sport.

The Hitler Youth gave young Germans a sense of meaning, belonging, and responsibility. Melita Maschmann, eventually a BDM functionary, wrote of joining: "I wanted to escape from my childish, narrow life and I wanted to attach myself to something that was great and fundamental." In part, young Germans achieved self-fulfillment through the notion of "youth must be led by youth." (In 1940, twenty-seven-year old Artur Axmann replaced Schirach, then thirty-three, as Reich Youth Leader.) Young people took charge of individuals just a few years younger than themselves. They often relished their newfound roles. But youth leadership was fraught with difficulties. Young leaders were inexperienced. They often abused their positions of power. In the Hitler Youth, corruption, sadism, and sexual promiscuity ran rampant.

The Nazis also empowered youth so as to undermine traditional sources of authority. The Nazis manipulated teenagers' natural tendency to rebellion so as to foster intergenerational tensions. Some Hitler Youth members even denounced their non-Nazi parents. The Hitler Youth also removed children from parental influence by scheduling numerous time-consuming activities. Many Hitler Youth activities were held on Sundays so as to undermine religious devotion. In some ways, however, youth policy contradicted other Nazi aims. Placing children in the hands of the Hitler Youth, for example, collided with the goal of having women stay at home to raise their children.

Schooling in Nazi Germany

Fundamentally anti-intellectual, Hitler disdained formal schooling. As he once exclaimed: "Put young men in the army, whence they will return refreshed and cleansed of eight years of scholastic slime." While the Nazis continued formal schooling, they revamped the German education system to fit their ideals. They subjected teachers to "coordination" (*Gleichschaltung*; see Chapter 3). By 1936, some 97% of all public school teachers belonged to the National Socialist Teachers' League. The Nazis also pared down the number of different kinds of schools. In 1938, they dropped a year of secondary education.

The Nazis also altered school curricula to propagate their racial ideology. They limited the hours of religious instruction. They devoted more school hours – up to five per week – to physical education. They changed the content of what was taught in traditional classes. In German lessons, for example, pupils focused more on folklore and literature that glorified Germany and its heroes. In history classes, they explored great German leaders, as well as the role of racial struggle in world-historical developments. In geography lessons, they learned about frontier regions and the plight of ethnic Germans living abroad. In biology classes, they focused on heredity, blood purity, craniology, and the classification of racial types. For some subjects, the Nazis introduced separate curricula for boys and girls. In physics and chemistry classes, for example, boys learned applications useful for military purposes, girls those for domestic science.

The Nazis even brought racial ideology into math classes. One math textbook problem, for example, read: "The construction of an insane asylum requires 6 million RM. How many housing units @ 15,000 RM could be built for the amount spent on insane asylums?" Students were encouraged to see caring for the sick as a waste of resources. Another math textbook questioned: "In Germany the people of foreign race are the Jews. In 1933 the German Reich had 66,060,000 inhabitants. Of those, 499,682 were practicing Jews. How much is that in percent?" Students were to learn that even a miniscule percentage of Jews posed a dire threat to the German nation.

The Nazis established elite educational facilities for future Nazi leaders. These boarding schools aimed to give students a total Nazi education. In addition to traditional academic subjects, they promoted the leadership principle, competitiveness, physical prowess, racial purity, and Germany's need for territorial acquisition. Thirty-seven National Political Institutes of Education (Napolas or Nationalpolitische Erziehungsanstalten) made up a network of state-run high schools established to train future government and army leaders. Twelve Adolf Hitler Schools prepared future party functionaries. Finally, four Order Castles (Ordensburgen) gave men in their twenties additional ideological training. They served as finishing schools for the rising Nazi elite.

Many teachers and parents were dismayed by educational developments in Nazi Germany. They were, however, loath to challenge the regime. Teachers did not want difficulties with school authorities. Parents were reluctant to jeopardize their children's future opportunities. Some young people chafed under Nazi demands of conformity and anti-intellectualism. Yet, while small numbers of young people resisted the regime (see Chapter 8), most dutifully followed its dictates.

To the end, many German youths showed great devotion to the Third Reich. This raises the question of youth responsibility for Nazism and its crimes. Hitler Youth leaders and functionaries clearly bear responsibility for the spread of Nazi values. They spouted Nazi ideology, modeled Nazi virtues, and never questioned Nazi ideals. These individuals – in varying degrees, of course – certainly bear a burden of guilt. But what about other young people? Since children could not escape Nazi propaganda, one might argue that they were blameless. Yet older children and certainly adolescents can think for themselves. In one way or another, many youths became complicit in the Nazi regime. Schooled in intolerance, they thought nothing of racial oppression. They also aided the war effort. Young soldiers carried out war crimes, albeit as part of the Nazi military system. Many "Aryan" youths were morally culpable for Nazi crimes.

Health Policies for "Aryans"

Eager for a population fit for war, the Nazis introduced numerous policies designed to improve the health of "Aryans" as a whole. To reduce health costs, they pioneered preventative health measures: regular physical examinations, annual cancer exams, and mass X-ray screenings to identify those with tuberculosis and other illnesses. They also urged Germans to adopt more natural lifestyles. In part, this reflected their "blood-and-soil" ideology – that the real Germany was rooted in the countryside, free from the unhealthy effects of modern urban life. In addition, the Nazis were concerned about industrial health hazards. They warned against asbestos, artificial food colorings, and heavy metals such as lead. They also promoted organic products and processes, such as folk remedies and homeopathic medicine. The SS even maintained a large herb garden for medicinal purposes at Dachau concentration camp.

Proper diet was necessary for lean, mean "Aryan" bodies. The Nazis exhorted Germans to eat healthier diets. Germans were told to eat fewer meats and fats and more fruits and vegetables. The Nazis touted the merits of whole-grain over refined white bread. They also tried to curb alcohol consumption. In changing German habits, the Nazis could point to the Führer. Hitler, a vegetarian, neither smoked nor drank. He also forbade others to smoke in his presence.

As Robert Proctor has shown, Nazi researchers were the first in the world to link smoking with lung cancer. Smoking was soon banned in many workplaces, including the air force (Luftwaffe), post offices, and hospitals and rest homes. During the war, the Nazis did not give pregnant women, or women under twenty-five and over fifty-five, tobacco rationing coupons. They made it illegal for minors to smoke in public. In spring 1944, they banned all smoking on city trains and buses.

In many ways, the Nazi organic vision appears progressive. It was, however, rooted in a coercive, racist ideology. The Nazis insisted that "Aryans" had a *duty* to lead healthy lives. They limited or banned unhealthy practices enjoyed by "Aryans." At the same time, they had little interest in the health of individual "Aryans"; the Nazis, for example, did not provide expensive end-of-life treatments to help terminally ill "Aryans." Finally, health measures were intended to improve only the "Aryan" population. Indeed, to protect "valuable" German workers, the Nazis had political prisoners or foreign laborers work in dangerous environments (such as uranium mining).

Nazi Policies toward "Community Aliens"

While the Nazis aimed to better "Aryans," they ruthlessly persecuted "community aliens." "Community aliens" were social and racial outsiders. The Nazis believed that many diseases, physical deformities, and even negative personality traits were genetic. By eliminating "community aliens," they hoped to remove disease, degeneracy, and racial otherness from the German population. The Nazis adopted measures toward "community aliens" that were often the very opposite of those for "Aryans" – sterilization, castration, abortion, incarceration, and, eventually, murder.

The Nazis believed that social outsiders' very existence betrayed the national community. Accordingly, they criminalized "community aliens." In addition, they merged the categories of political, racial, and criminal threats. While common criminals were lawbreakers, they were also racial threats because of their supposed hereditary "degeneracy." Homosexuals were charged with criminal offenses, but their real crime was racial, their refusal to produce "Aryan" children. The Nazis first saw the Roma as criminal elements, but by the late 1930s they classified Gypsies as "racial aliens." Finally, the Nazis saw Jews as a racial enemy, but, as the alleged standard-bearers of both liberalism and communism, Jews were political enemies, too.

By 1935, when most active regime opponents were in prison or exile, Himmler's police agencies were on the lookout for new "enemies." They turned to "community aliens." At the same time, the Nazi regime ordered the registration of various groups of "community aliens" with health offices or police agencies. This represented an extraordinary degree of state intrusion into private life. Registration also permitted heightened persecution. Many social outsiders soon found themselves in prisons and concentration camps.

Sterilization

In July 1933, the Nazis issued the Law for the Prevention of Progeny with Hereditary Diseases, also known as the Sterilization Law. It provided for compulsory sterilization for anyone with a hereditary disease if "there is a strong probability that his/her progeny will suffer from serious hereditary defects of a physical or mental nature." The law defined individuals as hereditarily ill if they suffered from any of the following: congenital feeble-mindedness, schizophrenia, manic depression, hereditary epilepsy, Huntington's chorea, hereditary blindness, hereditary deafness, and serious physical deformity. In addition, anyone suffering from chronic alcoholism could be sterilized. Some of these "diseases" had very elastic definitions.

To implement the Sterilization Law, the Nazis established some 181 genetic health courts and appellate genetic health courts. Doctors had to register all cases of hereditary disease. IQ tests were used to determine cases of "feeble-mindedness." It was usually doctors or social welfare workers who recommended individuals for sterilization. In most cases, the courts agreed to sterilization requests. Candidates for sterilization had the right to appeal, but appellate genetic health courts rarely ruled in their favor. Roughly two-thirds of those sterilized were deemed "feeble-minded."

Almost two-thirds of these were women. Many lived on the margins of society, while others were inmates of asylums and psychiatric institutions.

Most often, women were sterilized through tubal ligation and men through vasectomy. Because women's sterilization involved multi-day hospital stays, the Nazis were eager to experiment with less costly techniques of mass sterilization. Doctors, for example, injected carbon dioxide into women so as to scarify fallopian tube tissue. Roughly 2,000 individuals died from sterilization procedures. Current estimates suggest that upwards of 400,000 individuals were sterilized in Nazi Germany. Many sterilized persons and their families bitterly resented this state violation of their personal freedom.

"Rhineland bastards"

Among those sterilized were the "Rhineland bastards." These black children were the offspring of unions between African soldiers and German women during the French occupation of the Rhineland (see Chapter 1). There were roughly 500 young people in this category. In 1933, Hermann Göring ordered their registration with state health offices. In 1937, bypassing the Sterilization Law, Hitler secretly ordered that the teenagers be sterilized, but with their parents' permission. This was a brutal operation. Police officials abducted the youngsters from school or work. Doctors hastily evaluated their cases. Many parents gave "permission" only under Gestapo duress. Physicians often sterilized the teenagers within a day or two.

The harsh treatment of the small number of "Rhineland bastards" suggests that the Nazis saw the tiny German-African population as a terrible threat. According to commentaries on the 1935 Nuremberg Laws (see below), blacks were classified as "alien blood." Some Nazis even posited a racial link between Jews and blacks. They claimed that that the Jew was a "hybrid" between the "Negro" and the Oriental.

"Asocials"

The Nazis subscribed to criminal biology, a discipline that emerged in the late nineteenth century. Criminal biologists saw criminality rooted in racial inferiority – not in social environment or individual choice. The Nazis classified common criminals, such as thieves and murderers, as part of a larger group of "asocials." According to the Nazis, "asocials" were "unwilling to adapt to the life of the community." "Asocials" also included "beggars," "vagrants (Gypsies)," "prostitutes," "the work-shy," "alcoholics," and those with "contagious diseases, especially venereal diseases, who refuse treatment." All societies engage in sanctions against common criminals. The Nazis, however, criminalized the down and out. To them, "asocials" were a drain on welfare coffers. Their presence militated against Nazi law and order. They belied the Nazi image of a healthy, fit "Aryan" population.

Rather than provide welfare services, the Nazis deployed punitive measures. "Asocials" were criminalized for deviant, but not illegal, conduct. In September 1933, for example, the Nazis arrested thousands of vagrants and beggars. Most were soon released. In later years, the Nazis stepped up their persecution of "asocials." According to 1937 regulations, "asocials" could be taken into preventative custody and sent to concentration camps. In spring 1938, the Gestapo organized Operation Work Shy. Across Germany, police seized 11,000 able-bodied unemployed men and sent them to concentration camps. "Asocials" now endured back-breaking labor under lethal conditions. Arrests of "asocials" induced fear among those susceptible to that charge. The Nazis thus elicited social conformism.

In the Nazi worldview, criminals were born, not made; moreover, they produced "asocial" offspring. The 1933 Sterilization Law did not foresee the sterilization of criminals or "asocials." Hereditary health courts, however, invented a category of "social feeble-mindedness." Prison doctors drew on this category to sterilize some criminals. "Social feeble-mindedness" also served as a pretext to sterilize the "asocial," such as "whores" with many sexual partners or numerous illegitimate children.

In Nazi Germany, criminals and other "asocials" were deprived of basic legal rights. At the mercy of capricious police and judicial authorities, they were sentenced to long or even indefinite prison terms. In November 1933, for example, the Nazis issued a Law against Dangerous Habitual Criminals. It categorized criminals by character type. At a judge's discretion, persons with just two criminal convictions could be classified as "dangerous habitual criminals." For such individuals, the law foresaw security confinement – indefinite imprisonment in state penal institutions. The crimes involved were often quite minor, such as repeated theft of coats, bicycles, or small sums of money.

Homosexuals

Unlike other "deviancies," the Nazis did not think that homosexuality was hereditary. Instead, they believed that it was an epidemic spread by gay men "corrupting" young people. The Nazis were especially frustrated by the fact that gay men did not reproduce. In 1937, Himmler even claimed that Germany had a deficit of four million men – two million lost in World War I and two million lost to homosexuality. As he mused, "you can well imagine how this imbalance of two million homosexuals and two million war dead… has upset the sexual balance sheet of Germany and will result in catastrophe." To Himmler, every homosexual represented children lost to the nation. Radically homophobic, Himmler came to spearhead the Nazis' campaign against homosexuals.

When the Nazis came to power, "unnatural sex acts" between men – generally defined as anal, oral, and thigh intercourse – were already illegal according to Paragraph 175 of the German legal code. The Nazis stepped up enforcement of Paragraph 175. They shut down periodicals and organizations devoted to same-sex-desiring men. They raided homosexual bars and clubs. In 1935, in the aftermath of the Röhm affair, the Nazis revised Paragraph 175. They replaced the notion of an "unnatural sex act" with that of "indecency." "Indecency" was a very broad category. It embraced all manner of sexual conduct – from eye contact to intercourse. Homosexuals could be arrested on the slightest pretext.

In 1936, Himmler set up the Reich Office for Combating Homosexuality and Abortion; the link of the two suggests his major concern was battling those who allegedly stood in the way of higher German birthrates. This office tried to register all homosexuals in Germany. Police officials across the country arrested tens of thousands of same-sex-desiring men. Those found guilty of homosexual activity were sent to Nazi prisons. The Nazis hoped that prison would "reeducate" homosexual men to heterosexuality.

Most homosexuals in the Third Reich were never identified and thus never arrested. These men, however, spent twelve long years living in fear that they would be discovered. In the end, the Nazis arrested approximately 100,000 men for homosexuality. Many were released, but 50,000 served prison terms and 5,000–15,000 were sent to concentration camps (see Chapter 7).

Although there was some discussion of extending Paragraph 175 to women, the Nazis never systematically persecuted lesbians. Since women were excluded from positions of power, Nazi leaders did not view female homosexuality as a threat to the Third Reich. The Nazis also subscribed to stereotypes that lesbians were at most "pseudo-homosexual" and thus "curable." Furthermore, they believed that female homosexuality did not stand in the way of reproduction. Passive females, they thought, were always prepared to procreate. While the Nazis shut down lesbian clubs and infiltrated lesbian social networks, they did not criminalize lesbianism.

The Roma (Gypsies)

The Nazi treatment of the Roma, among all the groups mentioned in these pages, most resembled that of the Jews. In 1933, there were approximately 26,000 Roma in Germany. The Nazis, like those before them, called the Roma "Gypsies." (Today the term "Gypsy" has pejorative connotations and is often avoided.) Due to their wandering lifestyle, the Roma were long vilified as criminal outsiders. In 1926, for example, Bavaria passed a Law for the Combating of Gypsies, Travelers and the Work-Shy.

The Nazis stepped up traditional strictures on the Roma lifestyle. These included issuing permits for itinerancy (easily denied) and stipulations about where Roma could park their caravans. Shortly before the 1936 Olympics, Berlin authorities rounded up some 600 Roma and placed them in a Gypsy camp in Marzahn, on the outskirts of the city. The choice of camp location was particularly insensitive. In the immediate vicinity, there was a sewage site and graveyard, both of which violated Roma cultural taboos about where to rest caravans. The camp also had no electricity, just two toilets, and three water pumps. Other municipalities soon followed the Marzahn example.

At first, no Nazi law on criminality specifically targeted the Roma. Popular prejudice against Gypsies, however, meant that many individual Roma were victims of the Sterilization Law, the Law against Dangerous Habitual Criminals, and regulations concerning "asocials." Nazi doctors, for example, sterilized some 500 Roma. As part of Operation Work Shy, police officials also placed approximately 2,000 Roma in concentration camps.

In 1936, the Nazis established an Institute for Racial Hygiene and Population Biology to conduct "scientific" research into Germany's nonsedentary population. Dr. Robert Ritter, soon the leading Nazi authority on the Roma, headed the institute. Institute staff fanned out across Germany to collect personal and anthropological information. Curiously, Ritter (and soon Himmler) came to argue that Gypsies were originally an "Aryan" people with Indian origins. Ritter insisted, however, that very few pure Gypsies still existed in Germany. Most had long since intermarried with lower-class Germans. They had degenerated into "Gypsy mixed-bloods" (*Zigeunermischlinge*), a decidedly inferior racial breed.

In commentaries on the 1935 Nuremberg Laws, the Roma were designated, along with Jews and blacks, as "alien blood." They soon lost their citizenship rights. In May 1938, Himmler created a Reich Central Office for Combating the Gypsy Nuisance, housed within the criminal police. In December, the SS chief issued a decree on "Combating the Gypsy Plague." He now declared that the Gypsy problem was to be solved according to the "inner characteristics of that race." The decree called for the compulsory registration of all "Gypsies" and "Gypsy-like" itinerants with the Reich Central Office.

Historians have debated the similarities and differences between the Nazi persecution of Jews and of the Roma. While the Nazis never viewed the Roma as an evil comparable to the Jews, they did come to view the Roma as another race. In the 1930s, they deployed many discriminatory measures against the Roma that paralleled those targeting Jews. The Nazis, for example, prohibited the Roma from voting in elections, serving in the military, or marrying "Aryan" Germans. (For the fate of the Roma during World War II, see Chapter 7.)

Jews, 1933–1939

In 1933, Germany's 525,000 Jews made up less than 1% of the population. Still, Hitler raged against them. He claimed that the Jews were the cause of Germany's misfortunes. Jews, he insisted, had allegedly brought on Germany's defeat in World War I and the ensuing revolution of 1918–1919. Hitler also believed that "international Jewry" was conspiring to take over the world. He made no secret of the fact that he was eager to drive Jews from the German midst. Yet, for all the invective, Hitler moved against Jews gingerly. He did not yet know the "solution" to his "Jewish problem."

Before World War II, the Nazis treated Jews differently from social outcasts on the margins of society. Jews were much more integrated into mainstream German society. The Nazis never sterilized Jews just because they were Jews. Except for a brief period in 1938, they did not imprison Jews just because they were Jews. There were no camps or ghettos for Jews in Germany. Instead, the Nazis' initial goal was to separate Jews from Germans. They hoped to force Jews into "voluntary" emigration.

Right away in 1933, the Nazis imposed numerous degrading measures on Jews. In March, for example, the city of Cologne closed its sports facilities to Jews. On April 4, the German Boxing Association barred Jewish boxers. On April 7, the Nazis removed most Jews from civil-service positions (see Chapter 3). On April 19, authorities in Baden forbade the use of Yiddish in cattle markets. On April 24, the Nazis prohibited the use of Jewish names for spelling purposes in telephone communications. On April 27, Nazis in Frankfurt tore down the monument to Heinrich Heine, a celebrated German author of Jewish descent. Such actions – and there were so many more – signified that Jews were no longer welcome in German society.

In late March 1933, American citizens held rallies protesting Nazi policies in several US cities. The organizers called for an international boycott of German goods. In response, the Nazis launched a nationwide boycott of Jewish shops on April 1. Since there was little public enthusiasm for the boycott, it was not successful; German shoppers appreciated the competitive prices and services of Jewish shops. At the same time, the Nazis recognized that the failure of Jewish businesses would jeopardize economic recovery. Instead of boycotts, they turned to the "Aryanization" of the economy: pressuring Jewish owners to sell their businesses to Germans, often at a fraction of their true value.

On September 15, 1935, the Nazis decreed the Nuremberg Laws. The Reich Citizenship Law declared that "a citizen of the Reich may be only one who is of German or kindred blood." A second law, the Law for the Protection of German Blood and Honor, forbade marriage and even sexual relations between Jews and Germans. The Nuremberg Laws stripped Jews of their citizenship. Jews were no longer under the protection of a state authority and thus had no legal redress.

A supplementary decree to the Reich Citizenship Law defined Jews. Jews, Nazi authorities determined, were persons with three grandparents who were full Jews. Full Jews were defined by membership in a Jewish religious community. Jews were thus defined by religion, *not* by race. The Nazis could identify Jews by synagogue membership rolls but not by racial characteristics (since none exist). They also came up with classifications concerning the offspring of mixed

German-Jewish marriages contracted before 1933. Such persons were full Jews if they had two full Jewish grandparents *and* belonged to a Jewish religious community *or* were married to a Jew *or* were the offspring of extramarital relations with a Jew and born after July 31, 1936. By contrast, persons with one or two full Jewish grandparents, but who did not otherwise fulfill the stipulations of being a full Jew, were "mixed bloods" (*Mischlinge*). While *Mischlinge* faced some disadvantages in the Third Reich, they generally survived the regime.

The year 1938 marked a further escalation of measures against the Jews. In April, the Nazis ordered all Jews to register assets above 5,000 Reichsmarks. That same month, the Nazis designated 316 first names as officially "Jewish." Jews with other names had to add "Israel" or "Sarah" to their names. In early July, the Nazis banned Jews from numerous occupations, including working in real estate. Later that month, they revoked the medical licenses of all Jewish physicians. In October they expelled some 16,000 Polish Jews living in Germany to Poland. A seventeen-year-old Polish Jew living in Paris, Herschel Grynszpan, learned of his family's expulsion. On November 7, armed with a pistol, he went to the German Embassy in Paris, where he fatally wounded a German diplomat, Ernst vom Rath.

The Nazis used this murder as the pretext to carry out Kristallnacht ("Night of Broken Glass"). On the night of November 9–10, the anniversary of the November 1918 revolution and the 1923 Beer Hall Putsch, storm troopers, Nazi activists, and ordinary Germans went on a rampage. Across Germany, they torched or otherwise destroyed some 267 synagogues. They vandalized Torah scrolls and other Jewish ritual objects. They raided Jewish organizations. They looted and destroyed some 7,500 Jewish businesses. They attacked Jewish homes, robbing, beating, and raping their Jewish inhabitants. At least ninety-one Jews died in Kristallnacht. Some 30,000 Jewish men were seized and thrown into concentration camps. Most were soon released, but hundreds perished in the camps. In the aftermath of Kristallnacht, tens of thousands of Jews emigrated from Nazi Germany.

The Nazis now heaped new restrictions on the Jews. They levied a fine of one billion RM on the Jewish people – to cover the death of vom Rath and, perversely, property damages incurred during Kristallnacht. On November 12, Hermann Göring issued a law compelling Jews to sell their businesses and other valuables. On November 15, the Nazis expelled Jewish children from state schools (they could still attend Jewish schools). On November 19, the Nazis prohibited Jews from accessing the general welfare system. On December 3, they stripped Jews of their driver's licenses. On December 6, municipal authorities in Berlin banned Jews from theaters, cinemas, concert halls, museums, sports facilities, and other public places. The list could go on and on. As Marion Kaplan argues, Jews now experienced "social death." Under the complete control of the Nazi regime, Jews were cast out of the German community and relegated to a permanent state of dishonor.

Between 1933 and 1939, the Nazis aimed to rid Germany of Jews through emigration. They were quite successful in this: a majority of German Jews, over 300,000 individuals, left the Third Reich. Most fled to England and eventually the United States, but some went to far-flung destinations in the Far East or Latin America. Some 60,000 German Jews went to Palestine. Indeed, the Nazi regime even concluded a Transfer (Haavarah) Agreement with Jewish organizations, allowing Jews to transfer roughly 100 million Reichmarks to Palestine.

Why didn't all German Jews leave Nazi Germany? Many countries were reluctant to accept Jewish refugees. The United States, for example, refused to change its immigration quotas. It was thus extremely difficult for Jews to secure entry visas and other documents necessary for immigration. At the same time, many Jews were wary of starting new lives in foreign surroundings. Some remained in Germany to care for elderly parents. Mostly, though, Jews stayed because they never imagined that the Nazis would outright murder them. Until it happened, the Holocaust was all but unthinkable.

Culture and Science

Nazi racial policy affected not only people but also culture and science. The forced emigration of Jewish artists, musicians, and scientists fundamentally altered the arts and sciences in Germany. Nazi values also shaped artistic production in the Third Reich. At the same time, Nazi ideology made inroads into all academic disciplines, including the physical sciences. In Nazi Germany, the tentacles of the racial state reached into every field of endeavor.

Visual art

Hitler believed that art could inspire "Aryans" to embrace Nazi virtues. Art was to represent greatness. It was to showcase the beautiful. It was to model the Nazi way of life. The Nazis spent unprecedented sums on the visual arts. Art critics, however, argue that artists in the Third Reich produced conventional, mediocre art – in line with Hitler's tastes.

Hitler detested modern art. Unlike the realism of traditional art, modern art explored the symbolic and the subconscious, often in abstract or otherwise non-realist forms. To Hitler, however, modern art was "Jewish" and "international." In his words, modern art portrayed "misformed cripples and cretins, women who inspire only disgust, men who are more like wild beasts, children who, were they alive, must be regarded as cursed of God." Associating Jews with modern art, the Nazis persecuted Jewish artists and removed their work from museums and galleries.

Most modern artists in Nazi Germany were not in fact Jewish. Still, the Nazis purged all artists' works depicting mental anguish and social misery. In 1937, on Hitler's initiative, a "Degenerate Art Exhibition" was organized. Jumbled together in chaotic order, this show disparaged the works of modern artists such as Max Beckmann, Wassily Kandinsky, Otto Kirchner, Paul Klee, Oskar Kokoschka, and Emil Nolde. The Nazis sold some of these works abroad for hard currency. In 1939, they burned a large number of modern artworks in the courtyard of the Berlin fire station.

Hitler liked traditional art with conventional themes. Beginning in 1937, the Nazis exhibited the "best" new artworks in annual "Great German Art Exhibitions." Artists depicted nature and country life, showcasing farmers and their simple, natural ways. This reflected the Nazis' "blood-and-soil" ideology, which celebrated the German peasantry. In picturing broad landscapes, painters also suggested Nazi fantasies of colonial expansion, especially in Eastern Europe. Artists also extolled the harmonious "Aryan" family. They generally depicted women as fit helpmates or nurturing mothers, not as sensual or sexual objects. During World War II, artists turned to war themes. Then, however, they showed victory or heroic death, not the reality of mass slaughter and destruction. Some artists also specialized in portraits of Hitler and other leading Nazis.

Hitler privileged sculpture, not least because it was reminiscent of classical antiquity. The Führer believed that the Greeks and Romans were precursors to the Germans. Like the Greeks, Germans venerated beauty. Like the Romans, Germans had imperial ambitions. Sculpture was also the perfect medium with which to convey the ideal male body. The perfect "Aryan" had broad shoulders, narrow hips, and a muscle-rippled torso. Nude and classless, he was godlike in his disciplined strength and steely masculinity. Hitler's favorite sculptors, Arno Breker and Josef Thorak, cast massive sculptures of sinewy men and wild beasts that towered over humans. Their very size projected the immortality of the German people and their Third Reich.

Architecture

Of all the arts, Hitler most prized architecture. Monumental neoclassical architecture was to reflect the glory of the Third Reich. Hitler sketched plans and involved himself in the minutiae of major building projects. For Nuremberg, he had the architect Albert Speer oversee the design and building of the Party Rally Grounds. Speer planned the Zeppelin Field Stadium for 340,000 spectators; the German Stadium for 400,000 spectators; and the March Field, a huge parade ground, for 500,000 people.

As general building inspector for the Reich capital (GBI), Speer was also to transform Berlin into the capital city of a world empire, to be called Germania. He planned a monumental east–west axis with numerous government buildings,

Figure 4.3 Albert Speer's design for "Germania." *Source*: © ullstein bild / TopFoto.

a vast new train station, an immense triumphal arch, a huge national assembly building, and a cavernous domed hall for 180,000 spectators. Due to the war, very few of Speer's projects were actually built. Hitler promoted architectural projects for other cities, too. He took a particular interest in Linz, the city of his childhood and, he claimed, future retirement. He planned to build the largest art museum in the world there.

The monumental architectural projects were directly linked to Nazi persecution of "community aliens." As Himmler discovered, the SS could profit from using concentration-camp inmates as workers. It is no coincidence that Operation Work Shy took place in spring 1938, just when the SS founded the German Earth and Stone Works (Deutsche Erd- und Steinwerke). This SS business used concentration-camp inmates to produce brick and stone building materials. Its largest customer was Speer's GBI office. Two concentration camps, Flossenbürg and Mauthausen, were located close to stone quarries. Prisoners mining these quarries had a life expectancy of just six months.

Stone, with its connotations of strength, endurance, and tradition, was the material of choice for the new monumental German architecture. But its use also reflected regime priorities. By building with stone, these projects did not draw on precious steel and iron necessary for war materials. Moreover, camp inmates could produce stone building material at little cost. As Paul Jaskot has argued, Nazi architecture was an "architecture of oppression" not only for the values it conveyed but also for the tyrannical building methods it used.

Film

Like all areas of Nazi cultural life, the film industry was subject to "coordination." In July 1933, the regime banned Jews from working in the film industry, and some 2,000 Jewish actors, directors, producers, and cameramen soon left Germany. In February 1934 a new Reich Cinema Law increased censorship and created a new ratings system that gave tax breaks to films that furthered the regime's political aims. From 1937 onward, the Nazi state also bought up shares of the major film studios. State control over the entire production process soon meant that few films were actually censored; potentially subversive films were nipped in the bud long before they were ever made.

Despite state control of the film industry, the vast majority of the approximately 1,100 feature films made in the Third Reich had little obvious Nazi content. Indeed, just a handful of films featured Nazis as good guys or, for that matter, Jews as villains. This was because Joseph Goebbels, the Reich minister of propaganda, believed that film would best serve the regime if it provided good entertainment. In his words, "propaganda becomes ineffective the moment we are aware of it."

Even if film was first and foremost to entertain, it came to have other benefits for the Nazi regime. Many feature films conveyed Nazi values, albeit in often subtle ways. Adventure films, for example, promoted German domination of foreign lands and peoples as well as the need to maintain solidarity with fellow embattled Germans. Melodramas featuring fallen *femmes fatales* urged the sacrifice of erotic love for stable matrimony and procreation. Historical dramas illustrated patriotic loyalty to the nation. Nazi values such as obedience, the leadership principle, and individual sacrifice for the community were all expressed in films that ostensibly had nothing to do with contemporary events.

Film scholars note that movies allowed German audiences to enjoy wish fulfillment, escapism, and distraction. In watching films that dwelled on illicit romance, for example, Germans could play out fantasies that were otherwise squelched by the Nazi focus on family and children. Films that drew on traditional movie tropes such as the happy ending made Germans feel as though their world was safe, stable, and familiar. Feature films also gave Germans much-needed respite from their everyday cares and anxieties, especially during wartime.

The Nazi regime, of course, also produced some well-known propaganda films. Leni Riefenstahl's *Triumph of the Will* and *Olympia* top the list (see Chapter 3 and Chapter 5). Both films resolutely celebrated the Nazi regime and fascist aesthetics. Riefenstahl, however, used clever camera angles, innovative special effects, and ingenious editing to create truly extraordinary documentaries. While both films have drawn scathing criticism for their political message, they have earned grudging respect for their artistry. They raise a fascinating question: in the service of evil, can propaganda be true art?

Finally, a handful of feature films, all released after World War II began, directly addressed issues central to the racial state. *Robert und Bertram* made light of the expropriation of Jewish property, while *Die Rothschilds* portrayed Jews as excessively ambitious and greedy. Two other antisemitic films, *Jud Süss* (Süss the Jew) and *Der ewige Jude* (The Eternal Jew), are discussed in Chapter 7. *Feinde* (Enemies) and *Heimkehr* (Homecoming), released in 1940 and 1941, had anti-Polish plotlines; their subtext was that Germany should once again rule Polish lands. Finally, *Ich Klage an* (I Accuse), a 1941 film, argued that those suffering from terminal disease should undergo "euthanasia" (see Chapter 7). Through subliminal messaging and outright propaganda, as well as by providing opportunities for emotional release, film helped to consolidate the Third Reich and advance the aims of the Nazi racial state.

Music

Even before the Nazis came to power, many Germans believed that music was "the most German of the arts." Music fostered a sense of German national pride, identity, and belonging. Many Germans believed it reflected the national soul. For the Nazis, music was another proof of German superiority. All western music, they claimed, originated in ancient Germanic lands. Bach, Beethoven, and Brahms brought classical music to new heights. Wagner, Hitler's favorite composer, stood at the pinnacle of all German cultural achievement – he had transformed a musical form, opera, into a total work of art (*Gesamtkunstwerk*).

German musicologists tried to define "German" music. In this, they had little success. They claimed that "German" music projected heroism, depth, a drive to creation, introspection, and rootedness. It featured the triad, the tonal system, and "German" rhythms. By contrast, "Jewish" music, they claimed, was imitative and superficial. The Nazis immediately drove out Jews prominent in the German music world. Renowned conductors and composers, including Arnold Schoenberg, a pioneer of atonal music, fled the country. The Nazis, however, found it harder to police music than the other arts. They were confounded by the fact that many prominent "German" musicians either were Jews, had Jewish origins, or collaborated with Jews. Mendelssohn was of Jewish origins, Handel partly so. Mozart used a Jewish librettist. The Nazis imposed a total ban on the recording of works by Jewish musicians only in April 1938.

The Nazis had similar difficulties with chasing "modern" music from Germany. They railed against jazz, claiming it to be "Negro" music connected to Jews. One critic insisted that jazz was a "cancerous growth that has to be removed from Germany at all costs." Still, jazz survived in the Third Reich as "German" dance music, often played by German bands. It was too popular to ban altogether. When the Nazis mounted a "Degenerate Music" (*Entartete Musik*) exhibition, a scathing attack on "modern" and jazz music, it did not enjoy the same popularity as the parallel art exhibition.

In the Third Reich, youngsters sang German folksongs while hiking and camping. Music was also part of every Nazi ceremony. The Hitler Youth, the SS, and the Reich Labor Service (see Chapter 5) sported bands at all organizational levels. Even concentration camps had orchestras – staffed by Jews and other inmates. By adding joyous festivity and sublime beauty to life in the Third Reich, music helped to further consolidate the Nazi regime.

Science and scholarship

It is commonly assumed that certain human endeavors – such as the pursuit of knowledge – are apolitical or value-free. This, however, is rarely the case, and certainly not in the Third Reich. Right away, the Nazis insisted on the dismissal of all Jews in university and other research positions. The loss of Jewish academics had a dramatic impact, particularly on the natural sciences. Most pure mathematicians left the country. Many leading physicists, including Albert Einstein, emigrated. Some 2,900 medical doctors, including world-class specialists, departed Germany. Few German scientists protested their colleagues' removal.

The Third Reich saw some bogus science. In 1935, Himmler cofounded a research society, Ahnenerbe (Ancestral Heritage), to study the history of the Germanic race. Ahnenerbe eventually comprised some thirty-five research units. To prove an ancient German presence, Ahnenerbe staff searched for runes, old Germanic script, in caves and other locations. Moreover, Himmler sent an expedition to Tibet to collect material on an alleged Nordic race there. Himmler also ventured into the physical sciences. He trusted in the Cosmic Ice Theory (*Welteislehre*), a popular interwar theory claiming that antagonisms between suns and ice planets determined cosmic events. Ahnenerbe's Institute of Meteorology brought together scientists to prove the theory's validity. This wacky science found few adherents. Even Hitler scorned Himmler's scientific pretensions.

Some Nazi fanatics promoted "Aryan" branches of their disciplines. Two Nobel laureates in physics, Philipp Lenard and Johannes Stark, pushed "Aryan physics." "Aryan physics" questioned Einstein's theory of relativity, claiming it to be "Jewish physics." Advocates of "German mathematics" argued that German mathematicians focused on hard empirical realities, Jewish mathematicians on abstractions. Most German scientists, however, rejected "Aryan" science. While Hitler and other Nazi leaders initially supported "Aryan" knowledge, they soon sidelined its practitioners. They wanted useful science – science that could further Nazi aims.

Judged by the standards of the day, most science in the Third Reich was "good" science in that it followed appropriate research standards and procedures.

Nazi racial ideology, however, shaped scientific agendas. Research priorities shifted as funding poured into certain areas of research. Take biology. This field was indispensable to Nazi goals. Between 1932 and 1939, the German Research Association increased its funding for biology projects tenfold. It gave particular support to the subfields of genetics, applied botany, and breeding research. Some biologists now used "good" science to promote Nazi racial projects. Gerhard Heberer, an internationally acclaimed zoologist and anthropologist, tried to show the superiority of the "Aryan" race through population genetics and anthropology. A research team at the Kaiser Wilhelm Institute for Breeding Research worked to breed plants suitable for Eastern European climates so as to export the "German" landscape eastward. Biologists also developed biological weapons, including plague bacteria.

The humanities and social sciences also aided Nazi projects. This is best illustrated by research into the east (*Ostforschung*), an interdisciplinary field established in the years before and after World War I. Since the east was the target for expanded *Lebensraum*, research into that area provided scholarship that both prepared for and legitimated eventual German rule there. Geographers and landscape architects identified the demographic and climatic attributes of the region. Urban planners, statisticians, and economists mapped patterns of industry and transportation networks. Historians documented Germans' supposed ancient connections and thus rights to the area. They purported positive German and negative Slavic influences on the region. Beginning with the 1939 invasion of Poland, *Ostforschung* was put to sinister ends (see Chapter 6).

In Nazi Germany, knowledge served the state. Many distinguished scholars legitimized the regime's actions or furthered its goals. Scholars and scientists watched as their Jewish colleagues were hounded out of their jobs. They did research that allowed the Nazis to carry out vicious racial policies, both in the 1930s and during World War II (see Chapter 6, Chapter 7, and Chapter 8).

Germans and the Racial State

In forging a racial state, the Nazis depended on large numbers of Germans. Social workers, doctors, and criminologists categorized and classified the population. Police and judicial authorities arrested and sentenced "community aliens." Physicians and nurses X-rayed "Aryans" as a preventative health measure and willingly sterilized "community aliens." School teachers and Hitler Youth leaders indoctrinated "Aryan" youths while excluding non-"Aryans" from their activities. Visual artists, architects, and musicians conveyed Nazi values through their work. University professors, demographers, and urban planners used their expertise to generate plans for the Nazi domination of Europe. Scientists applied their knowledge to further Nazi racial aims.

The very participation of so many Germans in the racial state suggests widespread backing for the Third Reich. Germans showed their support of the Nazi regime by involving themselves in myriad elements of the racial state. They also implicated themselves in the regime by excluding "community aliens." Through participation in all the many different elements of the Nazi racial state, Germans bound themselves to Hitler's Third Reich. Moreover, while Chapter 5 examines various policies that generated support for the Nazi regime, none was more important than the forging of the racial state discussed here. For most Germans, the racial state was among the best features of the Nazi regime.

Citations for Quotations

Page   Source

70   "If it is said that the man's world…" and "Providence has entrusted…" Quoted in Jill Stephenson, *Women in Nazi Germany* (Edinburgh Gate: Pearson Education, 2001), 142.

71   "all things which take place…" Quoted in Michael Burleigh and Wolfgang Wippermann, *The Racial State: Germany 1933–1945* (New York: Cambridge University Press, 1991), 192–193.

71   "The woman has her own battlefield…" Quoted in Peter Adam, *Art of the Third Reich* (New York: Harry N. Abrams, 1992), 140.

71   "premature infertility" and "refusal to procreate." Quoted in Lisa Pine, *Nazi Family Policy 1933–1945* (Oxford: Berg, 1997), 18.

74   "the entire German youth." Quoted in Michael Kater, *Hitler Youth* (Cambridge, MA: Harvard University Press, 2004), 23.

75   "You have the duty to be healthy." Quoted in Lisa Pine, *Education in Nazi Germany* (Oxford: Berg, 2010), 124.

76   "I wanted to escape…" Melita Maschmann, *Account Rendered: A Dossier on my Former Self* (London: Abelard-Schuman, 1964), 12.

76   "youth must be led by youth." Quoted in Kater, *Hitler Youth*, 53.

76   "Put young men in the army, …" Quoted in Pine, *Education in Nazi Germany*, 13.

77   "The construction of an insane asylum…" Quoted in Robert N. Proctor, *Racial Hygiene: Medicine under the Nazis* (Cambridge, MA: Harvard University Press, 1988), 183–184.

77   "In Germany the people of foreign race…" Quoted in Kater, *Hitler Youth*, 65.

79   "there is a strong probability…" Quoted in Burleigh and Wippermann, *Racial State*, 137.

80   "hybrid." Quoted in Proctor, *Racial Hygiene*, 114.

80   "unwilling to adapt…" … "contagious diseases, …" Quoted in Guenter Lewy, *The Nazi Persecution of the Gypsies* (New York: Oxford University Press, 2000), 25–26.

81   "you can well imagine…" Quoted in Burleigh and Wippermann, *Racial State*, 192.

83   "inner characteristics of that race." Quoted in Lewy, *Nazi Persecution of the Gypsies*, 36.

84   "a citizen of the Reich…" Quoted in Louis L. Snyder, ed., *Hitler's Third Reich* (Chicago: Nelson-Hall, 1981), 211–212.

85 "social death." Quoted in Marion A. Kaplan, *Between Dignity and Despair: Jewish Life in Nazi Germany* (New York: Oxford University Press, 1998), 5.

86 "misformed cripples..." Quoted in Adam, *Art of the Third Reich*, 15.

88 "architecture of oppression." From title of Paul B. Jaskot, *The Architecture of Oppression: The SS, Forced Labor and the Nazi Monumental Building Economy* (London: Routledge, 1999).

89 "propaganda becomes ineffective..." Quoted in Susan Tegel, *Nazis and the Cinema* (London: Hambledon Continuum, 2007), 19.

90 "the most German of the arts." Quoted in Hans Rudolf Vaget, "Hitler's Wagner: Musical Discourse as a Cultural Space," in Michael H. Kater and Albrecht Rietmüller, eds., *Music and Nazism: Art under Tyranny, 1933–1945* (Laaber: Laaber-Verlag, 2003), 22.

90 "cancerous growth..." Quoted in Erik Levi, *Music in the Third Reich* (New York: St. Martin's Press, 1994), 121–122.

Bibliography

Adam, Peter. *Art of the Third Reich.* New York: Harry N. Abrams, 1992.

Barron, Stephanie, ed. *"Degenerate Art": The Fate of the Avant-Garde in Nazi Germany.* New York: Harry N. Abrams, 1991.

Bock, Gisela. "Antinatalism, Maternity and Paternity in National Socialist Racism." In David F. Crew, ed., *Nazism and German Society, 1933–1945.* London: Routledge, 1994, pp. 110–140.

Bridenthal, Renate, Atina Grossmann, and Marion Kaplan, eds. *When Biology Became Destiny: Women in Weimar and Nazi Germany.* New York: Monthly Review Press, 1984.

Burleigh, Michael. *Germany Turns Eastwards: A Study of Ostforschung in the Third Reich.* Cambridge: Cambridge University Press, 1988.

Burleigh, Michael and Wolfgang Wippermann. *The Racial State: Germany 1933–1945.* New York: Cambridge University Press, 1991.

Cornwell, John. *Hitler's Scientists: Science, War and the Devil's Pact.* New York: Viking, 2003.

Deichmann, Ute. *Biologists under Hitler.* Cambridge, MA: Harvard University Press, 1996.

Friedländer, Saul. *Nazi Germany and the Jews. Volume I: The Years of Persecution, 1933–1939.* New York: HarperCollins, 1997.

Gellately, Robert and Nathan Stoltzfus, eds. *Social Outsiders in Nazi Germany.* Princeton: Princeton University Press, 2001.

Grau, Günter, ed. *Hidden Holocaust? Gay and Lesbian Persecution in Germany 1933–45.* Chicago: Fitzroy Dearborn, 1995.

Guenther, Irene. *Nazi Chic? Fashioning Women in the Third Reich.* Oxford: Berg, 2004.

Heineman, Elizabeth. *What Difference Does a Husband Make? Women and Marital Status in Nazi and Postwar Germany.* Berkeley: University of California Press, 1999.

Jaskot, Paul B. *The Architecture of Oppression: The SS, Forced Labor and the Nazi Monumental Building Economy.* London: Routledge, 1999.

Kaplan, Marion A. *Between Dignity and Despair: Jewish Life in Nazi Germany.* New York: Oxford University Press, 1998.

Kater, Michael H. *The Twisted Muse: Musicians and Their Music in the Third Reich.* New York: Oxford University Press, 1997.

Kater, Michael H. *Hitler Youth.* Cambridge, MA: Harvard University Press, 2004.

Kater, Michael H. and Albrecht Rietmüller, eds. *Music and Nazism: Art under Tyranny, 1933–1945.* Laaber: Laaber-Verlag, 2003.

Koonz, Claudia. *Mothers in the Fatherland: Women, the Family and Nazi Politics.* New York: St. Martin's Press, 1987.

Lane, Barbara Miller. *Architecture and Politics in Germany, 1918–1945.* Cambridge, MA: Harvard University Press, 1968.

Levi, Erik. *Music in the Third Reich.* New York: St. Martin's Press, 1994.

Lewy, Guenter. *The Nazi Persecution of the Gypsies.* New York: Oxford University Press, 2000.

Maschmann, Melita. *Account Rendered: A Dossier on My Former Self.* London: Abelard-Schuman, 1964.

O'Brien, Mary-Elizabeth. *Nazi Cinema as Enchantment: The Politics of Entertainment in the Third Reich.* Rochester, NY: Camden House, 2004.

Petropoulos, Jonathan. *Art as Politics in the Third Reich.* Chapel Hill: University of North Carolina Press, 1996.

Pine, Lisa. *Nazi Family Policy 1933–1945.* Oxford: Berg, 1997.

Pine, Lisa. *Hitler's "National Community."* London: Hodder Arnold, 2007.

Pine, Lisa. *Education in Nazi Germany.* Oxford: Berg, 2010.

Plant, Richard. *The Pink Triangle: The Nazi War against Homosexuals.* New York: Henry Holt, 1986.

Potter, Pamela M. *Most German of the Arts: Musicology and Society from the Weimar Republic to the End of Hitler's Reich.* New Haven: Yale University Press, 1998.

Proctor, Robert N. *Racial Hygiene: Medicine under the Nazis.* Cambridge, MA: Harvard University Press, 1988.

Proctor, Robert N. *The Nazi War on Cancer.* Princeton: Princeton University Press, 1999.

Reese, Dagmar. *Growing up Female in Nazi Germany.* Ann Arbor: University of Michigan Press, 2006.

Renneberg, Monika and Mark Walker, eds. *Science, Technology and National Socialism.* Cambridge: Cambridge University Press, 1994.

Scobie, Alexander. *Hitler's State Architecture: The Impact of Classical Antiquity.* University Park: Pennsylvania State University Press, 1990.

Steinweis, Alan. *Kristallnacht 1938.* Cambridge, MA: Harvard University Press, 2009.

Stephenson, Jill. *Women in Nazi Germany.* Edinburgh Gate: Pearson Education, 2001.

Stibbe, Matthew. *Women in the Third Reich.* London: Arnold, 2003.

Szöllösi-Janze, Margit, ed. *Science in the Third Reich.* Oxford: Berg, 2001.

Tegel, Susan. *Nazis and the Cinema.* London: Hambledon Continuum, 2007.

Wachsmann, Nikolaus. *Hitler's Prisons: Legal Terror in Nazi Germany.* New Haven: Yale University Press, 2004.

Walker, Mark. *Nazi Science: Myth, Truth, and the German Atomic Bomb.* New York: Plenum, 1995.

5

Nazi Germany in the 1930s
A Popular Regime?

An economic miracle. Inexpensive cruises. A modern highway system. Progressive environmental legislation. Spectacular foreign-policy triumphs. In the 1930s, many Germans were quite satisfied with the Nazi regime. Hitler, after all, had ended the communist threat, put Germans back to work, implemented attractive domestic policies, and engineered a string of foreign-policy successes. Germany seemed headed toward a better future.

Such an image of Nazi Germany belies the common belief that Germans lived in constant fear during the Third Reich. Historians used to emphasize the role of coercion and terror in the Nazi dictatorship. Germans, they argued, lived as atomized, submissive individuals during the Nazi reign of terror. In recent decades, historians have taken the opposite tack. They emphasize the popularity of the regime, especially in the years 1933–1939. The Nazis, they argue, created a popular regime with considerable buy-in from the German population. Neither of these stark images, however, accords with reality. The Nazi dictatorship did not induce terror, except in those defined as "enemies." It also did not generate all-around enthusiastic support.

What, then, was the nature of German support for the Nazi regime? The following pages examine Nazi economic, social, and foreign policies. Many Germans found elements of these policies, and thus the regime, attractive. But some did not – although only a tiny minority of Germans engaged in resistance to Hitler's dictatorship. German support for the regime must also be placed in the context of Nazi coercion and racism, discussed in Chapter 3 and Chapter 4. While racism generally heightened the regime's appeal, coercion cut many

Nazi Germany: Confronting the Myths, First Edition. Catherine Epstein.
© 2015 John Wiley & Sons, Ltd. Published 2015 by John Wiley & Sons, Ltd.

ways. Many Germans appreciated the suppression of leftists yet disliked arbitrary Nazi terror. At the same time, the threat of coercion may have kept some from voicing discontent. As this chapter argues, even if most Germans were not enthusiastic Nazis, they nonetheless came to accept the Third Reich. They shared the fundamental values and goals of Nazism: racism, anti-Marxism, and German national revival.

The Economy

Nazi economic policy makes sense only if viewed in the context of Hitler's greater goal of securing Germany's future through the acquisition of *Lebensraum* (living space). The Führer was bent on making Germany an economic rival to the United States; otherwise, he feared, Germany would be enslaved to the world Jewish conspiracy. In his view, Germany could only rival America if it had a larger population and expanded territory. To secure *Lebensraum*, Hitler would have to go to war and, for that, he needed a strong armaments industry. But he faced a predicament: Germany's productive capabilities posed numerous challenges to his goal of national regeneration.

Hitler faced another conundrum, too. He wanted worker support for the eventual war he planned to launch. At the same time, though, he and the conservative elites that supported him were eager to alter industrial relations so as to weaken workers' influence. Already in spring 1933, Hitler had crushed the independent workers' movement (see Chapter 3). Moreover, the German economy remained decidedly capitalist, favoring the interests of the state and big business over those of workers. Hitler was thus anxious about maintaining the support of German workers.

An economic miracle?

Scholars used to think that Nazism brought an economic miracle. On June 1, 1933, the Nazi regime implemented the Reinhardt Plan, one billion Reichsmarks devoted to work creation. Unemployed Germans were put to work on infrastructural improvements, especially in underdeveloped regions. By fall 1933 the number of unemployed had fallen from six to four million. Nazi propaganda trumpeted regime successes in the "battle for work." In the next years, additional Nazi policies further lowered unemployment. In 1935, for example, the Nazis made service in the Reich Labor Service (Reicharbeitsdienst) mandatory for all young men. Among other projects, Reich Labor Service workers reclaimed some 1.8 million acres of marsh and other land for agricultural purposes. Still, economic recovery took longer than anticipated. Two million Germans had no work in winter 1935–1936.

The Nazis also tried to improve the lot of Germany's farmers. Not least, this reflected their "blood-and-soil" ideology – that peasants were the repository of the true Germany. In spring 1933, R. Walther Darré, the new Nazi minister of agriculture, introduced the Reich Food Estate (Reichsnährstand). It aimed to raise agricultural production by controlling agricultural prices, production quotas, and the import of foreign goods. In addition, a Law on Hereditary Landholding (Reichserbhofgesetz) protected farmers against foreclosures. Farmers, however, could no longer freely sell their land. They had to pass on their farms to a single male heir. Some chafed at the new restrictions. On the whole, however, German farmers benefited from Nazi policies. Prices for agricultural products were generally at least twice as high as those prevailing on the world market – good for farmers, but not consumers.

There was no economic miracle in Nazi Germany. While workers and farmers enjoyed better times, German economic performance during the Third Reich was impressive only if compared to the immediate postwar and Depression years. As shown below, German workers had good reason to complain. Moreover, since the German economy never performed as well as the Nazis hoped or needed, economic constraints posed a significant challenge to Hitler's ambitious rearmament goals.

Hitler's economic predicament

Almost immediately upon coming to power, Hitler initiated rearmament. At a meeting on February 9, 1933, he declared that "The future of Germany depends exclusively and only on the reconstruction of the Wehrmacht [armed forces]. All other tasks must cede precedence to the task of rearmament." Rearmament would allow Germany to conquer foreign lands for *Lebensraum*. In June 1933, the Nazis began a 35 billion Reichsmark rearmament program.

Rearmament came up against the structural constraints of the German economy. Since Germany was short on raw materials, its economy relied heavily on imports of steel, rubber, oil, cotton, and other raw materials not found or grown on its territory. To pay for these imports, Germany had to export manufactured goods. While Germany had a relatively strong record of exports, its population of some 66 million could produce only so much. At the same time, the country owed huge sums abroad, largely accrued to finance reparations payments. Adding to the Nazis' economic dilemmas, Britain and the United States had devalued their currencies in 1932 and 1933. But Hjalmar Schacht, the head of the Reichsbank, or national bank, refused to devalue the German currency – this would have made it much more expensive to repay German debt. The refusal to devalue meant that German exports were uncompetitive on world markets; foreign exchange rates made German exports too expensive for American and British consumers.

Schacht devised a number of measures to address the dire problem of insufficient foreign cash reserves. In September 1934, he implemented the "New Plan." This involved a complicated system of export subsidies, the regulation of German firms' access to foreign raw materials, and the realignment of foreign trade according to bilateral agreements. Trade was now calculated in the two countries' currencies, not in dollars or British pounds. By the mid-1930s, Germany had abandoned many of its traditional trading partners in North America and Western Europe. It found new ones in South America and Eastern and southeastern Europe.

In the drive for rearmament, Hitler's government placed huge orders for guns, ammunition, tanks, airplanes, battleships, and everything else necessary for war. To pay for this, Schacht engaged in financial wizardry. He introduced so-called "Mefo bills," IOUs issued by Mefo, a phantom company that awarded government contracts to private companies. Schacht forced major German industrial firms such as Krupp and Siemens to fund Mefo's capital. The Nazi government thus avoided paying for rearmament through cash outlays. Still, the "New Plan" and Mefo bills were not enough to ready Germany for war.

The Four-Year Plan: autarky

Hitler believed that Germany's reliance on foreign imports left it vulnerable to economic blockade in wartime (as had occurred during World War I). In 1936, the Nazis thus introduced the Four-Year Plan to make Germany autarkic (self-sufficient) in preparation for war. Hermann Göring, the second most powerful man in the Third Reich in the 1930s, developed a huge new bureaucracy to administer the Four-Year Plan. He directed German industry to manufacture synthetic fuels and textiles, including artificial rubber (Buna) and gasoline extracted from coal. IG Farben, the giant firm committed to synthetic chemistry, proved a key player in Germany's attempt to secure independence from imported oil and other raw materials. The costs of autarky were prohibitive. It was far more expensive to produce synthetic fuel than to buy imported oil. Similarly, it was far costlier to mine Germany's low-grade iron ore deposits than to buy Swedish iron. But, when industry balked at the Four-Year Plan, the government intervened even more in the German economy. The Reich works "Hermann Göring," for example, a huge state-owned conglomerate, organized domestic ore mining.

The Four-Year Plan saw some limited success. Between 1936 and 1938, Germany upped production of aluminum by 70%, lignite by 23%, coke by 22%, and coal by 18%. At the same time, it produced rayon and other artificial fibers for Germany's textile industry. While billions of marks poured into the Four-Year Plan, economic historians see it largely as a failure. By 1939, Germany had not significantly reduced its dependence on imported raw materials.

Autarky and rearmament were contradictory aims. Autarky demanded a sustained effort to create goods for domestic consumption. The arms build-up, however, called for large quantities of imported raw materials. Imports relied on foreign exchange reserves. But foreign exchange could be had only through German exports – a goal at odds with an economy geared toward autarky and rearmament. This was Hitler's predicament: the German economy didn't have the productive capacity necessary for his ambitious plans.

All along, the Nazi regime was forced into a difficult choice between guns or butter, rearmament or consumption. As the historian Tim Mason argued long ago, Hitler's drive for rearmament was somewhat tempered by his reluctance to alienate workers. In winter 1935–1936, for example, the Führer chose to avoid food rationing, opting for food imports at the expense of rearmament supplies. In 1939, however, when another shortage of imported raw materials derailed arms production plans, he took another tack. Hitler chose war (see Chapter 6).

Winners and losers in the Nazi economy

The German industrialist was a winner in the Nazi economy. This was true even though the Nazis imposed an extraordinary degree of regulation on a peacetime, capitalist economy. The Nazis closely controlled imports for industry, forced German industry to fund Mefo, and made companies push profits back into investment. But they also smashed workers' rights, oversaw a business recovery from the Depression, and compelled German industry to develop key technologies. Most important, they allowed soaring business profits, largely on government contracts associated with rearmament.

The small businessman, by contrast, was a loser. While owners of retail stores and small manufactories had been core supporters of the Nazi movement, they received little relief from and were deeply disappointed by Nazi economic policies. The Nazis did not follow through on promises to close department stores. Small producers also had difficulty accessing hard currency to cover their import needs. Squeezed by high taxes and shortages, both of which drove up their prices, shopkeepers became the targets of consumer wrath.

But the German consumer was the main loser in the Nazi economy. While most Germans had jobs (more or less full employment was reached by 1936), they had a relatively low standard of living. Real wage levels reached those of 1929 only in 1941 – and then were only slightly higher than in 1913. Compared to Britain and the United States, Germany was also a relatively poor country. Statistics on car ownership illustrate this point. In 1935, 1.6% of Germans owned cars, while the comparable number for Britons was 4.5% and for Americans 20.5%. For the average German consumer, big-ticket items such as a car or a refrigerator remained beyond reach. At the same time, most Germans continued to live in small, cramped apartments. They paid high prices for food and clothing.

From 1937 onward, many foodstuffs, including butter and other fats, were rationed. Although Germans complained bitterly about shortages and high prices, Hitler starved consumer demand so as to reorient the economy toward arms production. Between 1933 and 1938, the Nazis raised defense spending from 4% to 50% of all public expenditure. At every turn, German incomes were pushed down – whether through higher prices for goods, wage freezes, higher taxes, or forced savings (such as retirement plans).

Collective Consumption

In the long run, Hitler believed that Germans would enjoy consumer plenty through the conquest of *Lebensraum*. For now, though, he wished to maintain popular support. His challenge was to raise living standards without compromising rearmament. Nazi leaders tried to tamp down Germans' striving for personal material goods. They claimed that Germans could enjoy a higher quality of life through self-realization and the pursuit of collective goals.

Collective consumption means that the resources of society are put toward projects that benefit large numbers of individuals. Nazi leaders insisted that collective consumption – including rearmament, group leisure activities, motorization, and environmental legislation – would improve living standards. At the same time, these programs advanced other regime goals. They furthered a classless *Volksgemeinschaft* (people's community) and promoted the collective over the individual good. They also fostered *German* values, *German* superiority, and *German* uniqueness.

Collective consumption programs created buy-in for the present-day Nazi regime. Take rearmament. Rearmament played a major role in ending unemployment in Germany. Germans also saw it as a source of pride; they wanted their country to reassert itself on the international stage. In addition, rearmament allowed Germans to engage in modern pastimes. Many men first learned to drive in the Wehrmacht, and not a few learned to fly in the new air force (Luftwaffe). Rearmament also provided entertainment in the form of military parades and flyovers. Still, mass consumption, Nazi style, was a double-edged sword. The very promise of future prosperity afforded the Nazis substantial support. Yet, as the following pages indicate, many seemingly attractive programs involved coercion, indoctrination, and the invasion of privacy.

The German Labor Front

Many collective consumption programs were sponsored by the German Labor Front (Deutsche Arbeitsfront, or DAF), the Nazi organization that replaced independent trade unions. Robert Ley, a corrupt alcoholic, led the DAF.

All employers and employees were enrolled in the DAF. The DAF aimed to mediate workplace tensions by creating a people's community on the shop floor. In practice, however, employers retained the upper hand. Still, Ley was eager to show that Nazism improved the lives of working-class Germans. He deployed a rhetoric of "dignity of labor" and "German craftsmanship" to appeal to skilled workers' traditional pride. By fostering programs that would ennoble, energize, and relax German workers, Ley hoped to improve worker morale and productivity.

Beauty of Labor
Ley believed that all German workers should enjoy clean, healthy work environments. A DAF unit, Beauty of Labor (Schönheit der Arbeit), campaigned for workplace improvements. Beauty of Labor exhorted employers to clean up their factories, plant flowers, and create green spaces. It urged them to install modern canteens and recreation rooms, brighter lighting and better ventilation systems, new washrooms with showers, and recreation centers. According to its own statistics, Beauty of Labor oversaw the creation of some 15,000 canteens and recreation rooms, 20,000 washing and changing rooms, 13,000 green spaces, and more than 2,000 sports facilities in factories around Germany. A complementary program for the countryside, Beautiful Village (das schöne Dorf), sought to clean up dilapidated farms and villages, improve rural drainage systems, and construct communal buildings.

Coercion accompanied the benefits of Beauty of Labor and Beautiful Village. Beauty of Labor hectored employers to better their plants. Workers often paid for improvements in work time or salary reductions. The programs also brought further Nazi intervention into the private life of Germans. To reduce food imports, for example, canteens served meals with fewer fats and less meat. As of 1938, young workers had to exercise for a minimum of two hours per week.

Strength through Joy
Strength through Joy (Kraft durch Freude, or KdF), another DAF unit, sponsored leisure pastimes, including cultural events, sports activities, adult education, and tourism. By exposing workers to middle-class pursuits, the Nazis hoped to solidify the *Volksgemeinschaft*. Germans of all classes were to attend uplifting cultural events. All were to pursue recreational pursuits, even exclusive ones such as tennis and sailing. In 1934–1935, some three million Germans took part in sports offerings. By 1939, tens of millions of Germans had attended concerts, plays, operettas, folk evenings, and art exhibitions paid for or organized by Strength through Joy.

Strength through Joy is best known for its low-cost packaged tours. Some 43 million Germans went on KdF trips between 1934 and 1939. Many were day trips to local sites or weekend jaunts to major German cities. In the late 1930s,

Figure 5.1   Cruise organized by Strength through Joy. *Source:* SZ Photo / Süddeutsche Zeitung Photo.

however, over one million Germans annually took two- or three-week domestic vacations under KdF auspices. A much smaller number traveled abroad to Italy, Scandinavia, Portugal, and Libya. Strength through Joy also ran much-vaunted cruises. In 1939, some 140,000 Germans cruised to domestic and more exotic foreign destinations. The trips were generally popular with their clientele. Indeed, for many workers, these trips were their first vacation experience. To keep costs low, however, KdF often booked cheap accommodation; some travelers griped at their perceived second-class status.

In May 1936, Ley began the building of Prora, a massive KdF resort. Built on a beautiful stretch of beach on the Baltic island of Rügen, Prora was to accommodate 20,000 vacationers at a time. Plans included six-story residence halls, a huge communal hall, a pool (billiards) room, a movie theater, bowling alleys, a large restaurant, and two large swimming pools, one indoor and equipped with a wave-making machine. Prora suggests that the ideal Nazi vacation was regimented, filled with activity, and shared with the *Volksgemeinschaft*. Due to the war, however, Prora was never actually completed.

As the historian Shelley Baranowski has argued, Strength through Joy trips advanced numerous Nazi goals. By mixing participants, the trips were intended to overcome regional and class differences, thus solidifying the people's community.

Cruise ships were built or renovated so that all cabins and dining rooms were similar, eschewing the traditional three- or four-class cruise-ship model. Domestic trips often went to underdeveloped regions of Germany, bringing an influx of tourist monies to impoverished areas. They also went to threatened borderland areas such as Danzig, East Prussia, and Silesia so that participants could build attachment to the German east. Finally, tourists visited countries with living standards lower than Germany, thus feeding notions of German superiority.

The Volkswagen

Hitler was fascinated with making Germany a motorized society, but in 1933 few Germans could afford a car. The Führer enlisted the racing-car engineer Ferdinand Porsche to build a cheap prototype – the "people's car" or Volkswagen. It was to have a very low sales price of 1,000 Reichmarks. No private car maker in Germany would build a car at that price. The DAF thus took on the project, building a model car factory in Fallersleben. Workers could make weekly contributions toward the future purchase of a Volkswagen. By 1939, some 270,000 Germans had subscribed to the program. Not a single Volkwagen, however, ever rolled off the assembly lines for private use; the Fallersleben factory was soon converted to military production. The promise of a Volkswagen nonetheless appealed to many Germans.

The autobahn

Hitler also promoted the building of Germany's autobahn (highway) system. In May 1935 he opened the first leg, from Frankfurt to Darmstadt. The Nazis celebrated the completion of the 2,000th and 3,000th autobahn kilometers at Christmas 1937 and 1938. A key Nazi propaganda effort, the autobahn symbolized the Third Reich's promise of modernity.

The autobahn has long been a source of myth. Many believe that it had military applications. The military, though, played virtually no role in its design. Autobahn routes were clearly designed to transport people and goods across Germany. Most of the roads were far from border areas and could not serve as invasion routes. The autobahn's road surface was also too thin to support tanks and heavy transports. Furthermore, its bright, light surfaces defied military defense. During wartime, the autobahn proved so useful an orientation system to Allied pilots that it had to be camouflaged.

There is also a myth of the "green" autobahn. Nazi landscape architects believed that technology could meld with nature in positive, "German" ways. They placed native plantings in traffic dividers and along roadsides. They also planned sweeping, curvy autobahn routes that would blend into the German terrain (as opposed to straight roads that paralleled earlier railroad building). Fritz Todt, the inspector general of German roads, wanted German drivers to consume spectacular German scenery. He thus encouraged autobahn routes that traversed mountain peaks and lake shorelines. By ruining pristine nature, however, the autobahn proved an ecological travesty. Moreover, many mountainous routes proved unsafe and difficult to travel, especially in winter months. Even so, many Germans remained enamored with the autobahn's fast, sleek roads and vast, elegant bridges.

Environmental policies

Environmental protection is a form of collective consumption in that state resources are used to provide benefit – a healthy environment – to all. It may come as a surprise to learn that the Nazis introduced progressive environmental legislation. Göring, an avid hunter, spearheaded the 1935 Reich Nature Protection Law. The law sought comprehensive protection of landscapes and wildlife. It established a Reich Nature Protection Office, under Göring's aegis, to centralize nature protection throughout Germany. German conservationists were delighted with the new legislation.

Conservationists and Nazis alike couched their concern for the environment in ideological, racist rhetoric. The preservation of the organic German landscape, they claimed, was necessary to create a strong, healthy environment that would strengthen the German *Volk*. In 1934, for example, the Nazis made the "eternal forest" (*Dauerwald*) official silvicultural practice. The "eternal forest" mirrored the ideal of a perpetual, classless, and racially pure *Volksgemeinschaft*. The Nazis mandated the restoration of forest floor through mixed plantings and the growing of trees of various ages (so that they would be harvested at different times). They also insisted on the planting of deciduous and other native species. They decreed strict limits on the seeding and harvest of forests. All this was contrary to the then-current norm of single-tree stands and clear-cutting practices. The Nazis advanced what we today would call eco-forestry, biodiversity, and sustainability.

How "green" were the Nazis really? The Nazis created many nature preserves – more than in any other period of German history. They protected some stunning natural areas, including the Rhine Gorge. Their laws were ahead of the times. Indeed, the Reich Nature Protection Law remained in effect in West Germany until 1976. Still, the Nazis subordinated environmental concerns to economic development and military preparations. The Reich Labor Service's swamp-drainage and dam-construction programs devastated local ecosystems. The autobahn, Prora, and other large-scale building programs destroyed natural landscapes and animal habitats. Rearmament increased air pollution and factory waste. Industrial demand led to the relaxation of strict forestry laws. The military ruined landscapes with shooting ranges and drill fields. In the end, most historians agree, the Nazis caused more ecological harm than good.

While many Nazi domestic policies were appealing, they also had their draw-backs. Nazi promise outstripped reality. Collective consumption involved more sacrifice than benefit. Most Nazi programs had a coercive edge. Still, for many Germans, life under the Nazis did seem better. They had more economic security. They enjoyed intangible goods such as national renewal and the promise of modernity. For the first time, they could imagine family vacations in private cars, speeding along highways through gorgeous German scenery. Germans were both attracted to and ambivalent about Nazi domestic policies.

The Churches

Given the racist, coercive nature of Nazism, one might have thought that believing Protestants and Catholics would have opposed the Third Reich. After all, Christianity and National Socialism are theoretically incompatible. In the abstract, at least, Christian tenets include humility, forgiveness, and universalism. They also proclaim the equality of all believers before God and command the faithful to "love thy neighbor." Still, despite their religious beliefs, most church-men and believers supported Nazism in Germany.

The Protestant Church

In 1933, some 18,000 pastors ministered to roughly 41 million German Protestants. As part of Germany's conservative elite, most supported Hitler's nationalism, antisemitism, and anti-Marxism. During the Nazi era, the Protestant churches engaged in what was known as the "church struggle." This was *not* a church struggle *against* Nazism. Instead, it was an intra-confessional dispute over who should control the Protestant churches in Nazi Germany. Two main groups, the German Christians and the Confessing Church, stood opposed.

German Christians hoped to align Christianity with National Socialism. Their aim was to create a racist people's church that would work together with the Nazis for national regeneration. German Christians were particularly eager to remove all Jewish elements from their Christianity. They welcomed the dis-missal of non-Aryan Protestants from church positions. They sought to expunge the "Jewish" Old Testament from the Christian Bible. They simply ignored the fact of Jesus' Jewish origins. They espoused a manly Christianity whose members were tough soldiers for Jesus and Fatherland.

The German Christians numbered roughly 5,000 pastors and 600,000 layper-sons. In Protestant Church elections in summer 1933, they won two-thirds of leadership positions and took over almost all of Germany's regional churches. Hitler named a German Christian, Ludwig Müller, to a new position, Reich Bishop of Germany. Müller hoped to unite all German Protestants into one

"Reich church." Yet the movement's crude understanding of Christianity dismayed many mainstream Protestants. Unable to forge a unified state church, the German Christians soon lost official Nazi support.

The Confessing Church decried the attempt to introduce racist tenets into church doctrine and organization. In September 1933, Martin Niemöller founded the Pastors' Emergency League. Roughly one-third of German pastors joined the league. In 1934 Niemöller and others convened the first General Confessional Synod. It issued the Barmen Declaration, penned largely by the Swiss theologian Karl Barth. The Barmen Declaration insisted on church autonomy in spiritual affairs. It also stated that Jesus and the gospel were the only authentic sources of God's revelation – and not nature and history, too, as the German Christians believed.

The Nazis led a concerted attack on the Confessing Church. In 1934, for example, they placed Bishop Hans Meiser, who supported the Barmen Declaration, under house arrest and attempted to remove him from his bishopric. In response, Protestants held mass demonstrations that forced the regime to relent. While Protestants won this battle, Hitler created a Ministry for Church Affairs under Hanns Kerrl in 1935. Its very existence militated against church autonomy. Moreover, in 1937, the Nazis briefly arrested some 700 pastors for disobeying government proscriptions on their sermons. Soon thereafter, they shuttered denominational schools.

Despite the Nazi assault, most Confessing Church pastors sought accommodation with the regime. While they wished to defend church autonomy, they had little interest in outright resistance to Nazism. Few pastors spoke out against the regime's antisemitic policies or its aggressive expansion into central Europe. Only a small number of Confessing Church ministers openly challenged the Nazis. Niemöller excoriated Nazi intervention in church matters and the arrest of recalcitrant pastors. Yet, even though he was imprisoned from 1937 onward, he volunteered for navy service at the outbreak of war in 1939 (Hitler denied his request). Dietrich Bonhoeffer, a more determined church opponent of Nazism, preached against the regime's antisemitic and other violent policies. He was later executed in connection with the July 20, 1944, plot (see Chapter 8).

The Catholic Church

The Nazis meted out harsher treatment to Catholics and their church. They feared Catholic allegiance to a worldly power beyond Nazi control, the Vatican. They also worried about the influence of priests on their parishioners. Prior to 1933, Catholic clergy had successfully urged the faithful not to vote for the Nazis. After Hitler came to power, however, the Catholic hierarchy relented. Germany's 20 million Catholics did not want to be outsiders to the nation, as they had been during the Bismarck era (see Chapter 1). Moreover, they shared some basic Nazi values. Militantly anticommunist, they desired national renewal. They also harbored a traditional Christian antisemitism – the Jews were the people who had crucified Christ and rejected his teachings.

In the early days of the Nazi regime, both the Catholic Church and the Nazi government wished to come to an understanding. While the church hoped to secure the free exercise of Catholic religion, the Nazis aimed to end all Catholic political activity in Germany. In July 1933, Nazi Germany and the Vatican concluded an agreement, the Concordat. The Nazis guaranteed freedom of religion for Catholics and the continued activity of Catholic charitable, cultural, and educational institutions. The Vatican agreed to ban priests and members of religious orders from political activity. The Concordat was the first international treaty signed by the Nazi government. In a boon for Hitler, the Vatican signaled that the Third Reich was reputable and trustworthy.

The Nazis soon reneged on their Concordat promises. They pressured Catholic youth groups to disband. They shut Catholic primary schools and limited the hours of religious instruction in public schools. They closed Catholic welfare organizations and banned Catholic periodicals. They confiscated the property of religious orders. They even murdered important Catholic lay officials. Cardinal Eugenio Pacelli, Vatican Secretary of State (and later Pope Pius XII), lodged repeated complaints about violations of the Concordat. In March 1937, Pope Pius XI issued a papal encyclical, "With Burning Anxiety," a searing indictment of the Nazi government's failure to uphold the Concordat.

Vatican complaints only fortified Nazi antagonism toward the church. Schutzstaffel (SS) leader Heinrich Himmler and his deputy, Reinhard Heydrich, were fanatical opponents of the Catholic Church. Together with Goebbels they orchestrated a campaign to portray the church as corrupt and immoral. They charged Catholic priests with currency violations, not least so as to curtail contact with the Vatican. They also claimed that the clergy was engaged in widespread homosexuality and pederasty. By 1937, some 1,000 Catholic clergymen stood accused of sexual abuse or other misconduct. The Nazis held 250 widely publicized trials in which 200 Catholic order members were convicted of sexual crimes.

Despite persecution, Catholic opposition to the Nazi regime was narrowly focused on defending church independence against Nazi domination. In November 1937, for example, a regional minister of education in southern Oldenburg ordered the removal of all crucifixes and other religious symbols from public buildings, including schools. Thousands of Catholics protested by holding rallies, signing petitions, lighting up large crucifixes at night, and resigning from the National Socialist German Workers' Party (NSDAP). In the face of this determined opposition, the minister backed down.

Like the Protestant churches, the Catholic Church did not generally oppose Nazism. As discussed in Chapter 7, church officials did protest euthanasia policies. This, however, did not extend to Hitler's antisemitic policies. The influential prior of Saint Hedwig's Cathedral in Berlin, Bernhard Lichtenberg, was the sole Catholic priest to openly express sympathy with the Jews. Beginning in November 1938, Lichtenberg prayed aloud for Jews in every evening service (he was eventually arrested and died in Nazi captivity). He was, however, the exception; the Catholic Church never adopted a broad stance against the Nazi regime or its antisemitic policies.

Jehovah's Witnesses

In Nazi Germany, only Jehovah's Witnesses, also known as Bible Students, offered principled religious opposition to Nazism. Jehovah's Witnesses insist that their only loyalty is to Jehovah, God. In 1933, there were 25,000–30,000 Witnesses in Germany. As early as June 1933, they were banned. In the Third Reich, they were the only group persecuted solely on the grounds of religious belief.

Jehovah's Witnesses refused to go along with many Nazi practices. They did not give the obligatory Hitler salute, join Nazi associations, vote in elections, or participate in Nazi rallies. They refused to serve in the military. In 1937, they circulated leaflets critical of the regime. The Nazis, in turn, sent many Witnesses to prisons and concentration camps. Although they gave most the option of release if they renounced their religion, only six Witnesses chose to do so. Approximately 10,000 Jehovah's Witnesses were incarcerated during the Nazi era. Roughly 1,200 lost their lives.

Popular Opinion in the Third Reich

Resistance to the Nazi Regime, 1933–1939

Historians rightly debate what constituted "resistance" in Nazi Germany. Some believe that the term should have a narrow definition: moral-ethical opposition that involves organized action intended to bring down a regime. Others prefer to give the term a more capacious definition: any conduct that thwarts the regime's aim to infiltrate and control all aspects of society. In this text, "resistance" is used in the more narrow sense. Resistance brought almost certain arrest (and often death sentences), but few rewards – really just moral certainty and righteous feeling. "Nonconformist conduct" refers to a much wider range of behavior (see below), and usually brought lesser sanctions.

Left-wing resistance
At first, leftist resistance was the only organized opposition in the Third Reich. Just as before 1933, however, the left was unable to unite against Nazism. The communists hoped to turn Germans against the regime through mass underground

agitation. Between 1933 and 1935, they flooded German cities with literally millions of illicit leaflets, newspapers, and brochures. The mass character of the resistance, however, permitted easy police infiltration. Similarly, the large volume of printed material allowed the Gestapo to easily trace communist agitators. In 1935, the communists had to acknowledge the futility of their heroism. Virtually all party activists had been arrested or had fled abroad. Prior to World War II, roughly 150,000 communists endured Nazi concentration camps; 30,000 were executed.

The Social Democrats adopted a very different strategy. Their primary aim was to uphold party networks so as to have an intact party organization when the Nazi dictatorship ended. By late spring 1933 the party leadership had emigrated abroad. It arranged for the distribution of newspapers and other printed materials to the party faithful inside Germany. As one activist later recalled of this material, "It was not supposed to turn into a mass movement, but to be a shot in the arm for people who were already committed." The Gestapo was ruthless in arresting all members of the Social Democratic Party (SPD) and other independent socialists engaged in underground activity. These individuals, too, paid for their resistance with prison and even death sentences. Due to leftist disunity, harsh Gestapo methods, and the relative appeal of the regime, the left was unable to mobilize broad-based opposition to Nazism.

Conservative resistance

Initially, most conservatives were enthusiastic about Nazism. They rejected democracy and desired a strong, authoritarian state. But by the mid-1930s, some were bothered by Nazi despotism. Carl Goerdeler emerged as the civilian point man for national conservative opposition. He was mayor of Leipzig from 1930 to 1937 and Reich Commissioner of Prices from 1934 to 1935. He resigned as Reich Commissioner because he came to oppose Nazi economic policies, especially frenzied rearmament. He stepped down as Leipzig mayor after city officials razed a statue of the German-Jewish composer Felix Mendelssohn. Goerdeler established contacts with like-minded conservatives scattered throughout the various Berlin ministries. It took war, however, for these conservatives to turn to sustained resistance (see Chapter 8).

Pastor Martin Niemöller once famously stated: "First they took the Communists, but I was not a Communist, so I said nothing. Then they took the Social Democrats, but I was not a Social Democrat, so I did nothing. Then it was the trade unionists' turn, but I was not a trade unionist. And then they took the Jews, but I was not a Jew, so I did little. Then when they came and took me, there was no one left who could have stood up for me." As Niemöller's words suggest, the fact that the Nazis targeted groups disliked by many other Germans helps to explain the absence of a broad-based resistance. At the same time, the divided nature of German society prevented persecuted groups from finding solidarity across class or confessional lines. Individuals who had misgivings about Nazism thus looked in vain for like-minded persons.

A popular regime?

What did the absence of outright resistance to Nazism mean? Did most Germans consent to the regime? Were the Germans so terrorized that they could not express opposition? Or did most Germans have another reaction, perhaps passive acceptance? In the Third Reich, Germans could not express outright opposition to the regime. The Nazis censored the press, destroyed independent trade unions, banned all political parties (except the NSDAP), outlawed strikes, and cracked down on absenteeism and shirking at work. Moreover, the Sicherheitsdient (SD) and Gestapo ferreted out subversive activity, often aided by unsolicited denunciations. In such a situation, it makes sense to question whether Germans actually gave consent to the Nazi regime. Consent, one might argue, is meaningful only when genuine alternatives are possible.

During the Third Reich, many Germans displayed nonconformist behavior. Some left the Nazi party, while others refused to give the "Heil Hitler" greeting. Some staged illegal strikes and work slow-downs; others demonstrated for church autonomy and insisted on crucifixes in schools. Some Germans joked about the Führer, while others listened to foreign broadcasts or danced to American-style swing music. Some Germans used up precious fuel by driving private cars during wartime, while others refused to donate to the Winter Relief, a Nazi charity.

Historians have debated the meaning of such nonconformist conduct. In the 1980s, German historian Martin Broszat coined the term *Resistenz* to capture something very different from "resistance." Individuals who engaged in *Resistenz* did not do so out of a moral-ethical imperative but rather out of more mundane motivations, such as seeking profit or expressing their personal identities. For Broszat, *Resistenz* described behavior intended to ward off regime attempts to penetrate and control German society.

Other historians questioned the use of the concept. In their view, Broszat's notion of *Resistenz* was too easily conflated with resistance, and they did not want to confer the moral halo of resistance on those whose actions did not fundamentally challenge the Nazi regime. As the historian Ian Kershaw notes, it is unfortunate that *Resistenz* and resistance are such similar words. To him, though, the concept of *Resistenz* remains useful. The very ubiquity of nonconformist behavior points to underlying consent. When individuals grumble, they express discontent with perceived injustice in a legitimate status quo – not fundamental opposition to an illegitimate regime.

In the Third Reich, discontent was joined with basic support of Nazi goals. Germans widely shared the Nazi values of national regeneration, anti-Marxism, and antisemitism. Peasants and middle-class Germans were often frustrated with their economic situation, but they were pleased with the Nazi return of "order" and the crushing of Marxism. Workers complained about longer working hours and consumer shortages, but they were thankful to have jobs at all. They imagined future prosperity, already embodied in the autobahn, the Volkswagen, and Strength through Joy offerings. Conservative Germans disdained the plebian qualities of Nazi functionaries, but they supported Hitler's aggressive foreign policy (see below). Because Germans combined discontent with fundamental support of the Third Reich, dissenting behavior never posed a significant challenge to the Nazi dictatorship. Still, the existence of widespread dissent suggests the limits of Nazi popularity. While some fanatically supported the regime, most Germans merely accepted it. For them, Nazism was the new normal.

In determining the degree of Nazi popularity, one should not ignore Hitler's foreign-policy achievements. Most Germans viewed these very positively. Indeed, the Führer repeatedly used foreign-policy successes to divert attention from domestic problems. At a time when the popularity of Nazism suffered due to rising prices, flat wages, and ongoing unemployment, Hitler generated renewed regime support each time he circumvented another Versailles restriction.

Foreign Policy

Before 1933, Hitler promised to rid Germany of the Versailles Treaty. In office, he made good on his words. He removed many of the treaty's remaining restrictions. At the same time, he had grander ambitions: he wished to overturn the liberal tenets of the postwar order. The interwar western powers advocated disarmament, multilateral diplomacy, and international trade. Hitler, by contrast, espoused militarism, privileged bilateral pacts, and sought autarkic empire.

Hitler's chief aim was *Lebensraum* in the east. He always planned to conquer the Soviet Union. At the same time, though, he hoped to forge an alliance with Britain. In his preferred world order, Britain would rule the seas, Germany continental Europe. While seeking friendly relations with Britain, Hitler also worked to undermine relations between Britain, France, and Italy.

More so than in other realms, historians agree, Hitler played a decisive role in the foreign policy of the Third Reich. In terms of the intentionalist–structuralist debate (see Chapter 3), foreign policy provides much evidence for the intentionalist position. Hitler's prophecies in the 1920s became his actions in the 1930s. His obsessions – hatred of the communist Soviet Union, admiration for fascist Italy, respect for imperial Britain – fundamentally shaped Nazi foreign policy. His personal actions also mattered. Hitler took risks, manipulated tensions, and engaged in sheer opportunism. Still, he was dependent on others' reactions. He could not anticipate, much less dictate, what other states would do.

Overturning the Versailles Treaty, 1933–1936

First moves

After Hitler came to power, he insisted that Germany should have equal rights in armament. In October 1933, however, Britain proposed a four-year postponement to equalizing Germany's armaments. In response, Hitler pulled Germany from the Geneva Disarmament Conference, hosted by the League of Nations, and from the League itself. He thus signaled that he would not play by the old rules. He would challenge the status quo in international affairs.

Next, in January 1934, Hitler signed a ten-year Non-Aggression Pact with Poland. This reversed long-standing German policy that favored the Soviet Union over Poland, who were traditional enemies. For Hitler, the pact with Poland was a tactical maneuver. It emphasized his anticommunist credentials to the west, and particularly to Britain. It also undermined France's defense strategy of forging alliances with states that bordered on Germany. Hitler likely never intended to fulfill the pact. As he had reportedly stated a few months earlier, "I am prepared to guarantee all frontiers and to make non-aggression pacts and friendly alliances with anybody... There has never been a sworn treaty which has not sooner or later been broken or become untenable."

In July 1934, Hitler faced a foreign-policy setback when local Nazis attempted a coup in Austria. In the botched putsch attempt, Nazis murdered the Austrian chancellor, Engelbert Dollfuss. The Austrian elites rallied to uphold their country's independence. Perhaps most important, the coup exposed German–Italian tensions. Mussolini was adamant about maintaining an independent Austria as a buffer state between Italy and Germany. He was furious about the attempted coup, not least because Dollfuss' wife was just then vacationing in one of his villas. Coming on the heels of the Röhm affair (see Chapter 3), the Dollfuss incident made Nazi Germany seem a rogue terrorist state. In a meeting in the Italian town of Stresa, Britain, France, and Italy reaffirmed their intention to hold Germany in check.

Hitler soon recovered from the Austrian Nazi debacle. In January 1935, as mandated by the Versailles Treaty, the inhabitants of the Saar region were to vote on their future. They could rejoin the Saar to Germany, leave the Saar under League of Nations mandate, or join the Saar to France. In a free and fair election, over 90% of the Saar population voted to join Hitler's Germany. In a defeat for democracy, Germans showed that they *wanted* to join the Third Reich – a sign of Nazi legitimacy and, indeed, popularity.

Hitler was emboldened. On March 10, 1935, Göring announced the existence of a German air force. Six days later, Hitler announced the introduction of universal conscription. In addition, he set the size of the peacetime German army at 550,000 men. All were clear-cut violations of the Versailles Treaty. Britain and France lodged protests but took no further action. Indeed, just a few months later,

114

on June 18, Hitler secured an Anglo-German Naval Agreement. Britain allowed Germany naval forces at 35% of the strength of the Royal Navy, with parity in submarines. Hitler claimed this was "the happiest day" of his life. He was, so he thought, on his way to an Anglo-German alliance. British leaders, though, merely sought to appease Hitler. They wanted to satisfy "reasonable" German demands, mostly so as to secure a broad western front against Soviet Bolshevism.

The remilitarization of the Rhineland

By early 1936, Hitler was eager to remilitarize the Rhineland. This would allow Germany to defend itself against a French invasion, protect Ruhr industry, and permit conscription among the area's large population. Hitler exploited international tensions to accomplish his goal. In October 1935, Mussolini had invaded Abyssinia (Ethiopia). Britain and France, who opposed Italy's African adventure, were distracted by the Abyssinian crisis. Hitler, however, now insisted that a 1935 Franco-Soviet Pact – that allegedly undercut security guarantees in the Treaty of Locarno (see Chapter 1) – warranted a change in the Rhineland's status. On the morning of March 7, 1936, he sent 3,000 troops to reoccupy the Rhineland. This was risky business. France immediately placed its troops on alert. England, however, refused to take military action. France proved unwilling to fight Germany alone. Hitler later called the forty-eight hours following reoccupation the "most exciting of his life." But the risk paid off. While the western powers lodged protests, they took no action.

By the time Hitler reoccupied the Rhineland, he had circumvented many of the most onerous Versailles restrictions. Many Germans were enthusiastic about his foreign policy. After all, Hitler had fulfilled nationalist dreams of overturning much of the Versailles Treaty without going to war. At the same time, military leaders were thrilled with the arms build-up. Foreign ministry officials were impressed with Hitler's foreign-policy achievements. Businessmen reaped profits from rearmament. Ordinary Germans were proud of their country's heightened international stature. To drive home his foreign-policy triumphs, Hitler held plebiscites after withdrawal from the League of Nations and the reoccupation of the Rhineland. In both cases, 90% or more of Germans allegedly signaled approval. Still, underground SPD reports suggest that some Germans, at least, were wary of Hitler's foreign policy. Already, some worried about war.

The Berlin Olympics

In August 1936 the Olympics took place in Berlin, and were another foreign-policy triumph for the Nazis. Germany had been awarded the Olympics in 1931, well before the Nazis came to power. Hitler was initially skeptical about holding the Games. Olympic values flew in the face of Nazi ideology. The Games were international, championing equality and universalism. All athletes, regardless of race, religion, or ideology, could participate. Propaganda Minister Joseph Goebbels nonetheless convinced Hitler of the Games' potential. Hitler was soon set on staging the grandest Olympics yet.

American Olympic officials worried about how Nazi racism might affect the Games. They sent Avery Brundage, the head of the American Olympic Committee, to conduct an on-site inspection. On his trip to Germany, Brundage chose to ignore all evidence of Nazi discrimination against German-Jewish athletes. He wanted the Games to go on, regardless of the Nazi venue. Despite an intensive boycott campaign in the United States, Brundage ensured American participation in the 1936 Olympics.

At the Olympics, the Nazis displayed their penchant for pageantry. On August 1, 1936, in a refurbished Olympic Stadium, Hitler opened the Games before 110,000 spectators and 5,000 athletes from fifty national teams. The Nazis invented the tradition of lighting a torch in Olympia, Greece, and running it by relay to the host city to ignite the Olympic flame. In the first ever TV broadcast of any sporting event, they televised the Olympics to some twenty-five TV halls in Berlin and beyond. Leni Riefenstahl, director of *Triumph of the Will*, captured the Games in *Olympia*, one of the most impressive sports documentaries ever produced. *Olympia* is a paean to fascist notions of beauty, health, and virility.

The Berlin Olympics are best remembered for Jesse Owens' spectacular athletic performance. In the face of Nazi racism, Owens proved black athletic prowess. An African-American, Owens won four gold medals in track-and-field events. Contrary to popular myth, Hitler did not snub Owens. Although the Führer personally congratulated the first few event winners at the Games, by the time Owens won his medals, he had stopped doing so.

The Nazis used the Olympics to showcase the Third Reich at its best. In advance of the Games, they spruced up Berlin and ceased all antisemitic propaganda. They proved generous hosts. Goebbels held a lavish party for 2,000 guests at a fancy villa (recently confiscated from a Jewish family). The press corps enjoyed many amenities, including telephone and writing booths, darkrooms, and secretarial assistance. Journalists and other visitors were suitably impressed with the smooth organization of the Olympics. As Foreign Minister Konstantin von Neurath declared of the Games, "The whole world has come to pay respects to the new power of Germany." With this athletic extravaganza, the Nazis propped up their foreign image. The Olympics were a spectacular – and scandalous – propaganda coup.

The road to war, 1936–1939

In summer 1936, Hitler's foreign policy entered a new phase. Instead of working to overcome onerous restrictions in the Versailles Treaty, Hitler now focused on forging an alliance that would allow German conquest of

Lebensraum. In July 1936, General Francisco Franco led a revolt against the Spanish Republican government. While Germany remained officially neutral, Hitler aided Franco by sending the Condor Legion – some 5,000–6,000 volunteers equipped with airplanes, tanks, and antiaircraft guns – to Spain. Italy supported Franco with even more troops and military supplies. Mussolini's intervention further ruptured his relations with Britain and France, who practiced neutrality but hoped for Republican success. Meanwhile, the Soviet Union openly supported the Spanish Republican government. In November 1936, Germany and Japan signed the Anti-Comintern Pact, directed against their common enemy, the Soviet Union. That same month, Mussolini referred to a "Berlin–Rome axis." A year later, Italy joined the Anti-Comintern Pact. The future Axis powers during World War II – Germany, Italy, Japan – had begun to work together.

On November 5, 1937, in a conference with top officials, Hitler outlined his next foreign-policy steps. As recorded in the famous Hossbach Memorandum, the Führer emphasized Germany's need for *Lebensraum*. He would risk war for annexations. For Germany to take advantage of its edge in rearmament, he would begin war no later than 1943–1945. If, however, France appeared weakened, he would launch war sooner. Hitler would first target Austria and Czechoslovakia, two countries that would bring additional economic and manpower reserves. They would also serve as useful staging areas for eastward expansion.

After listening to Hitler, Generals Werner von Fritsch and Werner von Blomberg, along with Foreign Minister Neurath, voiced objections. A few months later, in February 1938, in the so-called Blomberg–Fritsch Affair, Hitler dismissed all three officials. At the same time, he removed twelve other generals, fifty-one senior officers, and four high-level diplomats. This was his final act of *Gleichschaltung* (coordination; see Chapter 3), now directed against the conservative elites. As he prepared for war, Hitler did not want naysayers to cramp his style. He appointed a sycophantic wine merchant, Joachim von Ribbentrop, as foreign minister. He named Wilhelm Keitel, a servile lackey, chief of the office that ran the Wehrmacht, the Supreme Command of the Armed Forces. Hitler himself took over direct command of the Wehrmacht and the functions of the minister of war.

Austria: the Anschluss

As suggested in the November 5, 1937, conference, Hitler next targeted Austria. The Treaty of Versailles expressly forbade German–Austrian union. Hitler, however, was eager to join his homeland – with almost seven million German-speakers – to the Third Reich. Austria had earlier relied on Mussolini's support to preserve its independence, but the Italian dictator now abandoned Austria in the hope of strengthening the Rome–Berlin Axis.

At the same time, the sluggish Austrian economy fueled support for an illegal Nazi movement there. Hitler was now in a position to pressure the Austrian government.

In February 1938, Hitler demanded that the Austrian government name Arthur Seyss-Inquart, an Austrian Nazi, minister of the interior. Seyss-Inquart was duly appointed. Some Austrians, however, including the chancellor, Kurt Schuschnigg, wished to maintain their country's independence. Schuschnigg thus planned a referendum on the matter. Hitler, however, threatened invasion if the referendum was held. Although Schuschnigg cancelled the plebiscite, Hitler sent German troops on a "friendly visit" to Austria on March 12. The next day, after jubilant crowds greeted him in Linz, Hitler decided on the *Anschluss*, the annexation of Austria. Mussolini quickly assented, as did the Austrian government (now headed by Seyss-Inquart). Britain and France voiced protests but soon recognized Germany's swallowing of Austria. On April 10, 1938, Hitler held the fourth and last plebiscite of the Nazi regime. Over 99% of German voters allegedly approved the union of Austria with Germany.

Czechoslovakia

Hitler next turned to Czechoslovakia. His pretext was the supposedly intolerable situation of the three million ethnic Germans who lived in the Sudetenland, part of the Czech state. On September 15, 1938, Neville Chamberlain, the British prime minister, came to Germany to negotiate with Hitler. The two men agreed on self-determination for the Sudeten Germans. Hitler, however, soon upped the ante. In their next meeting, on September 22, he threatened invasion if Czechoslovakia did not cede the Sudetenland to Germany by October 1. Chamberlain was understandably vexed. Soon thereafter, a British envoy warned Hitler that Britain and France would side with Czechoslovakia in the event of military action. Meanwhile, some high-ranking German military officials had serious reservations about the Führer's rash actions. If war ensued, General Ludwig Beck, recently dismissed as army chief of staff, and a number of active top army officers planned to carry out a coup against Hitler.

With war in the offing, Mussolini offered to mediate. Western appeasement now reached its zenith. At a four-power conference in Munich on September 29, Britain, France, and Italy agreed to German demands that Czechoslovakia cede the Sudetenland to Germany. Although Czechoslovakia was not party to the negotiations, the Munich Agreement forced the Czechs to hand over to Germany virtually all of their fortifications, much of their industry, and one-third of their population. Chamberlain returned home touting "peace in our time." Meanwhile, the agreement squashed preparations for the coup against Hitler. The British ambassador to Berlin, Sir Nevile Henderson, immediately recognized what the western powers had done: "By keeping the peace, we have saved Hitler and his regime." But, even though the west had caved in, Hitler was the one who was disappointed. Munich robbed him of a chance at war.

Just five months later, Hitler tore up the agreement. In March 1939, he manipulated tensions between Czechs and Slovaks so as to invade the country. Even before a satellite Slovak state had officially formed, it "invited" in German troops for protection. As the Führer remarked, "one cannot make history with lawyers." On March 15, Germany occupied the core Czech lands of Bohemia and Moravia. Immediately afterward, Hitler insisted that Lithuania cede tiny Memel, an ethnic German enclave, or suffer invasion. The Lithuanians handed over Memel on March 23. By now, though, the western powers had had enough. On March 31, Britain and France publicly guaranteed the independence of Poland, Hitler's presumed next target.

Why did the western powers take so long to counter Hitler? Although appeasement has negative connotations today, it was widely popular at the time. The last thing Britons wanted was another war. World War I had decimated a generation of British youth. At the same time, British statesmen questioned the fairness of the Versailles Treaty. They thought Germany justified in trying to mount credible defenses and recover self-respect. They also assumed that Hitler – as head of state – would make reasonable choices, follow diplomatic conventions, and avoid risky conduct that could lead to war. They could not fathom that what Hitler really wanted was war. By contrast, the French tolerated appeasement, largely because they were reluctant to go to war against Germany alone. Both Britain and France, however, viewed Czechoslovakia as the last straw. Although they never wanted to fight Germany, Hitler left them no choice. They could not accept a German tyrant running roughshod over the continent.

The German population had mixed reactions to Hitler's foreign-policy moves in the later 1930s. The *Anschluss* and annexation of the Sudetenland were popular. Hitler had achieved nationalist ambitions that had eluded even Bismarck! Yet, while many Germans delighted in the new Greater Germany, few wanted to achieve territorial gains through war. Indeed, during the Sudeten crisis, Hitler had a division of troops march through the streets of Berlin in the direction of the Czech frontier. No crowds of onlookers cheered. Similarly, the SPD underground reported widespread anxieties about Hitler's bellicose actions. While many Germans backed Hitler's aggressive moves, there was no universal support for them, and certainly not for war. Still, when Hitler did draw Germany into war, he could count on the support of the overwhelming majority of Germans.

Citations for Quotations

Page   Source

98   "battle for work." Quoted in Richard J. Evans, *The Third Reich in Power* (New York: Penguin, 2005), 333.

99   "The future of Germany…" Quoted in Adam Tooze, *The Wages of Destruction: The Making and Breaking of the Nazi Economy* (New York: Penguin, 2006), 38.

103   "dignity of labor" and "German craftsmanship." Quoted in Dick Geary, "Working-Class Identities in the Third Reich," in Neil Gregor, ed., *Nazism, War and Genocide: Essays in Honour of Jeremy Noakes* (Exeter: University of Exeter Press, 2005), 44.

111   "It was not supposed…" Quoted in Hartmut Mehringer, "Socialist Resistance," in Wolfgang Benz and Walter H. Pehle, eds., *Encyclopedia of German Resistance to the Nazi Movement* (Continuum: New York, 1997), 30.

111   "First they took the Communists, …" Quoted in Evans, *The Third Reich in Power*, 232–233.

114   "I am prepared…" Quoted in Christian Leitz, *Nazi Foreign Policy, 1933–1941: The Road to Global War* (London: Routledge, 2004), 68.

115   "the happiest day." Quoted in Leitz, *Nazi Foreign Policy*, 52.

115   "most exciting of his life." Quoted in Jonathan Wright, *Germany and the Origins of the Second World War* (Houndsmills: Palgrave Macmillan, 2007), 69.

116   "The whole world…" Quoted in Leitz, *Nazi Foreign Policy*, 70.

118   "friendly visit." Quoted in Wright, *Germany and the Origins of the Second World War*, 105.

119   "By keeping the peace…" Quoted in Peter Hoffmann, *German Resistance to Hitler* (Cambridge, MA: Harvard University Press, 1988), 88.

119   "one cannot make history with lawyers." Quoted in Wright, *Germany and the Origins of the Second World War*, 135.

Bibliography

Baranowski, Shelley. *The Confessing Church, Conservative Elites, and the Nazi State.* Lewiston: Edwin Mellen Press, 1986.

Baranowski, Shelley. *Strength through Joy: Consumerism and Mass Tourism in the Third Reich.* Cambridge: Cambridge University Press, 2004.

Benz, Wolfgang and Walter H. Pehle, eds. *Encyclopedia of German Resistance to the Nazi Movement.* New York: Continuum, 1997.

Bergen, Doris L. *Twisted Cross: The German Christian Movement in the Third Reich.* Chapel Hill: University of North Carolina Press, 1996.

Brüggemeier, Franz-Josef, Mark Cioc, and Thomas Zeller, eds. *How Green were the Nazis? Nature, Environment and Nation in the Third Reich.* Athens: Ohio University Press, 2005.

Conway, J.S. *The Nazi Persecution of the Churches 1933–45.* New York: Basic Books, 1968.

Evans, Richard J. *The Third Reich in Power.* New York: Penguin, 2005.

Garbe, Detlef. *Between Resistance & Martyrdom: Jehovah's Witnesses in the Third Reich.* Madison: University of Wisconsin Press, 2008.

Geary, Dick. "Working-Class Identities in The Third Reich." In Neil Gregor, ed., *Nazism, War and Genocide: Essays in Honour of Jeremy Noakes.* Exeter: University of Exeter Press, 2005, pp. 42–55.

Hockenos, Matthew D. *A Church Divided: German Protestants Confront the Nazi Past.* Bloomington: Indiana University Press, 2004.

Hoffmann, Peter. *German Resistance to Hitler.* Cambridge, MA: Harvard University Press, 1988.

Kershaw, Ian. *Popular Opinion and Political Dissent in the Third Reich: Bavaria 1933–1945.* Oxford: Clarendon Press, 1983.

Kershaw, Ian. *Hitler 1936–1945: Nemesis.* New York: W.W. Norton, 2000.

Kershaw, Ian. *The Nazi Dictatorship: Problems and Perspectives of Interpretation.* Fourth Edition. London: Arnold, 2000.

Kirk, Tim. *Nazi Germany.* Houndmills: Palgrave Macmillan, 2007.

Large, David Clay. *Nazi Games: The Olympics of 1936.* New York: W.W. Norton, 2007.

Leitz, Christian. *Nazi Foreign Policy, 1933–1941: The Road to Global War.* London: Routledge, 2004.

Lewy, Guenter. *The Catholic Church and Nazi Germany.* New York: McGraw-Hill, 1964.

Mandell, Richard. *The Nazi Olympics.* Urbana: University of Illinois Press, 1987.

Merson, Allan. *Communist Resistance in Nazi Germany.* London: Lawrence and Wishart, 1985.

Snyder, Louis L., ed. *Hitler's Third Reich.* Chicago: Nelson-Hall, 1981.

Steiner, Zara. *The Triumph of the Dark: European International History 1933–1939.* Oxford: Oxford University Press, 2011.

Tooze, Adam. *The Wages of Destruction: The Making and Breaking of the Nazi Economy.* New York: Penguin, 2006.

Uekoetter, Frank. *The Green and the Brown: A History of Conservation in Nazi Germany.* Cambridge: Cambridge University Press, 2006.

Wright, Jonathan. *Germany and the Origins of the Second World War.* Houndsmills: Palgrave Macmillan, 2007.

Zeller, Thomas. *Driving Germany: The Landscape of the German Autobahn, 1930–1970.* New York: Berghahn Books, 2007.

6

War and Occupation, 1939–1941

On September 1, 1939, Germany invaded Poland. Two days later, Britain and France declared war on Germany. While Hitler was eager for war, this was not the war he wanted. His sworn enemy, the Soviet Union, was initially on his side (see below). He was also fighting Britain, the country he had long sought as an ally. Regardless, Hitler was ready to stake all in his quest for *Lebensraum* (living space) and the global dominance that would ensue.

Many myths surround Nazi Germany in World War II. There is a common presumption that the German army was modern through and through. There is a misperception that *only* the early Russian winter kept German forces from seizing Moscow in fall 1941. There is a myth that the Wehrmacht (army) was "clean"; that is, that the Schutzstaffel (SS) – and *not* the army – perpetrated the Holocaust and other wartime atrocities. There is a presumption that the Nazi race war was directed solely at Jews – and *not* at Slavs or other "undesirables." Finally, there is a misperception that Britain and the United States – *instead of* the Soviet Union – were primarily responsible for Allied victory in Europe. Confronting these and other myths exposes important truths about Nazi Germany.

This chapter covers major developments in World War II up to the end of 1941: the invasions and occupations of Poland, Western Europe, and the Soviet Union. Hitler ultimately sought *Lebensraum* and raw materials in the Soviet Union. This, he believed, would allow Germany to evade an Anglo-American blockade and permit it to attack the United States in a bid for world domination. Hitler also hoped to Germanize Central and Eastern Europe – a process that involved everything from planting birch and oak trees

Nazi Germany: Confronting the Myths, First Edition. Catherine Epstein.
© 2015 John Wiley & Sons, Ltd. Published 2015 by John Wiley & Sons, Ltd.

to murdering Jews and Slavs. At its zenith, Nazi Germany imposed a brutal racial order that led to subjugation, segregation, deportation, and murder of many of Europe's inhabitants.

The Invasion of Poland

Decision for war

Hitler believed that only *Lebensraum* could solve his country's long-term economic and other problems. By March 1939, however, he had reached the territorial limits of what he could achieve without war. Britain and France staunchly opposed further German gains. While Hitler had always expected to fight the Soviet Union, he now realized that he would have to fight the western powers, too.

Economic reasons help to explain why Hitler launched war when he did. In fall 1938 Hermann Göring, backed by Hitler, had called for three times the current armaments production. This proved totally unrealistic. Göring's plan, like so many others, crumbled on Germany's acute balance-of-payments problem. Germany simply didn't have the revenue to import the necessary raw materials to produce so many weapons. The very fact, though, that it could not stockpile unlimited armaments made Hitler eager to start a war as soon as possible. For now, it seemed, Germany had the advantage. It had the largest, most prepared army in Europe. It had the best air force. Despite British and French rearmament initiatives, Germany was still ahead in the arms race. If Germany struck early, it could draw on the resources of a "Greater Germany" to fight a potentially long war of attrition.

To bolster his strategic position against Britain and France, Hitler realigned Germany's foreign relations. In early 1939, he invited Poland to join the Anti-Comintern Pact. Poland, however, did not wish to subordinate itself to Germany. A few months later, in May, Germany signed the "Pact of Steel" with Italy, a military alliance directed at Britain and France. Germany also courted Japan. But Japan was interested in a military alliance only if it was aimed at the Soviet Union (with whom it was fighting a war in Manchuria). With both Poland and Japan refusing military alliance on his terms, Hitler allowed a dramatic about-face in German foreign relations.

On August 23, Germany and the Soviet Union concluded a Non-Aggression Pact. Each side pledged not to attack the other. In a secret protocol, they planned the division of Eastern Europe between them. They also agreed on economic cooperation. The pact shocked the world. It flew in the face of Nazi anticommunism and Soviet antifascism. For Hitler, though, it was just a tactical move to avoid a two-front war. While he still planned to conquer the Soviet Union, he first needed to defeat the west. Meanwhile, Stalin believed that, by supplying Germany with oil, food, and other raw materials, he might convince Hitler not to attack the Soviet Union at all. In any event, he wanted to buy time against a potential German invasion. He also hoped that Germany and the west might engage in mutual destruction – to the benefit of the Soviet Union.

Despite British and French pledges to uphold Poland's independence, Hitler set about to provoke a war with his eastern neighbor. In April 1939, he had revoked the German–Polish Non-Aggression Pact. He had also demanded that Danzig be returned to Germany and that Germany be granted extra-territorial routes through the Polish Corridor to East Prussia. The Poles refused. As Hitler readied for military action, he feared that another Munich Conference might stymie his war plans. In late August, he reportedly told his military commanders that his only worry was that "some bastard [*Schweinehund*] would present a last-minute plan of conciliation." None did.

On the evening of August 31, in an operation dubbed "Canned Goods" (*Konserven*), the SS staged a Polish attack on a radio station in Gleiwitz, a German village near the German–Polish border. In the "attack," an anti-German message was broadcast (read, in fact, by German operatives). Concentration-camp victims, dressed up as Polish forces, were murdered to make it seem as though a nasty battle had taken place between insurgent Poles and Germans defending themselves. This fake attack was Hitler's immediate justification for war. Beginning at 4:45 the next morning, a German battleship shelled Polish naval installations in the Danzig harbor. One million German troops soon poured over the border into Poland.

Blitzkrieg

Although the translation of *Blitzkrieg* – "lightning war" – suggests speed, the concept really means the close coordination of airpower, tanks, and infantry in an attack. In September 1939, the Poles were overwhelmed by nascent *Blitzkrieg* tactics. The Germans sent in their most advanced mechanized columns. The German Luftwaffe (air force) pounded Polish cities. While valiant Polish forces put up some stiff resistance, their efforts were futile. By the end of the first week, Germany had all but secured Polish defeat.

Poland faced a hopeless military situation. It had no mountain ranges or other geographical features to defend its flat plains from German invasion. Given its ten-year Non-Aggression Treaty with Germany, Poland had not prepared for war with the Third Reich. Its military equipment was outdated and the country didn't have the resources to buy or produce modern weapons. Moreover, Britain and France, who still hoped to appease Hitler, insisted that Poland not provoke Germany by mobilizing its forces prior to a German attack. As a result, when Germany struck, Poland had only partially mobilized its troops. Meanwhile, although Britain and France declared war on Germany, they did nothing to defend their ally. Then, on September 17, the Soviet Union attacked Poland. Invaded by two much stronger neighbors, Poland ceased to exist. Polish leaders soon set up a government-in-exile in London.

The speed of German victory belied *Blitzkrieg* successes. In fact, the Polish campaign proved a poor display of such tactics. Air support for ground forces was not prioritized. While Germany deployed some fifty-four divisions, roughly 1.5 million men, against Poland, just fourteen were mechanized. All the other divisions involved infantry who marched into Poland on foot, relying on horses to transport their artillery and for other logistical needs. Swift triumph covered up Germany's lack of mechanized units.

No ordinary war

Despite imperfect *Blitzkrieg* tactics, the German invasion of Poland was stunningly ferocious. From the very beginning, the war in the east was no ordinary war. It combined territorial aggrandizement with a race war against not only Jews but *all* "non-Aryans." In the Nazi racial hierarchy, Slavs were near the bottom, just above Jews and Roma (Gypsies). The Nazis saw Poles as dirty, inferior, and foolish, but also as treacherous opponents.

In the five-week Polish campaign, SS mobile killing squads (*Einsatzgruppen*), sometimes aided by Wehrmacht troops, carried out numerous war crimes against alleged political opponents. Behind the front lines, SS Operation Tannenberg targeted the Polish elite: nobles, clergymen, politicians, and professionals such as lawyers, doctors, and educators. Some 16,000 leading Polish citizens were murdered. The aim was to "decapitate" Polish society, thereby destroying those who might foment resistance against Nazi rule. In the history of modern warfare, the murder of Poland's leading strata was as radical as it was unprecedented.

The German military also engaged in fierce reprisals against civilian Poles who put up armed or other resistance. German retaliation was out of all proportion to purported Polish actions. Reprisal killings claimed the lives of thousands of civilian Poles. German military officials also starved, beat, and murdered Polish prisoners of wars (POWs). Although Germany was a signatory to the 1929 Geneva Convention guaranteeing humane treatment of POWs, Wehrmacht officials did not adhere to the international standard – or even their own army regulations – on the treatment of Polish POWs.

The German treatment of Polish Jews was also outrageous. SS and army troops engaged in wanton destruction of synagogues and other Jewish communal buildings. They plundered Jewish stores and robbed Jews of their personal possessions. They beat and tortured Jews, not least by cutting off the beards of Orthodox men. They expelled some 22,000 Jews across the San river into

Soviet-occupied Poland. Finally, they burned some Jews alive in synagogues, and shot or otherwise killed thousands of others. Still, this was not (yet) genocide.

Some historians link German barbarity to the intensity of combat or the fact that inexperienced German soldiers were fighting on foreign territory. German brutality, however, appears to have been present from the start and thus premeditated. While some high-ranking army commanders refused to allow their units to participate in war crimes, many lower-ranking officers condoned vicious actions against Poles and Jews. They often harbored traditional anti-Polish and antisemitic prejudices, hardened by years of exposure to Nazi propaganda. At the same time, when told to commit atrocities, few German soldiers questioned the morality of their actions. In October 1939, Hitler issued a blanket amnesty for all Germans accused of committing crimes during the war in Poland. In subsequent campaigns, German military commanders had fewer qualms about their men committing atrocities. Poland thus proved a "dress rehearsal" for future German barbarity, especially in the Soviet Union.

The Nazi Occupation of Poland

At war's end in October 1939, Germany and the Soviet Union each occupied roughly half of Poland. Eastern Poland remained under Soviet control until June 1941. The Nazis divided their half of Poland into two major areas. Central Poland was known as the General Government and was headed by Hans Frank, once Hitler's private lawyer, with headquarters in Cracow. The General Government, with some 12 million inhabitants, was never formally part of the Third Reich. Meanwhile, the western areas of Poland, with some 16 million people, were annexed to the Third Reich (see Map 6.1). Most of this territory had once been part of the German Empire. It was now slated for immediate "Germanization": a radical demographic restructuring that would replace Poles and Jews with Germans.

Resettlement and deportation

With the conquest of Poland, the Nazis began the process of forging a German Empire in the east. This reflected the traditional German push to the east (*Drang nach Osten*), the notion that Germany's true destiny lay in the domination of Eastern Europe. In October 1939, Hitler appointed SS leader Heinrich Himmler in charge of "strengthening Germandom." The SS chief aimed to bring ethnic Germans to, while deporting "undesirable" races from, areas that were to be made "German." Ironically, although the Nazis claimed that the German people had insufficient *Lebensraum* for their numbers, there were actually not enough Germans either abroad or in the Third Reich to people the territories conquered by the Nazis. This, however, did not deter Himmler or his staff from imagining and attempting vast projects of demographic engineering.

The Warthegau, one part of western Poland annexed to the Third Reich, became the site of some of the most dramatic Germanization policies. Five million people lived in the Warthegau, but 85% were ethnic Poles. The Nazi leader (*Gauleiter*) of the Warthegau, Arthur Greiser, was nonetheless eager to create a Nazi "German" region (*Gau*). Between 1939 and 1941, Himmler's agencies arranged for some 575,000 ethnic Germans to come "home to the Reich," mainly from the Baltic countries, the Soviet Union, and Romania. Most of these "resettlers" ended up in the Warthegau. In another irony, the Nazis believed that resettlers had to be taught to be "German." Young officials of the League of German Girls (BDM), sent from the Reich, instructed them in German customs, songs, and child-rearing techniques.

To make way for the resettlers, Poles were forced out of their homes. (The Nazi regime did not yet privilege the removal of Jews above all other "undesirable" groups.) In four great deportation waves, nearly 300,000 Poles were rounded up, put on trains, and shipped to the General Government. Incoming Baltic and other ethnic Germans took over Polish apartments, businesses, and farms. In March 1941, however, all deportations eastwards were halted. Trains were needed to move German troops in advance of the invasion of the Soviet Union. Still, Poles continued to endure population transfers. From the Warthegau alone, some 450,000 Poles were sent westwards as forced laborers to replace German men, now soldiers, in factory and farm work.

The General Government was initially designated a dumping ground for those deemed "undesirable." In late 1941, however, Nazi officials changed course and decided to Germanize it, too. Germanization efforts in the General Government focused on the Lublin district, chosen for its fertile farmland and SS presence (due to concentration camps, factories, and an arms depot). By summer 1943, the SS had deported virtually all Jews and 100,000 Poles from 300 villages in the Zamość area of the Lublin district. In this area, 9,000 ethnic Germans and 4,000 Germans from the Reich took over emptied farms. This action, however, backfired. It sparked so much partisan activity that the Lublin district became virtually ungovernable (see Chapter 8).

Anti-Polish measures

Throughout Nazi-occupied Poland, Poles were deemed to be second-class persons. They were neither German nor Polish citizens. They lost all property rights and were subject to a special, stringent criminal code. To carry out these policies, however, the Nazis had to know who was "German" and who was "Polish." This was no easy matter in the ethnically mixed areas annexed to the Third Reich. To resolve the issue, Nazi authorities introduced an Ethnic German Registry.

Those who proved "German" descent (but not resettlers) were put on the registry and given German ID cards. All others were considered "Poles."

Registry policies varied significantly according to region. In Danzig-West Prussia and Upper Silesia, the *Gauleiters* claimed that most of the population was "German." Nazi attempts to racially categorize the population foundered on the absence of racial differences between Poles and Germans. As a result, more often than not, nonracial characteristics – such as German-language facility or the ability to provide useful labor – proved decisive in registry classifications. As with categorizing Jews, Nazi racial fanatics had to rely on nonracial criteria to make their determinations.

In the Warthegau, Greiser instituted the sharpest discriminatory measures against Poles. Germans and Poles were not permitted to marry. Germans and Poles attended separate schools and ate at separate restaurants. They sat on separate park benches. Poles were not allowed entry to museums, concerts, or theater shows, nor could they own cameras, binoculars, records, or record players. Poles were given lower rations than Germans, and at times could not buy butter, fruit, or wheat products. They were not permitted to use express trains or certain tram lines during rush hour. Poles were supposed to "greet" Germans by taking off their hats or otherwise acknowledging the presence of a "superior" being. Finally, since Catholicism was viewed – correctly – as a pillar of Polish national identity, German authorities closed Catholic schools and seminaries, shuttered most Catholic churches, limited the hours of masses, and arrested most Catholic priests.

Greiser also sought the biological elimination of the Polish population. He imposed a minimum marriage age of twenty-eight for Polish men and twenty-five for Polish women. He hoped that older marriage ages would reduce the number of children born of Polish unions. Together with Himmler, Greiser also implemented a program whereby Polish orphans deemed racially "valuable" were transferred – essentially kidnapped – to the *Lebensborn* program (see Chapter 4). If they passed racial muster, these children (several hundred in all) were placed with SS families and raised as Germans; in the process, they lost all contact with their Polish relatives. Greiser also hoped to have some 35,000 Poles with advanced tuberculosis murdered outright. Fearing an international outcry, Himmler rejected this plan.

"German" land

Nazi policies in western Poland offer a primer for ethnic cleansing. Immediately, the Nazis removed all Polish signs and inscriptions. They renamed cities, towns, villages, and streets. The large Polish city of Łódź, for example, became Litzmannstadt. The Nazis created or renovated institutions so as to project "German" culture. Poznań, renamed Posen, the capital of the Warthegau, soon sported a *German* castle, *German* university, *German* theater, and *German* museum. The Nazis also believed that Germans should enjoy "high" living standards in the east. They planned (and built in small numbers) new housing with modern conveniences such as running water and central heating. They wished to visually contrast "high" German living culture with "low" Polish slum dwellings.

Furthermore, the Nazis engaged in ambitious efforts to make the landscape "German." To Nazi eyes, western Poland seemed a vast "Asiatic" steppe. It did not have the trees or other greenery viewed essential for the health of the German psyche. As part of a vast planned Nazi reforestation program, forestry officials planted millions of trees. Local officials also constructed parks and hiking trails that were to build German attachment to the local landscape. Finally, in the Warthegau, the Nazis planned the largest reservoir in the world. Most of these projects barely got underway. Their planning, however, is a testament to Nazi ambitions to turn Eastern Europe into a German redoubt.

The Invasion of Western Europe

For Hitler, Poland was but a stepping stone to an invasion of the Soviet Union. In fall 1939, the Führer planned to attack Western Europe so as to neutralize opposition to additional German conquests. His military commanders, however, stalled. Claiming unfavorable weather, they repeatedly postponed attack orders. They had little confidence in Germany's ability to defeat the west; the Polish campaign had revealed military weaknesses. The Wehrmacht needed time to train troops and to replace lost or repair broken equipment.

Despite the declaration of war, neither Germany nor the western powers engaged in military operations in the winter of 1939–1940. This period is known as the "phony war." On November 30, however, the Soviet Union attacked Finland. In the Winter War, the Finns put up stiff resistance, embarrassing the much larger Soviet forces. But they could not win. In March, Finland agreed to a peace treaty in which it ceded territory and economic assets to the Soviet Union. The Winter War made Finland fiercely anti-Soviet, and thus inclined to cooperate with Nazi Germany.

In spring 1940 Hitler moved to secure the rest of Scandinavia for German aims. He wanted Norwegian naval bases for use in an eventual war with England. He also desired the continued supply of Swedish iron ore, vital for German industrial production. Moreover, during the winter months, Swedish iron ore was usually shipped via Norway to Germany. On April 9, Germany attacked both Denmark and Norway. Denmark surrendered in hours. Norway, however, resisted for almost two months. British, French, and Polish forces rushed to its aid. While Germany managed to defeat Norway, it lost much of its surface fleet in the process. After German victory, Vidkun Quisling headed a Norwegian collaborationist regime. In Denmark, in turn, Hitler permitted a relatively benign occupation. Denmark sent large quantities of dairy products, meat, and fish to the Third Reich. Sweden remained officially neutral but continued to deliver iron ore and much else to Germany.

On May 10, just weeks after attacking Denmark and Norway, Germany invaded Belgium, France, Holland, and Luxembourg. To conquer France, the Germans adopted a daring battle plan recently devised by General Erich von Manstein. The new plan was actually a product of German carelessness. German operational orders fell into Allied hands after officers carrying the plans were shot down over French territory. The whole incident, however, ultimately helped the Germans. French military strategy was based on the captured *earlier* German plans, not the *later* plans actually implemented.

Manstein's plan foresaw the bulk of German invasion forces coming via a southerly route, through the heavily wooded Ardennes Forest, thought to be impassible for tanks. Since the French had not anticipated this, the area was barely defended. The Germans, however, also invaded Belgium in the north, just as the French had expected, but with a relatively small force. To meet that force, the French moved virtually all of their available troops northwards – never realizing the greater danger to the south. Meanwhile, tank (panzer) units, commanded by General Erwin Rommel and others, punched through the Ardennes and raced toward the Channel. *Blitzkrieg* tactics were devastatingly effective; the Luftwaffe provided air cover for the rapidly advancing ground forces. The speed of the invasion was halted not by the Allies but by the Germans' inability to maintain supply lines to forward positions.

German military maneuvers trapped some 1.7 million Allied troops in a wedge of Belgian and French territory. Since the Germans had troops to both the north and south, Belgian, British, Dutch, and French soldiers were squeezed toward the Channel coast. Allied troops were at serious risk of capture. But the British engineered a remarkable evacuation – the Miracle of Dunkirk. In late May, Britain deployed naval, merchant, and private ships to pluck soldiers from the beaches of Dunkirk and ferry them across the Channel to England. Some 220,000 British soldiers and about 120,000 French soldiers were saved to fight another day. Still, France and its allies had suffered a catastrophic military rout.

What explains the German defeat of France in 1940? The *Blitzkrieg* myth masked unpleasant truths about both French and German military operations. The French thought that they had been overwhelmed by a superior military force. There was, however, nothing inevitable about the French defeat. Indeed, piece for piece the French had better military equipment than the Germans. The French loss stemmed from poor army morale, faulty military strategy, and a lack of coordination among Allied troops. Meanwhile, the Germans deployed the teaching of the famed nineteenth-century military thinker Carl von Clausewitz to great effect: concentrate all forces at the enemy's weakest point.

The stunning German victory in France was not repeatable, however. The Germans focused virtually all of their forces on one risky maneuver. Had the Allies marshaled a different response, the outcome might have been otherwise. In addition, the costs of *Blitzkrieg* were high. Three weeks into the invasion, Germany had lost 30% of its planes. Finally, the *Blitzkrieg* mystique applied to only about a dozen assault divisions. As in Poland, most German troops invaded on foot, while their supplies were moved to railheads and then by horse and cart to battlefield destinations.

Historians often assert that the Wehrmacht carried out a "correct" war in the west – that is, that German troops did not engage in the wanton crimes that had characterized the Polish campaign. In large part, this is true. There was no counterpart to Operation Tannenberg. The vast majority of the two million captured French POWs survived Nazi incarceration. In May and June 1940, however, some Wehrmacht units singled out and massacred 1,500–3,000 Tirailleurs Sénégalais, black colonial soldiers serving in the French army. Some of these Wehrmacht units were the very same ones that had carried out war crimes in Poland. The Nazis thus brought the race war from Poland to Western Europe. These massacres illustrate the Wehrmacht's growing Nazification.

Thirty-five days after invading France, Hitler controlled a large Western European land empire. The Nazis implemented a "new order" in Europe – not least, one that brought them economic advantage. Ostensibly independent countries such as Finland (rich with nickel), Hungary, Italy, and Romania (rich with oil) soon aligned themselves with Germany. Neutral countries such as Spain, Sweden, and Switzerland could not escape the German orbit. German hegemony stretched from the Atlantic to the Black Sea, encompassing 30% of global GDP and some 290 million people (20% of the world's population). Germany's new stature exceeded the wildest dreams of the most ardent Nazi nationalists. Hitler basked in his military success. He and his regime were vindicated in every possible way.

The Nazi Occupation of Western Europe

France

At Compiègne on June 25, 1940, in the very same railway car in which Germany had surrendered in 1918, the elderly French World War I hero, Marshal Philippe Pétain, signed a humiliating armistice. France ceded Alsace-Lorraine to Germany. The Germans occupied the northern two-thirds of the country, including Paris and the Channel and Atlantic ports. In the unoccupied southern zone, Pétain established a government in the town of Vichy. In November 1942, after the

Allied invasion of North Africa, the Germans extended their occupation to the southern zone, too.

Pétain instituted a quasi-fascist state, aiming to appease the Third Reich and achieve French autonomy. He believed that he was "saving" France by instituting a "new order." In his view, excessive democracy had weakened France and allowed its defeat. Vichy thus replaced traditional French values of "Liberty, Equality, Fraternity" with those of "Work, Family, Fatherland." Pétain's authoritarian regime eliminated all political parties and other democratic institutions. Many French citizens, dismayed by military defeat and eager for national renewal, supported the marshal. Pétain's strategy, however, bore little fruit. Germany had no reason to grant concessions. Instead, the Germans demanded that the French pay "occupation costs." These amounted to some 25 billion Reichsmarks by the end of 1943 – a sum far exceeding the costs of German occupation. France delivered food, chemicals, cars, textiles, and much else to Germany.

Everyday life in occupied France was hard, often very hard. Because France had to send food to the Third Reich, the French endured terrible food shortages. Ration cards initially covered 1,800 calories per day, but they eventually fell to 1,300 and then to as few as 900 calories per day. To ward off hunger, French citizens resorted to the black market. They also ate pets or stray animals – so much so that the Parisian authorities warned residents of the dangers of eating stewed cat. The Nazis also demanded French workers for German industry. Many of the two million French POWs captured in 1940 labored in Germany until war's end. In addition, Vichy introduced the Compulsory Labor Service in 1943, forcing 650,000 Frenchmen to leave their homeland for work in Germany. Finally, the French people endured the intangible sufferings of foreign occupation. In a blow to French masculinity, some French women chose German occupation soldiers for lovers.

Historians have long debated the role of the French during wartime. Did the Germans foist Nazi policies on the unwilling French? Or did Vichy officials initiate Nazi policies on their own, with or without the support of the French population? Put starkly, was France a nation of resistors or collaborators? There is no simple answer. Vichy certainly initiated antisemitic policies independent of Germany. These culminated in the death of some 75,000 Jews from France. Yet approximately 225,000 Jews survived inside the country, largely due to the efforts of the French population.

The French record of resistance is also mixed. While many citizens engaged in oppositional practices, only a small minority was truly committed to resistance. Particularly after the introduction of compulsory labor, many Frenchmen joined the Maquis, resistance groups in the countryside. 30,000 French civilians eventually lost their lives as hostages or resistance members, and another 60,000 were sent to German concentration camps. General Charles de Gaulle also led a small Free French movement in London and then Algiers. Such resistance activity, however, must be placed alongside the widespread acceptance of Vichy. The latter compromised the moral integrity of France, a country long associated with liberty and equality.

The low countries

Similar dynamics developed in the other western countries under German occupation. The Germans placed Holland under German civil administration and Belgium under military control. They *de facto* annexed Luxembourg. While few citizens in these countries "liked" the Germans, most resigned themselves to Nazi occupation policies. They continued to produce large quantities of industrial goods for the insatiable German war machine. At the same time, citizens of the Low Countries went along with Nazi racial policies. A Dutch informer, for example, turned in Anne Frank, who was hiding in Amsterdam in 1944. Still, while Western Europe endured a wretched occupation, it was generally not murderous (as in Eastern Europe). The Nazis ranked Western Europeans racially higher than Slavs.

The Battle of Britain

After conquering Western Europe in spring 1940, Hitler was all the more bent on Germany's conquest of Soviet territory. Britain, however, stood in the way. Its dominance of the oceans thwarted Nazi strategic aims; in August 1940, for example, Britain began a naval blockade against Germany. At the same time, in any military conflict with Germany, Britain could hope to draw on the United States, an economic powerhouse. To neutralize Britain, Hitler planned an amphibious invasion of the island nation, codenamed Operation Sea Lion. Since Germany had lost most of its surface fleet in the battle for Norway, this was no easy matter. It was now essential for Germany to destroy the British Royal Air Force (RAF): in any amphibious assault, the Luftwaffe would need control of the skies to provide tactical air support to an invasion force.

In July 1940, the Luftwaffe began the Battle of Britain. It pounded the English Channel, forcing Britain to divert ships away from the Channel. In August, it targeted British airfields and radar stations, as well as RAF fighter planes on the ground and in the air. The Luftwaffe attacks were devastating: the RAF lost pilots, planes, airfields, and radar stations at frightening rates. Still, the British were able – just barely – to hang on. On August 24, German pilots accidentally bombed London. In turn, the RAF retaliated by bombing Berlin. An enraged Hitler now ordered the bombing of London. A sustained aerial attack on the capital, he thought, would terrify British citizens, leading them to beg their government to sue for peace.

Shifting the focus from RAF targets to London proved a major German strategic blunder. The "Blitz" only heightened British resolve. It also allowed the RAF respite to quickly train new pilots, repair damaged planes, and resupply its depleted force. Already by mid-September the RAF was repulsing incoming Luftwaffe planes – so much so that staggering German losses made Hitler reconsider his aims. He now decided to save Luftwaffe planes for his planned attack on the Soviet Union. On September 17 Hitler indefinitely postponed an invasion of Britain.

The Battle of Britain was Hitler's first military failure. Britain had proved that it could and would stand up to Nazi Germany. As British Prime Minister Winston Churchill famously stated of the 500 RAF pilots who perished over Channel waters, "Never in the field of human conflict was so much owed by so many to so few." Britain's ability to stay in the war allowed it to marshal imperial and American resources for a long war against Nazi Germany.

By then, the United States, concerned by the defeat of France and imminent danger to Britain, had already begun an extraordinary military build-up. In summer 1940, President Franklin D. Roosevelt laid plans for the United States to produce 50,000 aircraft per year. Congress approved the Two Ocean Navy Expansion Act, which foresaw the building of 1,325,000 tons of warships. In September, Britain and the United States concluded the destroyers-for-bases deal – in return for fifty destroyers, Britain leased seven bases rent-free for ninety-nine years to the Americans. Roosevelt also secretly authorized an atomic weapons program. In summer 1940, although technically neutral, the United States planted the seeds for Germany's final defeat.

The Battle of Britain should have given Hitler pause. The west had shown resolve. The Luftwaffe had suffered defeat. Hitler, however, had already decided to attack the Soviet Union. Given the enormous German land victories in France, he thought it would be easy to defeat Russia, weakened as it was by a "Judeo-Bolshevik" leadership. Conquering the Soviet Union would render the British blockade meaningless – Germany would have all the resources it needed. Indeed, Hitler calculated, plundered Soviet resources would allow Germany to take on Britain and the United States.

This raises the question of long-term Nazi aims. Did the Third Reich desire European or global domination? Historians long presumed that Hitler's aim was a land empire based on *Lebensraum* in the Soviet Union. More recently, however, scholars have argued that Hitler sought more. Norman Goda, for example, shows that after the defeat of France the Third Reich tried to secure bases in Northwest Africa. For what purpose? According to Goda, Hitler contemplated offensive operations against the United States. In spring 1941, the Führer also planned a great shift in resources away from the army to the air force and navy, the latter two vital for fighting Britain and the United States. In the heady early months of 1941, Hitler thought that he could defeat the world.

The Balkans

In advance of the invasion of Russia, Hitler wished to secure his Balkan flank and solidify the Axis position in the Mediterranean. In October 1940, Mussolini had invaded Greece, but the Greeks had repulsed the Italians, not least through aid from Britain. In March 1941, a coup deposed a pro-Nazi Yugoslav government. Hitler now feared that the new Yugoslav government would side with Britain. This, he worried, might give Britain an opening to attack the Ploeşti oil fields in Romania, essential for the German war machine. Hitler was also concerned that Britain might make gains in North Africa at Italy's expense, thus threatening Axis positions around the Mediterranean.

To shore up its position in the Balkans, Germany invaded Yugoslavia and Greece on April 6, 1941. Yugoslavia fell in eleven days. Despite the aid of 50,000 British imperial forces, Greece surrendered soon after. Germany next attacked the Greek island of Crete, valuable to Britain as a Mediterranean air base. In the first airborne invasion in military history, Germany managed to force British troops to withdraw from the island and the Greeks to surrender Crete. The Luftwaffe, however, sustained such high losses that the Third Reich never launched another airborne assault.

Still, the Balkan campaign was an Axis success. Britain was defeated, again. Romania's oil was safe. The Axis position in the Mediterranean was bolstered. The Germans now imposed a brutal occupation on the Balkans. In Yugoslavia, the Wehrmacht initiated vicious reprisals against partisan activity, leading to the murder of many Jews and Roma. In Greece, exploitative economic practices led to widespread starvation, particularly around Athens.

There is a myth that the Balkan campaign cost Hitler World War II. Hitler had initially planned to invade the Soviet Union on May 15, 1941. Historians have argued that the diversion of troops to the Balkans delayed that invasion. As a result, they claimed, the Wehrmacht had too little time to capture Moscow before winter set in. More recently, however, historians have shown that logistical predicaments and a late spring thaw led Hitler to postpone the attack on the Soviet Union. Furthermore, as argued below, logistical and strategic shortcomings – and not winter weather conditions – explain why the German offensive stalled outside Moscow in fall 1941.

Operation Barbarossa: The Invasion of the Soviet Union

On Sunday, June 22, 1941, Germany launched Operation Barbarossa, the invasion of Soviet Russia. Hitler hoped to grab great swathes of *Lebensraum* in order to establish the preconditions for German global dominance. Operation Barbarossa was named after the legendary Frederick I, the twelfth-century

Holy Roman Emperor who crusaded against Muslims. It involved the largest invasion force in history. Roughly 3.3 million German troops and another 500,000 Axis troops rushed into the Soviet Union. The German forces were equipped with 3,350 tanks, 2,770 Luftwaffe planes, and over 600,000 horses. This huge invasion force was organized into three army groups. Army Group North was to strike the Baltic countries and Leningrad. Army Group Central was to push toward Minsk and then on to Smolensk and Moscow. Army Group South thrust toward Ukraine. The Germans opened an enormous front that ran almost 1,800 miles from the Barents Sea in the north to the Black Sea in the south.

Prior to June 22, Stalin was desperate to avoid war with Hitler. The Soviet Union had continued to deliver huge amounts of rubber, oil, copper, tin, and grain to Germany. The Third Reich, however, had delayed sending promised manufactured goods in return. Stalin also chose to ignore the many intelligence reports that warned of an impending invasion. He did not think that Hitler would engage in a two-front war. Once Germany did attack, Stalin fell into depression and hid in his home for days. On July 3, however, he emerged to give a rousing radio address. Calling on the Soviet people to save their country, he urged them to fight a great patriotic war against the German invader. Stalin's ability to maintain a stable Soviet regime – not to be taken for granted – was crucial to Russian successes in 1941.

German war plans called for destroying the Red Army in the western parts of the Soviet Union and preventing its remnants from escaping eastwards. Hitler expected that the Soviet government would collapse under the weight of the Wehrmacht onslaught. In fact, in the first days and weeks of the war, the Wehrmacht dealt a crushing blow to the Soviet military. In June and July, it surged forward in great pincer movements, encircling whole Soviet armies. By June 29 the Germans had taken Minsk, by July 16 Smolensk. The Germans thought that they had won the war. On July 3, General Franz Halder, the army chief of staff, noted that "the campaign against Russia has been won within two weeks."

Yet, despite extraordinary German military triumphs, the Soviet regime did not fall. Moreover, it soon became clear that the Germans had underestimated Soviet potential. To be sure, the Red Army was totally unprepared for war with Germany. Stalin had murdered much of the officer corps in the Great Purges of the late 1930s. Inexperienced officers led soldiers with little training. The Red Army made some dreadful mistakes. Aircraft, for example, were lined up in neat rows on Russian airfields – easy targets for the Luftwaffe. Still, the Red Army had more and better military equipment than German intelligence had presumed. The Soviet regime could also mobilize huge numbers of soldiers. By the end of the first week of the war, it had called up some 5.3 million army reservists. In the face of dire peril, Red Army commanders inspired their soldiers to fight against the fascist threat. Soviet soldiers confounded German troops with their unexpected and dogged ferocity.

The Wehrmacht now faced a host of challenges. It was not the modern army of *Blitzkrieg* myth. Only 33 of the army's 160 divisions were fully motorized. Moreover, panzer units faced extraordinary attrition as vehicles broke down on inferior Soviet roads. In just five weeks, General Heinz Guderian's Panzer Group lost 70% of its tanks. Meanwhile, German soldiers *marched* – they did not drive – through the western parts of the Soviet Union. They arrived at the front exhausted. The Wehrmacht also faced a logistical nightmare. Its plans called for trucks to resupply its troops. This system was sustainable within a 300-mile range of the German border. Deep inside Soviet territory, however, roads were poor and fuel costs prohibitive. The Russian railroad network proved too thin to support Wehrmacht needs.

Most important, the Germans lacked strategy. In Russia, as in France, they staked all on one risky maneuver: defeating the Red Army close to Germany. When *Blitzkrieg* failed, the Germans had no back-up strategy to defeat the Soviet Union. Making matters worse, Hitler and his generals could not agree on what to do next. General Halder wished to move on Moscow, in the vain belief that taking the capital would destroy the Soviet system. Late in August, however, Hitler insisted on pushing south toward Ukraine, hoping to capture natural resources such as the Caucasus oil fields. The turn southwards, however, further exhausted German troops and supplies.

In late September, Hitler changed tack, now ordering Operation Typhoon, an overly ambitious plan to take Moscow. In the first two weeks of October, the Nazis did win stunning victories in the battles of Vyazma and Briansk. Now Stalin even considered surrender. But Marshal Georgi Zhukov, the hero of a Soviet victory over Japan in Manchuria, managed to raise huge reserve armies from Siberia and the Far East. In late October, German offensive operations were hampered by steady rains, making fields muddy and roads impassable. When the Wehrmacht resumed its attack in November, freezing winter conditions, dwindling supplies, and a lack of reserve troops stalled the advance. Some German advance units nonetheless reached within twelve miles of the Soviet capital. On December 5, however, Zhukov began a counteroffensive, pushing the Germans 175 miles in retreat. For the Third Reich, this was calamitous. Zhukov's attack brought on a crisis from which Nazi Germany never recovered.

Observers have often claimed that "General Winter" defeated the Germans outside Moscow. With temperatures dropping to minus forty degrees Fahrenheit, the cold certainly made things more difficult for the Germans. Winter weather, however, affects both sides in a conflict. Unlike the Soviets, the Germans were not prepared to fight in winter. When temperatures fell, they had no winter clothing. When the cold congealed engine oil or gun lubricants, they had no antifreeze. When snow covered railways, they had no equipment to clear their long supply lines. The Germans had overstretched and insufficiently prepared their advance. Not winter but faulty strategy and logistics left the Wehrmacht mired in Russia in late fall 1941.

The Soviet Union and its Red Army deserve enormous credit for halting the Germans near Moscow and later dislodging the Germans from occupied Soviet territory. Soviet officials oversaw the transfer of some 1,523 industrial plants to the Urals, Siberia, central Asia, and other areas far away from German invaders. This allowed Soviet industry to supply the Red Army. At the same time, the Soviet leadership mobilized huge armies from its enormous population. These armies fought tooth and nail over every inch of Soviet soil. The Soviet Union thus remained standing – the only bulwark against Hitler dominating Europe, and perhaps the world.

The Nazi Occupation of Soviet Lands

Even though the Soviets halted the Germans outside Moscow, the Nazis now occupied vast tracts of western Soviet territory; they would hold on to these areas until 1944. Initially, the Nazis had every opportunity to turn disaffected Soviet citizens into collaborators against Bolshevism. When German troops marched into the Soviet Union, they were often met by local citizens bearing traditional welcoming gifts of flowers, bread, and salt. Many Soviet citizens saw the Germans as liberators freeing them from Bolshevik repression. But the Nazis squandered this opportunity. Their racial ideology prevented them from capitalizing on anti-Bolshevik sentiment.

War of annihilation

As Hitler and other top Nazis proclaimed, the war with the Soviet Union was a war of ideologies (*Weltanschauungskrieg*). To preserve the German race, they claimed, it was necessary to eradicate Bolshevik ideology and the lower races associated with it. Nazi propaganda dehumanized the peoples of the east as "Jewish-Bolshevik *Untermenschen* [subhumans]" and "Mongol hordes." Moreover, in a war with racial inferiors, Hitler insisted, all possible means of war – however inhumane – were justified.

Wehrmacht commanders echoed Nazi propaganda. In October 1941, Field Marshal Walther von Reichenau issued a notorious order: "The essential goal of the campaign against the Jewish-Bolshevik system is the complete destruction of the sources of power and the eradication of the Asian influence on the European cultural sphere... The soldier in the East is not only a fighter by the rules of war, but also the carrier of an inexorable racial concept and the avenger

139

of all bestialities inflicted upon the Germans... For this reason the soldier must have complete understanding for the necessity of harsh, but just measures against Jewish sub-humanity." Reichenau's order belies any notion that the Wehrmacht was somehow "clean" or "above" carrying out Nazi atrocities.

Before and during the invasion, the Wehrmacht issued various criminal orders. Hitler's infamous Commissar Order demanded that all captured Red Army political commissars be shot as agents of communism. The so-called Barbarossa Order called for draconian retribution for resistance in Nazi-occupied territories. The army was empowered to shoot individuals engaged in partisan actions. If no guilty party was found for a given action, the military was to carry out ruthless collective measures against the civilian population. Yet another order, Guidelines for the Conduct of Troops in Russia, insisted that the fight against Bolshevism "demands ruthless and energetic measures against Bolshevik agitators, irregulars, saboteurs and Jews, and the total eradication of any active or passive resistance." Finally, SS murder units (mobile killing squads) were given free rein in areas controlled by the army.

Soviet prisoners of war (POWs)

The first victims of Operation Barbarossa, Soviet POWs, endured a terrible fate. Since the Soviet Union was not a signatory to the Geneva Convention, the Third Reich did not recognize a protected status for Soviet POWs. In 1941, the Wehrmacht captured some 3.3 million Soviet soldiers. Roughly two million were dead by February 1942. Of these, 600,000 were shot on the basis of the Commissar Order. Most, though, died from criminal mistreatment. Once captured, Soviet POWs were marched to barbed-wire holding pens that served as makeshift camps. They had no shelter, were given miniscule rations, and received little medical attention. Physically run-down, few could perform labor – in turn, a death sentence. As German Quartermaster-General Eduard Wagner declared, "prisoners incapable of work in the prison camps are to starve." This maltreatment did not result from unforeseen circumstances (as some Wehrmacht commanders later claimed). It was deliberate. German war strategy presumed the capture of millions of Soviet POWs – with no provision for their survival.

Some Wehrmacht commanders recognized the boomerang effect of German POW policies. Knowing their fate if captured, Soviet soldiers redoubled their fierce combat efforts. German military authorities eventually raised POW food rations. Still, the mortality statistics for Soviet POWs are hair-raising. Of the total 5.7 million captured by the end of the war, some 3.3 million, or 57.5% of the total, perished in German hands. By contrast, of the 232,000 Englishmen and Americans captured, just 8,348, or 3.5%, died in German captivity. In fall 1941 more than 8,348 Soviet POWs in German captivity were dying *every day*. The rapid physical elimination of whole Soviet armies in captivity was unprecedented in modern history. Indeed, had the war ended in spring 1942, we would have remembered the deaths of two million Soviet POWs as *the* atrocity of World War II.

The civilian population

Wehrmacht troops also subsumed civilians into the "enemy" and turned occupied territories into imaginary battlefields. To the Nazis, Jews by definition were partisans – they were engaged in a worldwide conspiracy against the "Aryan" race. This justified their massacre (see Chapter 7). On even the slightest suspicion of resistance activity, Wehrmacht troops also moved against alleged communist or other partisans and the communities that supposedly sheltered them. German soldiers massacred whole villages, shooting the inhabitants in nearby woods or ditches, or burning them alive in community or other structures.

The Wehrmacht terrorized the civilian population in other ways, too. Due to supply problems, troops were instructed to live off the land. Soldiers foraged for food and plundered livestock. They requisitioned homes and farms. They stripped the population of its winter furs, boots, and bedding, as well as snowshoes and sledges. They also dragooned local inhabitants into back-breaking labor or deported them westwards to work in occupied Poland or Germany. By summer 1942, these actions had galvanized a partisan movement that posed a genuine threat to German military operations (see Chapter 8).

As Omer Bartov has argued, a number of factors came together to explain the barbarization of the Wehrmacht on the eastern front. German soldiers fought under abysmal conditions. They had insufficient food and military equipment. Sleeping in the open or in primitive shelters, they endured lice and frostbite, as well as constant exposure to the noise of artillery barrage. Units suffered casualty rates of 200% or 300% – as soldiers and then their replacements perished. Still, Wehrmacht soldiers continued to fight for the Nazi cause. Why? Many junior officers were Nazi believers who raised troop morale by circulating propaganda and holding pep talks. Soldiers had also long been exposed to Nazi propaganda demonizing Jews and Slavs. Their ruthless struggle with Soviet troops only confirmed the seeming truth of Nazi ideology. In the situation in which they found themselves, Wehrmacht troops did what they thought was right: they annihilated their enemy.

Civilian administration

The Nazis established a welter of occupation administrations in Soviet lands. While eastern Ukraine and Crimea remained under military administration, western Ukraine, the Baltic countries, and Belarus were ruled by Nazi civilian administrations. Hitler appointed Alfred Rosenberg, a longtime Nazi Baltic

German ideologue, to head up the Reich Ministry for the Occupied Eastern Territories. Erich Koch, the *Gauleiter* of East Prussia, headed the German administration in Ukraine. He referred to Ukrainians as "niggers" and once declared that "If I find a Ukrainian who is worthy of sitting at the same table with me, I must have him shot." Hinrich Lohse, another long-serving Nazi, took over Ostland, a Nazi administrative unit covering the Baltic countries and much of Belarus. Finally, Himmler saw the east as the preserve of the SS. In 1942, the SS leader moved his headquarters to Zhytomyr in Ukraine. Constant turf wars between Nazi civilian and SS institutions added to the hardship and terror of the German occupation of Soviet lands.

Like its military counterpart, civilian administration was brutal. Fearing inefficiencies from the breakup of collective farms, Nazi officials refused to privatize land. They thus lost their best chance to generate support among the local population. In summer 1942 Nazi authorities began a draconian food-confiscation drive. They searched peasant homes, outbuildings, mills, yards, and gardens and confiscated every sack of grain they found. In other brutal measures, Koch banned all educational institutions except four-year primary schools. Fritz Sauckel, Hitler's General Plenipotentiary for Labor Mobilization, resorted to savage measures to round up much-needed workers for the Third Reich. Police officials threw cordons around churches, dance halls, and movie theaters. Those caught in the dragnet were sent to work in Germany.

The Nazis had even more nefarious plans for the Soviet Union. Hitler planned to wipe Soviet cities from the face of the earth. In May 1941 Herbert Backe, soon Reich minister of food, formulated a "Hunger Plan." It foresaw starving some 30 million "useless eaters" in Soviet cities and diverting the food to German soldiers and civilians. In fall 1941, the Nazis lay siege to Leningrad, eventually killing 700,000 inhabitants, mostly from starvation (today, Leningrad is known by its pre-1914 name, St. Petersburg). Nazi administrators also tried to starve the Ukrainian cities of Kiev and Kharkiv. They never, however, fully implemented the Hunger Plan. They worried that it would spark too much resistance. They did not want to battle the Red Army *and* quell uprisings behind the front lines.

As Joseph Goebbels cynically noted, Germans were "digesting" the occupied areas. Germans, mostly soldiers, consumed prodigious quantities of food produced in the east. At least nine million tons of grain and tens of millions of cattle, pigs, sheep, and goats raised there ended up in German stomachs. This, in turn, meant that German civilians never experienced hunger during wartime. Meanwhile, some 4.2 million individuals in Soviet lands starved to death under German occupation (including Soviet POWs, excluding Jews).

The Nazis also harbored grand colonization plans. Nazi propaganda claimed that Eastern Europe was "black earth that could be a paradise, a California of Europe." An army of Nazi racial experts, demographers,

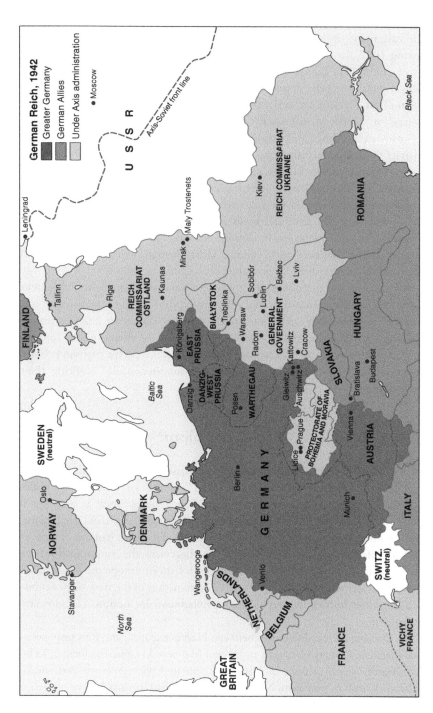

Map 6.1 German Reich (1942).

agronomists, city planners, and landscape architects set out to Germanize the east; many drew on academic research into the east (see Chapter 4). In spring 1942, for example, SS planner Konrad Meyer put forth the notorious General Plan East (Generalplan Ost). To make way for German settlers, Meyer envisioned the deportation, resettlement, and "liquidation" of some 30 million Slavs, Jews, and other peoples. His plan foresaw three major zones of German colonization: "Ingermanland" (Leningrad region), "Gothegau" (Crimea and southern Ukraine), and Memel-Narev (Białystok district and western Lithuania). These zones would feature model German towns (with German homes and gardens growing German plants), linked together by railroads and superhighways. In the countryside between towns, millions of sturdy German peasants, mostly SS and Wehrmacht veterans, would till the land and build a human wall against "Asian hordes" – "blood-and-soil" ideology in action. And the native inhabitants? Some would remain, enslaved to Germans. Most, though, would be expelled to Arctic areas to perish in labor camps.

Because the war did not go their way, the Nazis were unable to implement most of their Germanization plans. Himmler, though, did establish the colony of Hegewald ("preservation forest") near his Zhytomyr headquarters in Ukraine. SS officials settled over 10,000 ethnic Germans while forcibly removing at least 17,000 Ukrainians from the area. Constant partisan activity, however, prevented the German settlers from successfully working their new farms.

Nazi Colonialism?

In recent years, historians have engaged in passionate debate about whether Nazi practices in Eastern Europe constituted "colonialism." Remarks by Hitler and other top Nazis suggest that the Third Reich viewed itself as an imperial power. In September 1941, for example, the Führer declared that "the Russian space is our India, and just as the English have ruled it with a handful of men, so will we rule this colonial space of ours." For historians, the issue is really about the singularity of Nazism. Were Nazi crimes in Eastern Europe the product of a unique, sinister regime? Or were they the culmination of the dark side of modern European history, the perversion of Enlightenment notions of rationality and order?

By focusing on the differences between Nazi occupation and European colonial practices, Robert Gerwarth and Stefan Malinowski argue the former. To be sure, European colonialism in Africa was saturated with violence. But, unlike modern British imperialism, Nazi rule in Eastern Europe involved no pretence of "a civilizing mission," the notion that Westernization would improve the lives of indigenous peoples. The Nazis never aimed to develop indigenous elites and thus never employed indirect rule. Nazi violence was also not directed at upholding or restoring order. It was purely destructive in intent and practice. All this suggests the unprecedented nature of the Nazi occupation – it was a phenomenon apart from European colonialism.

But other scholars, notably A. Dirk Moses and Jürgen Zimmerer, suggest important parallels between Nazi practices in the east and European colonialism. The Nazis imposed a racial order on a territorial space allegedly inhabited by primitive peoples. Their regime was based on a binary opposition of German occupiers and native helots. The Nazis presumed that the entire native population, racially inferior as it was, could simply be done away with. Like colonial wars, German military operations in the east constituted predatory war. Moreover, while native unrest felled other colonialisms, partisan activity seriously undermined the Nazi empire (though Allied armies ultimately destroyed it). Finally, Germans in the Third Reich – like citizens of the European democracies – held a positive view of colonialism. Many Germans recognized that violent methods were necessary to uphold colonial rule; they did not find Nazi methods extreme. Nor did they balk at carrying them out. For scholars such as Moses and Zimmerer, Nazism was a radical form of colonialism.

Global War

President Roosevelt, who despised Nazism, was deeply concerned about Hitler's war gains. Throughout 1941 he tried to counter isolationist sentiment in the United States. In March he convinced Congress to pass the Lend-Lease Act, permitting the United States to give, lend, or sell materials to belligerent nations – Britain and soon the Soviet Union. Roosevelt also authorized US Navy escorts to protect merchant ships carrying those supplies. By the end of the year, after repeated attacks by German submarines, the president had secured congressional repeal of the Neutrality Acts. Even before, in August, Roosevelt and Churchill had proclaimed the Atlantic Charter. The charter was a declaration of war aims – but the United States was not yet in the war! Britain and the United States declared they were not fighting the war to seek territorial gains. Rather, the two countries sought to protect peoples' right to self-determination and to secure a liberal postwar world.

Some Nazi leaders were alarmed by American actions. Hitler, however, viewed war with the United States with some indifference. He certainly recognized America's economic potential. He believed, though, that the US could not mobilize quickly enough to make a difference in the current war. Moreover, although Hitler viewed Roosevelt as a dangerous agent of "international Jewry," he believed that racial corruption was sapping the US of its strength. As he once stated, "Everything about [America is] half Judaised, the other half negrified. How can one expect a state like that to hold together?"

In fall 1941 Hitler hoped that Japan would distract the western powers with war while Germany finished its conquest of Soviet lands. Hitler had verbally promised Japanese leaders that he would declare war on the United States if they did so. Four days after Japan carried out its surprise attack on Pearl Harbor on December 7, Hitler declared war on the United States. This was a major mistake on Hitler's part. Roosevelt might not have secured a congressional vote to declare war on Germany. Moreover, the president could now portray the Axis as a united enemy, allowing him to pursue a "Germany first" strategy – the United States would first defeat Germany, then Japan.

Why did Hitler declare war on the United States? Besides his racial views on American society, the Führer believed that the United States would soon declare war on Germany. After all, US forces were already attacking German U-boats in the Atlantic. At the same time, Hitler wished to bolster his commitment to his Tokyo ally; he believed that Japan was stronger than it really was. Hitler even hoped that, after a quick defeat of the United States, Japan would help him finish off Soviet Russia.

In many ways, 1941 proved a watershed year for the Third Reich. Hitler went from triumph in the west to quagmire in the east. He drew Germany from a one-front into a two-front war. He pushed Germany from a European into a global war. Nazi leaders implemented ever more draconian policies, especially in Eastern Europe. Nowhere was this more evident than in the murder of Jews. By December 1941 the Nazis had already massacred some 500,000 Jews in the Soviet Union. But now, just when the Nazis faced great military challenges, they also focused on the "Final Solution."

Citations for Quotations

Page   Source

125   "some bastard…" Quoted in Christian Leitz, *Nazi Foreign Policy, 1933–1941: The Road to Global War* (London: Routledge, 2004), 73.

127   "dress rehearsal." Alexander B. Rossino, *Hitler Strikes Poland: Blitzkrieg, Ideology, and Atrocity* (Lawrence: University Press of Kansas, 2003), 234.

135   "Never in the field…" Quoted in Marvin Perry, *World War II in Europe: A Concise History* (Boston: Wadsworth, 2013), 48.

137   "the campaign against Russia…" Quoted in Gerhard L. Weinberg, *A World at Arms: A Global History of World War II*, New Edition (Cambridge: Cambridge University Press, 2005), 266.

139   "Jewish-Bolshevik *Untermenschen*" and "Mongol hordes." Quoted in Omer Bartov, *The Eastern Front, 1941–45: German Troops and the Barbarisation of Warfare*, Second Edition (Houndsmills: Palgrave, 2001), 83.

139 "The essential goal…" Quoted in Bartov, *The Eastern Front, 1941–45,* 84–85.
140 "demands ruthless…" Quoted in Mark Mazower, *Hitler's Empire: Nazi Rule in Occupied Europe* (London: Allen Lane, 2008), 142.
140 "prisoners incapable…" Quoted in Collingham, *The Taste of War,* 194.
142 "niggers." Quoted in Mazower, *Hitler's Empire,* 152.
142 "If I find a Ukrainian…" Quoted in Karel C. Berkhoff, *Harvest of Despair: Life and Death in Ukraine under Nazi Rule* (Cambridge, MA: Harvard University Press, 2004), 37.
142 "useless eaters." Quoted in Lizzie Collingham, *The Taste of War: World War II and the Battle for Food* (New York: Penguin, 2012), 196.
142 "digesting." Quoted in Collingham, *The Taste of War,* 217.
142 "black earth…" Quoted in David Furber and Wendy Lower, "Colonialism and Genocide in Nazi-Occupied Poland and Ukraine," in A. Dirk Moses, ed., *Empire, Colony, Genocide: Conquest, Occupation, and Subaltern Resistance in World History* (New York: Berghahn Books, 2008), 385.
144 "the Russian space…" Quoted in Robert Gerwarth, *Hitler's Hangman: The Life of Heydrich* (New Haven: Yale University Press, 2011), 247.
146 "Everything about [America is] half Judaised, …" Quoted in Norman J.W. Goda, *Tomorrow the World: Hitler, Northwest Africa, and the Path toward America* (College Station: Texas A&M University Press, 1998), xviii–xix.

Bibliography

Baranowski, Shelley. *Nazi Empire: German Colonialism and Imperialism from Bismarck to Hitler.* Cambridge: Cambridge University Press, 2011.

Bartov, Omer. *The Eastern Front, 1941–45: German Troops and the Barbarisation of Warfare.* Second Edition. Houndsmills: Palgrave, 2001.

Berkhoff, Karel C. *Harvest of Despair: Life and Death in Ukraine under Nazi Rule.* Cambridge, MA: Harvard University Press, 2004.

Bryant, Chad. *Prague in Black: Nazi Rule and Czech Nationalism.* Cambridge, MA: Harvard University Press, 2007.

Collingham, Lizzie. *The Taste of War: World War II and the Battle for Food.* New York: Penguin, 2012.

Epstein, Catherine. *Model Nazi: Arthur Greiser and the Occupation of Western Poland.* Oxford: Oxford University Press, 2010.

Furber, David and Wendy Lower. "Colonialism and Genocide in Nazi-Occupied Poland and Ukraine." In A. Dirk Moses, ed., *Empire, Colony, Genocide: Conquest, Occupation, and Subaltern Resistance in World History.* New York: Berghahn Books, 2008, pp. 372–400.

Gerwarth, Robert. *Hitler's Hangman: The Life of Heydrich.* New Haven: Yale University Press, 2011.

Gerwarth, Robert and Stephan Malinowski. "Hannah Arendt's Ghosts: Reflections on the Disputable Path from Windhoek to Auschwitz." *Central European History* 41, no. 2 (2009): 279–300.

Gildea, Robert. *Marianne in Chains: In Search of the German Occupation 1940–1945.* London: Macmillan, 2002.

Goda, Norman J.W. *Tomorrow the World: Hitler, Northwest Africa, and the Path toward America.* College Station: Texas A&M University Press, 1998.

Harvey, Elizabeth. *Women and the Nazi East: Agents and Witnesses of Germanization.* New Haven: Yale University Press, 2003.

Jackson, Julian. *France: The Dark Years, 1940–1944.* Oxford: Oxford University Press, 2001.

Kay, Alex J. *Exploitation, Resettlement, Mass Murder: Political and Economic Planning for German Occupation Policy in the Soviet Union, 1940–1941.* Oxford: Berghahn Books, 2006.

Laub, Thomas J. *After the Fall: German Policy in Occupied France, 1940–1944.* Oxford: Oxford University Press, 2010.

Leitz, Christian. *Nazi Foreign Policy, 1933–1941: The Road to Global War.* London: Routledge, 2004.

Lower, Wendy. *Nazi Empire-Building and the Holocaust in Ukraine.* Chapel Hill: University of North Carolina Press, 2005.

Marrus, Michael R. and Robert O. Paxton. *Vichy France and the Jews.* New York: Basic Books, 1981.

Mazower, Mark. *Hitler's Empire: Nazi Rule in Occupied Europe.* London: Allen Lane, 2008.

Murray, Williamson and Allan R. Millett. *A War to Be Won: Fighting the Second World War.* Cambridge, MA: Belknap Press of Harvard University Press, 2000.

Paxton, Robert O. *Vichy France: Old Guard and New Order, 1940–1944.* New York: Knopf, 1972.

Perry, Marvin. *World War II in Europe: A Concise History.* Boston: Wadsworth, 2013.

Rossino, Alexander B. *Hitler Strikes Poland: Blitzkrieg, Ideology, and Atrocity.* Lawrence: University Press of Kansas, 2003.

Rutherford, Phillip T. *Prelude to the Final Solution: The Nazi Program for Deporting Ethnic Poles, 1939–1941.* Lawrence: University Press of Kansas, 2007.

Scheck, Raffael. *Hitler's African Victims: The German Army Massacres of Black French Soldiers in 1940.* Cambridge: Cambridge University Press, 2006.

Schulte, Theo. *The German Army and Nazi Policies in Occupied Russia.* Oxford: Oxford University Press, 1989.

Shepherd, Ben. *War in the Wild East: The German Army and Soviet Partisans.* Cambridge, MA: Harvard University Press, 2004.

Vinen, Richard. *The Unfree French: Life under the Occupation.* New Haven: Yale University Press, 2006.

Weinberg, Gerhard L. *A World at Arms: A Global History of World War II.* New Edition. Cambridge: Cambridge University Press, 2005.

Zeiler, Thomas W. *Annihilation: A Global History of World War II.* Oxford: Oxford University Press, 2012.

Zimmerer, Jürgen. "The Birth of the Ostland out of the Spirit of Colonialism: A Postcolonial Perspective on the Nazi Policy of Conquest and Extermination." In A. Dirk Moses and Dan Stone, eds., *Colonialism and Genocide.* Abingdon: Routledge, 2007, pp. 101–123.

7

Genocide

The Third Reich is best known for the Holocaust, the murder of almost six million Jews. While this genocide was embedded in Germany's war effort as well as its aim to "Germanize" the east, the Nazis pursued it with singular zeal and unparalleled success. They not only murdered millions of Jews but also destroyed a Jewish world that had existed for centuries. How was this possible? How did the process unfold? As we shall see, the Holocaust developed gradually and in an often uncoordinated manner. The Nazis tried various strategies and methods before settling on the "Final Solution."

The Holocaust has spawned many myths. There is a common presumption that Hitler issued an order for the murder of Europe's Jews and that he alone was responsible for radicalizing antisemitic policies. There is a stereotype that the Holocaust was all about industrial murder – Jews were put on trains, brought to death camps, gassed in "shower rooms," and burned in crematoria. There is a common belief that German Jews were the primary victims of the Holocaust or that Jews were the only victims of Nazi genocidal practices. There is a myth that Jews went to their deaths "like lambs to their slaughter." It is often assumed that German perpetrators were sadists, lunatics, or otherwise deranged persons.

But, if Hitler issued a clear-cut order for the Final Solution, historians have not found it. Instead, other top Nazis and many lower-ranking functionaries were "working towards the Führer" to implement radical antisemitic policies (see Chapter 3). While many Holocaust victims were gassed, the Germans shot or otherwise massacred many Jews far away from death camps. The majority of victims were Polish and Soviet Jews, *not* German Jews (most of whom emigrated before World War II). Jews also did not passively await death. Some tried armed

Nazi Germany: Confronting the Myths, First Edition. Catherine Epstein.
© 2015 John Wiley & Sons, Ltd. Published 2015 by John Wiley & Sons, Ltd.

resistance, others inventive ways to thwart Nazi aims. The Nazis also committed genocide against disabled individuals and the Roma (Gypsies). Finally, the perpetrators were "ordinary" men, many of whom were well educated and professionally secure.

Writers often deploy the term "Final Solution" as a synonym for the Holocaust. This is the translation of the Nazi term *Endlösung*. It is the language of perpetrators. It conveys an impersonal, bureaucratic approach to the murder of Europe's Jews. When writing of the Nazis' motivations, intentions, or plans, I often use that term. "Holocaust" stems from ancient Greek roots meaning "whole" and "burned." It invokes the tragedy that befell victims. I use this term when writing about the general phenomenon of the genocide of Europe's Jews.

Murderous Antisemitism

Why kill Jews? Hitler was convinced that Jews aimed to destroy Germany. As he saw it, Jews' penetration of German society was leading to the nation's downfall. Jews, he believed, were undermining the racial purity of the German people (*Volk*) by assimilation practices such as intermarriage. Moreover, by looking and acting like Germans, Jews masked their identities and were able to carry on their nefarious activities. For Germany to reclaim its national essence, Hitler believed, Jews had to be purged from its midst. The Nazi regime spared no effort to convince the public of the danger posed by Jews. In their everyday lives, Germans constantly encountered antisemitic posters, banners, and newsstand publications. At school, children were taught the alleged evil influence of Jews.

The Nazis released several antisemitic films widely seen by Germans. *Jud Süss* (Süss the Jew, 1940) was perhaps the most notorious. Made by Veit Harlan, the Third Reich's leading director, *Jud Süss* was a lavish production that retold the eighteenth-century story of Karl Alexander, the Duke of Württemberg, and a wealthy Jew, Joseph Süss Oppenheimer. In the film, Süss worms his way into the duke's confidence, eventually taking over the duchy's finances for his own gain. After Süss commits various nefarious acts, including the rape of a Christian woman, the people rise up against his tyranny and he is hanged. It was a blockbuster hit, and an estimated 20 million Germans saw *Jud Süss*. A short time later, the Nazis released *Der ewige Jude* (The Eternal Jew). Made to look like a documentary, this film contains vicious untruths about Jews in the guise of objective information. Although much less popular than *Jud Süss* – no more than 4.75 million Germans saw the film during the Nazi years – *Der ewige Jude* was screened for Wehrmacht soldiers and Schutzstaffel (SS) recruits. While it is impossible to know the exact impact of antisemitic films and other propaganda, there can be little doubt that many Germans were convinced that Jews posed a dangerous threat.

Figure 7.1 This Nazi poster reads: "He is to blame for the war!" (1943). *Source*: Courtesy Library of Congress.

In the lead-up to war, Hitler raged on about the Jews. As he famously told the Reichstag on January 30, 1939, "Today I will… be a prophet: if the international Jewish financiers in and outside Europe should succeed in plunging the nations once more into a world war, then the result will not be the Bolshevizing of the earth, and thus the victory of Jewry, but the annihilation of the Jewish race in Europe!" With this warning, Hitler had raised the possibility of extermination. He also imputed his own fantasies of world domination to Jews. Indeed, he insisted that a Jewish cabal was poised to take over the world. Both the communist leadership of Soviet Russia and US President Franklin D. Roosevelt, he claimed, were part of this worldwide Jewish conspiracy. To Hitler, the very fact that the Soviet Union and the United States – two such ideologically opposed regimes – stood united against Germany proved the conspiratorial reach of "international Jewry." It made no difference that all rational evidence belied his assertions. Hitler believed that he was unmasking important truths about the nature of the world.

If you put yourself into Hitler's mindset, Nazi polices had a certain logic. Since the Führer believed that he was defending Germany from the Jews, it made sense to him to declare war on the United States – after all, in his logic, America, controlled by Jews, would soon battle Germany. In addition, since Hitler saw Britain and the United States as agents of "international Jewry," he believed that the Jews were responsible for bombing German cities (see Chapter 8). It thus made sense to massacre Jews in Eastern Europe in retaliation for Anglo-American bombings.

As the historian Jeffrey Herf has argued, the Nazis believed the annihilation of Jews to be an urgent *political* task. For them, World War II and the Final Solution were one interconnected war in which Germany was fighting "international Jewry." This helps to explain the singular zeal with which they pursued the Final Solution. Exterminating Jews, the Nazis believed, was necessary to win the war. They continued to murder Jews even when it hampered German war operations.

Some historians emphasize "rational" reasons why the Nazis murdered Jews. Christian Gerlach and others contend that the Nazis murdered Jews so as to reduce the number of "useless" eaters in Eastern Europe and increase food supplies for the German population. Götz Aly argues that the Nazis perpetrated the Holocaust to plunder Jewish property, thereby securing much-needed funds. In this chapter, I argue that these were ancillary "benefits" but *not* the Nazis' primary motive for killing Jews. First and foremost, the Final Solution was an ideological project rooted in Nazi antisemitism.

Euthanasia

Murderous Nazi policies began with the disabled. Drawing on longtime notions of "racial hygiene" (see Chapter 1 and Chapter 4), the Nazis stepped up propaganda against the severely disabled. Disabled patients, they insisted, compromised the racial health and purity of the German community (*Volksgemeinschaft*). Society, they claimed, should not waste resources on the care of those considered "unworthy of life." "Euthanasia," they said, constituted "mercy deaths." Nazi "euthanasia," however, had nothing to do with what we today understand by the term – a humane ending to the lives of individuals suffering from terminal illness. Nazi "euthanasia" was a euphemism for murder.

In 1938, Hitler was approached about a baby born to the Knauer family. The infant, sex unknown, was missing a leg and part of an arm and was possibly blind and/or mentally challenged. Doctors in Leipzig refused to give the baby a "mercy death." The parents appealed the decision to Hitler. The Führer sent his personal physician, Karl Brandt, to investigate. Once Brandt had confirmed the baby's medical details, the infant was killed. Thereafter, Hitler charged staff in his private Chancellory of the Führer (Kanzlei des Führers) with organizing a broader euthanasia campaign. By using his private Chancellory, he hoped to preclude intervention by state agencies. Philipp Bouhler, head of that Chancellory, assigned Viktor Brack to handle the day-to-day management of the campaign.

Bouhler, Brandt, and Brack organized teams of physicians to check all hospitals for children eligible for the euthanasia program. In the next two years, doctors and nurses murdered roughly 5,000 children through starvation or lethal overdoses. In January 1940, the program was expanded to adults. This was the T4 operation (*Aktion* T4), codenamed after the address of its Berlin headquarters, Tiergarten Strasse 4. Medical personnel killed some 75,000 adult inmates of psychiatric or other asylums, many of whom were *not* terminally or incurably ill. T4 specifically targeted disabled Jewish patients in state hospitals – the first group of Jews systematically killed by the Nazis.

With T4, the Nazis gained important experience with killing operations. T4 personnel invented the gas chamber. As T4 staff discovered through experimentation, injecting poisonous gas into closed rooms proved efficient, rapid, and secret. T4 staff recognized that it was easier to bring victims to killing centers (rather than killers to victims); accordingly, they set up murder facilities inside six hospitals. Through T4, the Nazis learned the importance of subterfuge in killing operations. Patients were told that they were being transferred to a new hospital. Just before their murder, they entered what they believed to be shower rooms. The Nazis also found out that it was easy to recruit professional killers. Many doctors were willing to carry out "mercy deaths," especially if absolved of legal culpability. The Nazis had no difficulty finding nurses and other staff for the killing facilities.

News of the "euthanasia" deaths leaked out. Not least, parents and guardians were suspicious about the sudden deaths of their loved ones. In August 1941, Clemens August Cardinal von Galen, Bishop of Münster, preached a widely circulated sermon against euthanasia. Hitler now officially ended the program. (In fact, the Nazis continued to murder the disabled, albeit less systematically.) Historians are divided on the impact of von Galen's sermon. Some argue that it did not factor into Hitler's decision. They believe that a main objective in the euthanasia campaign – to clear hospital space for wounded soldiers – had been met. Others argue that Hitler, always wary of losing public support, ceased the euthanasia campaign because too many Germans knew about and disliked it. Yet others believe that von Galen's sermon was the key factor. If, however, von Galen's sermon made a difference, historians question whether Germans could have successfully protested other murderous Nazi policies (see below).

The euthanasia campaign shared an ideological motivation, method of murder, and personnel with the Final Solution. T4 staff soon moved on from gassing the disabled to murdering other groups deemed "undesirable." In spring 1941, they gassed concentration-camp inmates unable to perform labor. This operation, known as Special Treatment 14f13, killed 10,000 to 20,000 inmates. Later, Bouhler subcontracted T4 officials to build and run the death camps in which many Polish Jews were murdered. A clear line of continuity stretched from the murder of the Knauer baby to the Holocaust.

Ghettoization

After the Nazis defeated Poland in 1939, some 2.2 million Polish Jews came under their control. Initially, Nazi policy toward Jews in Poland was an extension of Reich policy toward Jews. The Nazis identified and segregated Jews by forcing them to wear the Yellow Star (even before this happened in Germany). They deprived Jews of their livelihoods and made them do forced labor such as snow shoveling and road building. They destroyed or repurposed Jewish communal property. In Poznań, for example, they turned the synagogue into a swimming pool. Still, there were no concrete plans for the wholesale extermination of Jews. It took two years for Nazi policy to evolve from segregation and expulsion to outright murder.

The Germans established ghettos so as to segregate and control Jews. On May 1, 1940, they sealed off the ghetto in Łódź, the first major ghetto in Poland. 163,000 Jews were trapped inside. German authorities could force Jews to do their bidding by withholding food, medicine, and fuel. In November, they established the Warsaw ghetto, the largest in Nazi-occupied Europe. At its peak in May 1941, the Warsaw ghetto incarcerated 445,000 Jews. An average of 7.2 individuals shared one room. Jewish ghettos were always located in the worst city slums. In the Łódź ghetto, for example, just forty-nine apartments had a drain, toilet, and bath; over 30,000 apartments had none of these conveniences.

To combat terrible conditions, Jews tried to carry on with a semblance of normality. Jewish municipal authorities – Jewish Councils (see below) – organized welfare measures. They cared for the neediest, set up schools and apprentice programs, and established a rudimentary healthcare system. Jews also continued a vibrant cultural life. They wrote poetry and short stories, staged theatrical productions, and made art out of whatever supplies they could find. Jews also held concerts and readings, and organized lectures and clandestine libraries. Many Jews also continued their prewar political associations.

Despite Jewish self-help, reports about ghetto life are hair-raising. The Polish Underground, for example, reported of the Warsaw ghetto: "Further crowding has resulted in conditions of ill-health, hunger and monstrous poverty that defy description. Groups of pale and emaciated people wander aimlessly through the overcrowded streets. Beggars sit and lie along the walls and the sight of people collapsing from starvation is common... Every day a few more people die on the street." In the Warsaw ghetto, approximately 100,000 Jews died between November 1940 and July 1942 (when deportations to the Treblinka death camp began). Roughly one in four inmates died in the Łódź ghetto.

German observers had a very different take on Jews in ghettos. In April 1940, for example, Ingrid Greiser, the daughter of Arthur Greiser (see Chapter 6), wrote her fiancé about the Łódź ghetto: "There are epidemics there, and terrible air since everything is spilled into the drainage pipes [the ghetto had no underground sewage system]. There is no water, the Jews have to buy it for ten pennies a bucket, and so they surely wash themselves less frequently than usual. Just seeing this can make one sick." She continued: "You know, one really can't have any sympathy for these people. I think that they feel very differently from us and therefore don't feel this humiliation and everything." German onlookers do not seem to have registered that it was Nazi policies that turned Jews into the miserable figures of their anti-Jewish stereotypes. Their views illustrate the effectiveness of Nazi propaganda – and suggest why Germans might have found it plausible to kill Jews.

Jewish Councils

In every ghetto, the Germans appointed Jewish Councils: municipal administrations that implemented Nazi rules and regulations. Among other tasks, the councils staffed police forces that rounded up ghetto inhabitants for forced labor and, ultimately, deportation. Scholars have engaged in heated debate about these councils. Some, including Hannah Arendt, have argued that the Jewish Councils collaborated with the Nazis in the Holocaust. Without the help of the Jewish Councils, she and others believed, the Nazis would have had much greater difficulty carrying out their murderous policies. Many other scholars, however, argue that the Jewish Councils helped alleviate the misery imposed by the Nazis. Moreover, Jewish communal leaders' decision to submit to a noxious ruler reflected successful past Jewish conduct. The Jews did not know that this time it would prove disastrous.

Evolving "Solutions"

The ghettos were intended as a temporary measure against Jews. But what was to be Jews' ultimate fate? Nazi authorities weighed options for a "territorial" solution, expelling Jews to eastern areas. In October 1939, SS officials came up with the Nisko Plan, according to which they would send Jews to a "reservation" in the Lublin district of the General Government. In late October 1939, 4,700 Jews from Vienna and newly annexed Polish areas were deported to Nisko. Upon arrival, Jews were dispersed into the countryside; no provisions were made for their work or shelter.

After just two transports, SS Chief Heinrich Himmler halted the Nisko Plan. The army needed train capacity to move troops from Poland to the west. The plan also interfered with Himmler's Germanization schemes. His priority was to resettle ethnic Germans in newly annexed areas. This necessitated the removal of Poles – and not Jews – from the annexed areas to the General Government (see Chapter 6). Finally, it was soon evident that the Nisko Plan would be expensive: it would involve a massive security operation and the subsidization of Jews in an inhospitable climate.

In June 1940, following the defeat of France, Nazi functionaries found another "territorial" solution. Now, they thought, they would ship all Jews to the French colony of Madagascar, an island in the Indian Ocean. There, Jews would serve as hostages (as would have been the case in the Nisko Plan, too). As Franz Rademacher, a high-ranking official in the Foreign Ministry, noted: "The Jews [in Madagascar] will remain in German hands as a pledge for the future good conduct of the members of their race in America." Due to Madagascar's tropical microbes, many Jews would have died of disease there. It would also have been very expensive to ship Jews to the island. Regardless, this option soon slipped away. Since Germany did not defeat Britain in 1940, Britain continued to control the seas. Germany could not rely on having the open sea lanes necessary to implement the plan. Although seriously considered by Nazi officials, Madagascar was a phantasmagoria.

Massacres in the Soviet Union

After the invasion of the Soviet Union in June 1941, some four million additional Jews came under Nazi rule in eastern Poland and the western Soviet Union. (Roughly 1.5 million of these Jews escaped Nazi clutches, largely fleeing eastwards.) Since Hitler believed that Jews were a mainstay of Bolshevism, they were, by definition, "enemies." In summer 1941, four mobile killing squads (*Einsatzgruppen* A, B, C, and D), made up of 3,000 SS men, set out to murder Jews and other "enemies."

The killing squads initially targeted Jewish men as Soviet officials or partisans. But, already in late July 1941, some SS units were murdering women and children as "alleged enemies." They enlisted the help of native populations – Poles, Ukrainians, and others – to carry out pogroms. The pace and character of the massacres, however, remained uneven. In summer 1941, the murder of Soviet Jews was not yet part of a centralized "Final Solution."

Himmler played a major role in initiating mass murder. He traveled widely in newly occupied Soviet territories, apparently ordering the escalation of murderous practices. Following his visits, local commanders often massacred entire Jewish communities. After his visit to Baranowicze on July 31, for example, a radio order went out to a cavalry division stationed there: "Express command of the RFSS [Himmler]. All Jews must be shot. Jewish women to be herded into the marshes." This was a death sentence for all. The women would drown in the marshes, with their children in tow.

For Himmler, killing Jews was the first step in his vast ethnic-cleansing program for the German east (see Chapter 6). Later, Himmler explained his decision to have women and children murdered: "I decided... in this case also to find a clear solution. I did not see myself as justified in eradicating the men – by that I mean in killing them or having them killed – only to let their children grow up to avenge them by killing our sons and grandsons." In Himmler's mind, the murder of women and children was essential to prevent a resurgence of Jews in the German east.

Throughout fall 1941 operational groups, often aided by the Wehrmacht, carried out mass shootings of Jews in Soviet territory. In just two days, September 29–30, for example, 33,771 Jews in Kiev were killed. The Jews were marched out to a ravine in Babi Yar, told to undress, and shot into pits. Some were buried alive in the mounting pile of corpses. Similar harrowing executions took place in Serbia, where the Wehrmacht took the lead in killing Jews. The following year, in summer and fall 1942, SS mobile killing squads, in conjunction with the army, carried out another huge wave of massacres in occupied Soviet lands. All told, some 1.3 million Soviet Jews were murdered. That so many Jews died in open-air executions adds a gruesome dimension to the Holocaust that is often unacknowledged. At the same time, the active role of the Wehrmacht belies any notion that the German army was "clean" (see Chapter 6).

Killing with gas

When Himmler witnessed a mass execution in Minsk on August 15, 1941, the executioners complained of "mental and nervous strain." The SS chief was anxious about the killers' state of mind. He and others also worried about what it would mean for German society to have so many brutal killers in its midst. He now initiated a search for a murder method less taxing on killers. In the Warthegau, an SS official, Herbert Lange, experimented with boiling Jews in slaked lime. Near Minsk, Arthur Nebe, head of Mobile Killing Squad B, tried dynamiting mental patients in their asylum.

Lange, Nebe, and others soon found gassing more promising. In the Warthegau, Lange had long used mobile gas vans to kill mental patients in occupied Poland. Now, more efficient vans were developed, and some thirty were soon in use in

Eastern and southeastern Europe. At Auschwitz, camp authorities experimented with a poison gas, Zyklon B, to kill Soviet prisoners of war (POWs) and sick prisoners. In Mogilev, Nebe had mental patients gassed with carbon monoxide in hermetically sealed rooms. Other SS officials learned of these experiments. In mid-October, Odilo Globocnik, the SS and police leader in the Lublin district, sought Himmler's permission to construct a death camp with stationary gas chambers. This camp, Bełżec, proved a milestone in the evolution of Nazi killing methods.

The "Final Solution"

Until late 1941, official policy in Germany remained the expulsion – and *not* the murder – of Jews. After the 1938 annexation of Austria, for example, Adolf Eichmann, a security service (Sicherheitsdienst, SD) official, went to Vienna to organize the expulsion of Austrian Jews. His Central Office for Jewish Emigration, staffed by Austrian antisemites, was brutally successful. Between August 1938 and June 1939, some 110,000 Austrian Jews left the country. Top SS officials viewed Eichmann's "Vienna Model" as so successful that a similar Reich-wide office was set up in Berlin. But, to Nazi officials, the pace of Jewish emigration still seemed too slow.

In fall 1941, after massacres of Jews in Soviet territories were ongoing, the Nazis significantly escalated the persecution of Jews in Germany. As of September 19, all Jews over the age of six had to wear the Yellow Star. As of October 18, Jews were no longer permitted to emigrate. On November 25, all German Jews living abroad (including in ghettos and camps) lost their citizenship and property.

When did Hitler decide on the Final Solution, the murder of all Jews in Germany's grasp? Since historians have never found a clear-cut Führer order, the timing of Hitler's decision is hotly debated. Most historians believe that Hitler decided on the murder of all European Jews sometime between October and December 1941. The process, though, appears to have been gradual and incremental. At the same time, Hitler was not alone in pushing forward the Final Solution. Himmler was deeply involved. A broad stratum of Nazi leaders also believed that a "solution" to the "Jewish Problem" had to be found. Hitler and Himmler thus allowed regional officials considerable latitude in initiating their own "solutions." This elicited a dynamic of "cumulative radicalization," in which central and regional Nazi officials together spurred on ever more murderous solutions.

Christopher Browning believes Hitler decided on the Final Solution in the wake of the October military successes in the Soviet Union. In mid-September Hitler had ordered the deportation of German Jews eastwards – to ghettos, not death camps (none yet existed). In mid-October, after military victories in the Soviet Union, trains filled with German Jews rolled eastwards to Łódź and other ghettos. Almost simultaneously, regional authorities began to plan and build death camps. In late October, for the first time, Hitler publicly mentioned the murder of Jews: "By exterminating this pest, we shall do humanity a service of which our soldiers can have no idea."

Other historians believe that the murder of Polish Jews began as regional initiatives intended to solve local demographic "problems." In both the Warthegau and Lublin, where the first two death camps were built, officials were involved with carrying out Germanization policies that involved large-scale demographic movements (see Chapter 6). Murdering Jews – to shuffle around the Polish and German populations – was one piece of this demographic "puzzle." In fall 1941, officials in the Warthegau readied Chełmno, a primitive death camp using three mobile gas vans. Beginning on December 8, Polish Jews "unfit for work" were murdered there – the first gassing of Europe's Jews.

According to Christian Gerlach, Hitler decided on the Final Solution only after Chełmno began operations. Early in December, the Red Army pushed the Wehrmacht into retreat. The Nazis no longer had the option of expelling Jews and other undesirable populations deep inside conquered Soviet territories. In addition, once Germany entered war with the United States mid-month, there was no reason to keep Jews as "hostages" to influence relations with America. With "territorial" options foreclosed and no reason to keep Jews alive, Gerlach argues, Hitler decided on murder.

While good evidence favors each possible dating scenario, none aligns perfectly with all available evidence. By year's end, however, the Germans had massacred at least half a million Soviet Jews. One death camp in Poland was in operation, another planned. Some 40,000 German Jews had been deported eastwards. These initiatives coalesced into what soon became the Final Solution.

The Wannsee Conference

On January 20, 1942, Reinhard Heydrich, the head of the Reich Security Main Office (RSHA), convened a conference of fifteen senior Nazi officials, many of whom worked on Jewish affairs in civilian ministries. The conference took place in an elegant villa on the Wannsee lake in suburban Berlin. Historians used to think that the Final Solution was decided there. Now they believe that Heydrich held the conference to consolidate SS authority over the murder of Europe's Jews. Indeed, the SS was coming off a string of failures as concerned anti-Jewish policy. The Nisko and Madagascar Plans had gone nowhere. Local murder initiatives threatened to spin out of central SS control. Heydrich now wished to show his authority. At the conference, he told participants just what was to happen: the Jews of Europe would be deported to occupied Soviet areas where they would be killed through a combination of arduous forced labor and outright murder.

In the ensuing discussion, Josef Bühler, the representative of the General Government, proposed an alternative: that the Final Solution begin in occupied

Poland. Transport and manpower there, he argued, would be less complicated than further east. In spring 1942, this alternative was adopted. The Final Solution thus took place on two tracks. While mobile killing squads carried out mass executions in occupied Soviet areas and southeastern Europe, much of the rest of the Final Solution took place in death camps in occupied Poland. The focus of the Final Solution thus shifted from the Soviet Union to Poland.

Jewish Slave Labor

Historians debate whether and to what degree the Nazi regime privileged ideology over economic and military needs. A case in point is Jewish slave labor. Once World War II began, the Nazis were desperately short on manpower. Between 1939 and 1942, state agencies, municipalities, and private industry used Jewish labor throughout Nazi-occupied Europe. Jews built highways, dug anti-tank ditches, and worked on water-control projects. In Upper Silesia, SS official Albrecht Schmelt oversaw a network of labor camps that deployed Jews in factories or local building projects.

Among high-level Nazis, the use of Jewish labor was controversial, especially once murder was an option. Some preferred to exploit Jews, while others sought the immediate elimination of this "enemy." For a time, acceding to demands for wartime labor, Himmler advocated the use of Jewish slave labor. Under ghastly conditions, Jews worked on building Transit Road IV, a major supply line for Army Group South and a key road for the Germanization of Ukraine. In addition, from 1942 onward, the SS Business and Administration Main Office (WVHA), under Oswald Pohl, worked closely with armaments companies to use concentration-camp labor (see Chapter 8).

Although historians used to think that Jewish labor was economically pointless and just another way to torture Jews, most work done by Jews actually furthered the regime's economic or military goals. Accordingly, at the start of 1943, there were still 400,000 Jews at work in Germany and occupied Poland. Facing serious labor shortages, many local Nazi officials wished to retain their Jewish workers. Himmler, however, generally preferred extermination to exploitation. Increasingly, he urged the deportation of Jews. Accordingly, in February 1943, the Gestapo carried out the "Factory Action" in Berlin. Most Jews still in the capital, including armaments workers, were now deported.

After the Warsaw Ghetto Uprising in April 1943 (see below), Himmler was even more adamant about ending the use of Jewish slave labor. Virtually all working Jews were now deported, the vast majority murdered. Still, due to the exigencies of war, the SS never entirely gave up Jewish slave labor. Instead, it came to focus on both maintaining a workforce *and* exterminating Jews. This process was known as "destruction through labor" and was made possible through constant "selections." Due to a steady influx of newly deported Jews, the SS could "select" those exhausted by labor and murder them. The SS believed that it was balancing ideological and economic imperatives. While SS policy allowed some few Jews to survive, antisemitic ideology ultimately trumped the economic and military needs of the Third Reich.

Death Camps

Many use the terms "concentration camp" and "death camp" interchangeably. In fact, they mean very different things. A "concentration camp" was first and foremost a labor camp, run by the SS. In addition, there were many other labor camps independent of SS control, run by municipalities or even private companies. At last count, researchers had documented some 42,500 labor camps in Nazi-occupied Europe. By contrast, the SS built just six death camps – Auschwitz, Bełżec, Chełmno, Majdanek, Sobibór, and Treblinka. Auschwitz and Majdanek contained concentration camps, but the other four were solely death camps.

In spring 1942, Hitler, Himmler, and Heydrich held a series of meetings to implement the Final Solution. In turn, Eichmann and his staff, known as RSHA section IV B 4 (Jewish Affairs), arranged a wave of deportations from Austria, France, Germany, and Slovakia. Some of these Jews ended up in ghettos while others were immediately murdered in death camps. In some cases, local Jews in ghettos were murdered so as to make way for the arrivals from Western Europe.

In late spring 1942, Himmler escalated the murder campaign by sending most German and Western European Jews directly to concentration or death camps, bypassing ghettos. In his view, the Jews had proven themselves a terrible security risk. In May, Herbert Baum, a Jewish communist who led a resistance group of Jews and non-Jews, organized a bomb attack on an anti-Soviet exhibition in Berlin. The attack caused little damage, but the Nazi leadership was dismayed by the audacity of Jewish resistance. Then, on June 4, Heydrich died of wounds incurred in an assassination attempt outside Prague. To Himmler, Czech assassins, sent in from Britain, must be allied with the nefarious Jewish enemy (even though no Jewish connections to the assassination have ever been established). Finally, Germany was facing a looming food shortage. To the Nazis, this resulted from alleged Jewish black marketeering. Since large numbers of civilian Polish and Russian workers were now available to replace Jewish workers (see Chapter 8), Himmler believed that the Nazis could dispense with German and Western European Jews.

At the same time, the SS chief urged the quick murder of Polish Jews in the General Government. This program was codenamed Operation Reinhard, a posthumous honor for Heydrich. T4 euthanasia specialists set up and ran all three Operation Reinhard camps: Bełżec (opened in March 1942), Sobibór (late April), and Treblinka (early summer). Altogether, some 1.7 million Jews died in these three camps. Keep in mind: each of these individuals was a living and breathing person, each a mother or son, father or daughter, spouse or sibling. In just over a year, the SS completed Operation Reinhard; virtually all Polish Jews in the General Government had been killed (except those in camps or hiding). Bełżec had already closed in December 1942; Sobibór and Treblinka closed in summer and fall 1943, respectively.

Eichmann now worked to quicken deportations from countries allied with Nazi Germany. While some countries complied (the Netherlands), others tried to evade Nazi pressure (Denmark). By compelling countries to participate in the Final Solution, Nazi Germany further bound them to its "New Order." The more, however, that Germany suffered military setbacks, the less these countries were willing to collaborate in the deportation of Jews. Conversely, when Nazi Germany directly occupied countries – Greece in 1941, Italy in 1943, and Hungary in 1944 – the consequences were devastating for Jews. Hundreds of thousands of Jews from these countries were quickly sent to death camps.

In rounding up or transporting Jews to their deaths, the Germans engaged in excessive cruelty. They threw babies against walls or roads, and laughed when the brains splattered out. They seized children by the legs and tore apart their limbs. When the sick, elderly, or young lagged behind, they shot them point-blank. They used truncheons to beat Jews unconscious. They abused Jewish women, sometimes slicing off their breasts. To weaken Jews prior to deportation, they locked them in synagogues or other community buildings without food or water for days.

Figure 7.2 Child at gun point (Warsaw, 1943). This photo was included in *The Stroop Report*, a Nazi account of the suppression of the Warsaw Ghetto Uprising. *Source*: akg images.

At the death camps, prisoners arrived by train. The camps were disguised as train stations, and Jews were told that they had arrived at a transit point. If "selections" took place there (often these had occurred earlier or en route), Jews "fit for work" were separated from the others. The elderly, mothers with small children, and children under age ten remained behind. They were told to deposit their valuables and to undress for showers. Once naked, they were herded into a chute that led directly to gas chambers. Pushed into the chambers, they soon suffered an agonizing death. Afterward, Jewish work commandos shoveled out the corpses and burned or buried them.

Many think that the deportations and murders went off without difficulty. In fact, Nazi officials encountered myriad obstacles. In early summer 1942, for example, there was a transport ban due to a Nazi offensive in the Soviet Union. At times, gas chambers became overburdened and malfunctioned. At Treblinka there were so many unburied corpses and other signs of disorder that the camp was temporarily shut and then reopened under new leadership. At Chełmno the gasses from buried bodies were so noxious that the corpses had to be dug up and burned. Local SS and other officials, however, showed considerable ingenuity in overcoming these and other obstacles. In summer 1942, for instance, a main railroad line to the Sobibór death camp was under repair. Rather than interrupt murder operations, Globocnik simply used units of the Order Police to massacre Jews close to their homes. As this and numerous other similar initiatives suggest, the Holocaust was possible because so many Nazi officials on the ground were "working towards the Führer."

Auschwitz

Auschwitz remains the iconic Holocaust death camp. It did not, however, become the central site of the Holocaust until late 1943. Its history suggests the Third Reich's evolving priorities. In June 1940, the camp opened as a concentration camp for Polish prisoners. The following spring, IG Farben, the giant chemical company, decided to locate a factory in Auschwitz. For IG Farben, Auschwitz was attractive due to the presence of prison labor, good railway connections, and raw materials such as coal and lime. The company also benefited from generous tax breaks granted to factories situated in the east. In the next four years, the company built a huge plant to make Buna, artificial rubber. The factory was just nearing completion in 1945.

IG Farben changed both the camp and the town of Auschwitz (Oświęcim in Polish). The plant was the linchpin of a plan to "Germanize" the Upper Silesian region, an area of Poland annexed to Nazi Germany in 1939. Some 500 German companies were involved in building the IG Farben complex or its subsidiary operations. In addition, other German manufacturing companies came to Auschwitz to exploit prison labor. To accommodate the influx of German managers and their families, Himmler wished to make Auschwitz a model "German" town. Urban architects drew up plans for large municipal and Party buildings, parade grounds, schools, recreational facilities, and residential areas. Himmler supported "German" landscaping and sophisticated recycling operations in the region. Germans worked and played with the stench of death in the air.

After the invasion of the Soviet Union, the Nazis briefly envisioned Auschwitz as a huge work camp for Soviet POWs. Already by spring 1942, however, the vast majority of prisoners were Jews. They endured terrible conditions in the main camp and in the thirty or so sub-camps that provided labor to various companies. While slave labor cost companies little, productivity was also very low – sometimes just 20% of a well-fed German workforce. Although many Jews died from the terrible work conditions, camp officials were unconcerned. There was always a ready supply of new prisoners.

While the Nazis forced prisoners to work, they also aimed to dehumanize them. They stripped camp inmates of their individuality and human dignity. They forced inmates to wear prison garb, and identified inmates by number rather than name. (Auschwitz was the only camp where prisoners were tattooed with numbers.) Nazi camp authorities also starved prisoners with too little moldy bread and watery soup. They made prisoners sleep in overcrowded barracks with few sanitation facilities. Moreover, as Primo Levi, an Italian Jew, described in his remarkable memoir, *Survival in Auschwitz*, the Nazis compelled prisoners to compromise their morality in their quest for survival. To survive, prisoners often acted according to base instincts; placing their own interests above others, inmates often stole from or otherwise exploited fellow prisoners.

Adjacent to Auschwitz, camp authorities built Birkenau, a death camp. After the Operation Reinhard camps closed in fall 1943, Auschwitz-Birkenau became the leading death camp. From then on, Jews from all over Europe were killed there. From May to July 1944, for example, some 438,000 Hungarian Jews arrived. Roughly 85% were murdered immediately. At the height of operations, camp crematoria could burn up to 4,756 corpses per day. In turn, the SS profited from the body parts of murdered Jews. Gold from tooth fillings was melted down and sent to the Reichsbank, the central German bank. Human hair was spun into thread and used to manufacture felt, rope, and mattresses. Ashes and bonemeal were sold for use as fertilizer.

Roma (Gypsies)

Like the Jews, the Roma endured new restrictions after war began in 1939. They were no longer permitted to move around Germany, and some were subject to compulsory labor. Heydrich planned to remove all 30,000 Roma in Germany and Austria to the General Government. In May 1940, some 2,500 Roma were deported. But, since Himmler had other priorities, no further deportations of Roma took place at this time. Still, the Roma endured ever tightening restrictions. In March 1941, for example, Roma children were no longer permitted to attend state schools.

For unknown reasons, some 5,000 Sinti and Lalleri Gypsies from Austria were sent to the Łódź ghetto in fall 1941. They remained in the ghetto only briefly. After an outbreak of typhus, ghetto authorities decided to liquidate the Gypsy camp. In January 1942, the Roma still alive in the ghetto were gassed at Chełmno. They were among the first victims of that death camp.

In December 1942, Himmler issued the so-called Auschwitz Decree, according to which all Roma were to be sent to Auschwitz. There were, however, numerous exemptions. The SS chief believed that some full-blooded Roma were "Aryan," and these individuals were not to be deported. There were also many exceptions among the allegedly inferior mixed-blooded Roma. Roma who had settled and held steady jobs were exempt from deportation. So, too, were those married to Germans. The Roma who remained in Germany, however, were to be sterilized – and many were, against their will.

Starting in February 1943, 13,080 Roma from Germany and Austria were deported to Auschwitz. Another 10,000 Roma from other parts of Europe were brought to the camp. Unlike other prisoners, the Roma were not subject to selections or slave labor. In addition, they were housed in a Gypsy family camp, wore civilian clothing, and received somewhat better food rations than other prison inmates at Auschwitz. SS doctor Josef Mengele, known as the "Angel of Death," took a particular interest in Roma. On his initiative, a kindergarten, serving hundreds of children, was established in the Gypsy camp. Mengele's attention, however, was a double-edged sword. He performed gruesome medical experiments on some Roma (see below). Moreover, despite the somewhat better conditions in the Gypsy camp, disease was still rampant. Among other epidemics, the camp saw an outbreak of noma, a gangrenous condition that leaves gaping holes in the cheeks.

In summer 1944, the decision was made to eliminate the Gypsy camp. It is not clear why. Perhaps the camp was emptied to make room for arriving Hungarian Jews. By then, some 14,000 Roma had already died from disease or other maltreatment at Auschwitz. Now, roughly 3,500 Roma deemed capable of work were transferred to other concentration camps. As guards moved in to push the remaining Roma into gas chambers, the Roma engaged in an armed uprising. Some 5,600 Roma were nonetheless gassed. Besides killing Roma in the death camps of Auschwitz and Chełmno, the Nazis massacred many other Roma in Serbia, the Soviet Union, and other parts of Nazi-occupied Europe.

The Nazis did not pursue the Roma with the same zeal as they did the Jews. Many Roma – perhaps even the majority – were never even deported. The 2,500 Roma sent to the General Government were not murdered outright, although many died as a result of terrible living conditions. The Gypsy camp in Auschwitz existed for seventeen months, suggesting that the Nazis had not decided the Romas' fate. Nonetheless, most historians agree that the Nazis perpetrated genocide against the Roma. Besides the disabled and Jews, the Roma were the only group who were murdered because of who they were as opposed to what they did. In addition, enforced sterilization constituted a "delayed genocide" in that it reduced the number of future Roma. Of a prewar population of close to one million in Europe, the Nazis killed as many as 220,000 Roma. In the Roma language, this was *Parajmos* (the Devouring).

Homosexuals

During the war, Nazi persecution of homosexuals escalated. In 1940, for example, Himmler decreed that same-sex-desiring men convicted of more than one homosexual act were to be sent to concentration camps after completing their prison sentences. This amounted to indefinite incarceration, if not death. Beginning in 1942, some homosexuals classified as "habitual criminals" were transferred to camps and subjected to "extermination through work."

In concentration camps, homosexuals were stigmatized by pink triangles sewn onto their camp garb. They were often shunned by other prisoners' support networks. Some were promised early release if they agreed to voluntary castration. As of 1942, camp commanders could also order compulsory castration. A few homosexual men – perhaps no more than ten – were subject to a medical experiment to "cure" homosexuality. At Buchenwald, they were implanted with a hormone preparation that allowed for the slow release of hormones intended to cause a "reversal of hormonal polarity."

Some observers claim that the Nazis perpetrated a "homocaust." This is inappropriate language. The Nazis did not try to hunt down and murder every last homosexual in Germany and beyond, as they did Jews. While they sent some 5,000–15,000 homosexuals to concentration camps, we do not know how many of these men perished during the Nazi years.

Human Experiments

In 1942, Hitler decided that human experimentation was permissible if it benefited the state. As a result, prisoners in various concentration camps endured horrific medical experiments. Some experiments were intended to facilitate regime goals such as the sterilization of "inferior" peoples. One doctor, for example, injected chemicals into women's uteruses in the hope of finding a cheap, quick method to sterilize victims during "routine" physical examinations. Another tried to sterilize prisoners by aiming X-rays at their genitalia; this not only effectively castrated prisoners but caused burns so severe that prisoners were unable to work. Other medical experiments furthered doctors' pet research agendas. Most notoriously, Josef Mengele carried out genetics "experiments." He focused on dwarfs and twins, often Roma or children. Among other atrocities, he injected dyes into victims' eyes to determine whether eye color could be changed. He also killed twins on a dissecting table and then compared their bodies, part for part.

Due to soldiers' concerns about poor medical care, the Wehrmacht and SS supported experiments aimed at helping military personnel in emergency situations. At Dachau, researchers forced prisoners to spend hours in low-pressure chambers to study the needs of pilots bailing out at high altitudes. They also submerged prisoners in ice water to study the impact of hypothermia on pilots downed in ocean water. They forced prisoners to drink seawater to test how long soldiers stranded at sea could survive without fresh water. Doctors also tested vaccines against cholera, malaria, smallpox, typhus, and other diseases that German troops encountered in foreign areas. Other researchers focused on the treatment of combat injuries. At Ravensbrück, for example, doctors wounded women, injected them with infectious bacteria, and then treated them with sulfonamide, a new antibacterial drug. Researchers also focused on nerve regeneration and bone and limb transplants. Finally, they tested ways to counteract mustard and phosgene gas warfare.

Most historians believe that the medical experiments at Auschwitz were sadistic endeavors with no scientific value. Scholars are more divided on the value of the military experiments at Dachau and other camps. Some argue that these experiments, especially those on hypothermia, had some scientific validity. Since ethical concerns preclude their repetition, they believe that the research findings should be disseminated, albeit only with mention of the circumstances in which the data were acquired. Many other scholars, however, argue that the experiments were methodologically flawed and the results close to useless. Moreover, they insist that it is morally wrong – and disrespectful to victims – to use evidence attained in unethical ways.

Perpetrators

Why did the perpetrators carry out their horrendous crimes? In a October 4, 1943, speech to SS group leaders in Posen, Himmler praised the killers: "Most of you will know what it means when 100 bodies lie together, when 500 are there or when there are 1000. And... to have seen this through... to have remained decent, has made us hard and is a page of glory never mentioned and never to be mentioned." In Himmler's view, the killers carried out a difficult, yet heroic duty. History, of course, has judged them very differently.

Immediately after World War II, observers presumed that Nazi criminals were misfits, sadists, psychopaths, or worse. This was comforting. Nazi perpetrators seemed heinous but separate from the rest of humankind. In the 1950s and 1960s, however, totalitarian accounts of Nazism became influential. Inspired in part by Arendt's notion of the "banality of evil," scholars came to believe that perpetrators were cogs in a totalitarian machine, thoughtless automatons with no will of their own. This vision of perpetrators was more disturbing: vicious crimes seemed to arise from mere thoughtlessness.

Neither vision accords with what we now know about Nazi perpetrators. In fact, many high-ranking SS officials in the RSHA – those who planned and implemented the Holocaust and other Germanization schemes – were fanatic nationalists or antisemites. They were young, smart, and urbane, many even trained lawyers. Their lives, however, were indelibly shaped by the upheaval following Germany's defeat in World War I. In Michael Wildt's phrase, they made up an "uncompromising generation." They espoused a steely nationalism. They were determined to cleanse "inferior races" from Germany and the east and thereby restore Germany to greatness. Most had blood on their hands. Otto Ohlendorf, for example, was an SS economist with a law degree. He commanded Mobile Killing Squad D, the unit that massacred Jews throughout southern Ukraine and Russia.

The Nazis drafted SS men, soldiers, and policemen to staff killing squads. (They also used foreign auxiliaries, often Ukrainians or Lithuanians.) Scholars offer various interpretations for why these men executed innocent civilians. Daniel Jonah Goldhagen suggests that Germans had come to believe that it was necessary to remove Jews from their midst. In *Hitler's Willing Executioners*, he argues that they killed because they were imbued with an "eliminationist antisemitism." Most historians believe that Goldhagen overstates his case. Jews were too integrated into mainstream society for all Germans to be consumed with "eliminationist antisemitism." Still, some perpetrators likely killed because they hated Jews. After all, by the early 1940s, they had been exposed to years of anti-semitic propaganda.

If many German perpetrators were not fanatical antisemites, why did they kill? In *Ordinary Men*, Browning argues that situational factors best explain the men's actions. Germany was at war. Jews were the enemy, the men were told. In military or police units, individuals are expected to follow orders. Furthermore, the men were living in foreign surroundings, amidst a hostile population. If they did not participate in the killings, they thought, they would let down their peers and perhaps endure ostracism. Moreover, after they had participated in a massacre or two, they became accustomed to the task. At the same time, once the death camps were operational, many men no longer did the actual killing. Instead, they rounded up Jews and shoved them onto trains headed to the death camps. Although Jews died due to their actions, this segmentation of tasks eased the perpetrators' consciences. If the men didn't actually pull the trigger or the switch, they told themselves, they did not kill. According to Browning, most individuals – even you and I – would become perpetrators in this situation. While it is profoundly unsettling, many historians concur with his assessment.

Jewish Resistance

The war gave the Nazis the cover they needed to carry out genocide. No state power protected the Jews. Jews were also isolated from each other and the outside world. It was all but impossible to publicize the ongoing murders. The international mail service was erratic. No foreign journalists were present. Few foreign diplomats were stationed in Nazi-occupied Europe.

Why didn't Jews rise up against their Nazi tormentors? Jews who advocated armed resistance faced formidable obstacles. They had virtually no weapons. In the ghettos and camps, it was also hard to break the apathy and resignation of fellow Jews. Weak and starving, many Jews could barely muster the energy necessary to do everyday tasks, let alone engage in resistance actions. Additionally, most Jewish leaders believed that submission, not resistance, offered the best chance for survival; armed resistance, they feared, would bring on reprisal killings. They did not realize that the Germans intended to kill every last Jew in Europe.

It was also difficult for Jews to hide from the Nazis. Food was available only through official ration cards. Jews could not easily mix into the local Slav populations. They looked different, and their first language was often Yiddish, not a Slavic language. At the same time, many Eastern Europeans were antisemitic and unwilling to aid Jews. Moreover, the Nazis threatened those who did help Jews with draconian punishments. One diarist, Elisheva, despaired of survival: "Is being alive after the war worth so much suffering and pain? I doubt it. But I don't want to die like an animal."

Jews still found ways to resist. On December 31, 1941, a young poet, Abba Kovner, encouraged youth groups in the Vilna ghetto to challenge the Nazis: "We will not be led like sheep to the slaughter... Brothers! It is better to die fighting like free men than to live at the mercy of the murderers. Arise! Arise with your last breadth!" Kovner's appeal galvanized the founding of the first Jewish resistance organization in Nazi-occupied Europe, the United Partisans Organization. The group eventually carried out guerilla attacks against the Germans. Altogether some 20,000–30,000 Jewish Partisans managed to hide in the forests or marshes of Eastern Europe. One group, the Bielski brothers, dedicated its efforts to saving Jews. Tuvia Bielski and his three brothers spirited some 1,500 Jews into the dense forests of western Belorussia. Against all odds, they survived in the wild.

The 1943 Warsaw Ghetto Uprising is the most famous case of armed Jewish resistance during the Holocaust. Between July and October 1942, 265,000 Jews from the Warsaw ghetto had been murdered in Treblinka. In the ghetto, however, the Jewish Combat Organization (ZOB), led by Mordechai Anielewicz, managed to buy or steal weapons. Its members knew they had little chance of victory. But, if they had to die, they wanted to choose how. They wished to die fighting rather than passively accept death. In January 1943, when Germans entered the ghetto to round up the remaining 55,000 Jews, the ZOB attacked. While the Germans hurriedly left then, they returned on April 19, the first night of Passover that year. The ZOB and several other groups now engaged in street battles with German units. After about a week of fighting, the Jews retreated into underground bunkers. SS General Jürgen Stroop then ordered his troops to flood the sewers to prevent Jews from escaping to other parts of Warsaw. He also had his men burn the ghetto, building by building, to smoke out Jews in hiding. The Nazis suffered several dozen fatalities and took four weeks to quell the uprising. While few Jews survived, their legendary resistance has stoked Jewish identity ever since.

Jews rebelled against the liquidation of other ghettos, too. Moreover, inside death camps, they carried out armed uprisings. They rose up against their Nazi tormentors in Sobibór on August 14 and Treblinka on October 1, 1943, and in Auschwitz on October 7, 1944. Few Jews managed to escape the camps, and most who did were later caught. Still, the uprisings led to the abrupt closing of both Sobibór and Treblinka death camps. In Auschwitz, the rebellion destroyed Crematorium IV.

Finally, Jews thwarted Nazi aims in ways not usually classified as resistance. In the camps, Jews insisted on maintaining their dignity in the face of Nazi dehumanization. They found ways to keep clean and to pursue artistic and intellectual endeavors. Outside the camps, Jews wrote diaries or otherwise recorded Nazi crimes. Viktor Klemperer, a noted German-Jewish diarist, insisted on the importance of recording "the everyday life of tyranny." In the Warsaw ghetto, Emanuel Ringelblum organized Oyneg Shabes, a group that collected and buried documents about the ongoing destruction of Jewry. The Nazis certainly did not want Jews to frame or narrate the story of the Holocaust. When Jews bore witness to Nazi crimes, they ensured the Third Reich's lasting infamy.

Reaction at Home and Abroad

Domestic inaction

Many Germans later claimed that they knew nothing about the Holocaust. Of course, no German media sources reported the murders. Still, Germans could surmise something was amiss – if they chose to. They saw Jews gathered at assembly points, or noticed that nearby apartments were suddenly vacant. Some heard BBC broadcasts about the killing of Jews. Germans also learned about the murders from those who participated in or witnessed the Holocaust. Germans, after all, ran the railroad operations that brought Jews to the east, constructed and guarded death camps, and provisioned camps with poison gas and other products. German soldiers also aided the SS mobile death squads in their murderous tasks. On home leave, they and others talked about what they had seen or done.

Despite widespread knowledge of ongoing murders, not one organized group in Nazi Germany voiced solidarity with the Jews. No social group, no church, no professional organization, no scholarly association. While widespread German antisemitism may explain this lack of solidarity, it is more likely that Germans were just indifferent to the fate of the small Jewish minority. Germans were preoccupied with their own troubles, whether worrying about family members at the front or dealing with the aftereffects of Allied bombings. As Ian Kershaw has famously stated, "the road to Auschwitz was built by hate, but paved with indifference."

Small numbers of Germans *were* dismayed by anti-Jewish measures. Not least, this was true of those with Jewish relatives. In late February 1943, during the Factory Action, the Gestapo rounded up some 2,000 Jewish spouses, mostly men. The men were brought to a Jewish community building on Rosenstrasse in Berlin. Their "Aryan" wives soon hurried to Rosenstrasse to demand their return. For the next week the women held constant vigil. After a week of demonstrations, the Nazis freed the Jewish men.

Why did the regime relent? Nathan Stoltzfus suggests that, in the wake of Stalingrad (see Chapter 8), Propaganda Minister Goebbels was concerned about public morale. He did not want to antagonize any part of the German population, even German spouses of Jews. Wolf Gruner, however, argues that there were no plans to deport those in mixed marriages and that the men would soon have been released even without the protests. Regardless of what actually happened in the Rosenstrasse incident, mixed marriage *was* the surest way for Jews to survive in Nazi Germany. In September 1944 there were 13,217 Jews officially registered in Germany, 98% of whom lived in mixed marriages.

Could German protests have stopped the murder of Jews? The "Aryan" women's protest may have prevented the deportation of their Jewish husbands. Public outrage may also have led Hitler to halt the euthanasia campaign (see above). According to Henry Friedlander, however, these two seemingly successful protests shared an important feature: *German* relatives stood up for their loved ones. Always conscious of public opinion, Hitler wished to avoid alienating any part of the German community. Unlike the disabled or spouses, however, most Jews didn't have German friends or relatives willing to stand up for them. The Nazis' assiduous promotion of Jews' "social death" proved highly effective.

It should be noted that Germans did help the estimated 5,000 German Jews who survived in hiding or by adopting false identities, mostly in Berlin. Jews underground needed Germans to procure food and shelter for them. Those living under false identities needed Germans to help forge papers and create plausible cover stories. Germans who aided Jews put themselves at serious risk of imprisonment, although not of death. Their actions belied the later widespread German legend that nothing could be done in the face of Nazi terror.

Foreign inaction

Jews also found little support abroad. Many observers criticize the Vatican and Allied governments for inaction during the Holocaust. They question, for example, why Pope Pius XII refused to use his enormous moral stature to speak out on Jews' behalf. While the pope quietly aided some Jews and privately voiced concerns about their fate, he never publicly denounced Hitler or the Holocaust. Some historians think that Pius' reticence stemmed from antisemitic or pro-Nazi attitudes. There is little concrete evidence to support these contentions. Rather, it seems that Pius believed that any public denunciation of Nazism would make things only worse for Jews and especially Catholics. Indeed, his major concern was to protect Germany's 20 million Catholics. If he antagonized Hitler, Pius feared, the Nazis might further undermine the Concordat and send even more priests to concentration camps (see Chapter 5). The controversy surrounding Pope Pius XII continues. Did the pope's caution save some Jews and protect many Catholics? Or did it simply compromise the church's moral mission?

By August 1942, Allied government officials knew about the ongoing murder of Jews. By year's end, the mass killings were public knowledge. The Polish government-in-exile and Jewish groups begged the Allied governments to somehow intervene. To no avail. Historians have pilloried the 1944 Allied decision to not bomb train tracks leading to Auschwitz or the camp's extermination facilities. While some historians see antisemitism as the cause of Allied inaction, other factors are perhaps more telling. As the Allies knew from aerial raids on Germany, ruined railway lines are easily repaired. Strategic bombing was also notoriously inaccurate. Bombing the extermination facilities would have endangered the 130,000 Jews imprisoned in nearby camps. Then, too, the murder of Jews was not seen as the singular crime it is today. Allied government officials and Jewish leaders alike believed that rapid military victory was the surest way to end Hitler's tyranny – and bring a stop to *all* Nazi crimes. Any diversion could delay winning the war. Although the refusal to bomb Auschwitz seems a case of moral indifference, it was, in fact, reasoned strategy.

The Legacy

Roughly 5.8 million Jews died in the Holocaust. Some 60% died by gassing, 40% by other means, including open-air executions and starvation in the ghettos. Holocaust victims included some three million Jews in Poland, one million in the Soviet Union, 500,000 in Hungary, 270,000 in Romania, 160,000 in Germany, 140,000 in Lithuania, 106,000 in the Netherlands, 83,000 in France, and smaller numbers of Jews from many other countries. The death tolls for Jews in certain death camps, particularly Auschwitz (960,000) and Treblinka (870,000), are staggering. While just six persons survived Chełmno death camp, roughly 100,000 individuals survived Auschwitz concentration camp. These survivors were still "capable of work" and had not yet been "selected" for death.

The Final Solution tells us much about Hitler's Third Reich. An extraordinary antisemitism was at the regime's core. For Hitler, the Final Solution was a matter of Germany's life or death, a goal worth pursuing even in the face of defeat. For all the chaos in the Nazi administration, the Third Reich was singularly effective in carrying out its mission to destroy Jews. This was only possible because Hitler and his minions were able to prevail upon their allies to deliver Jews and to mobilize their countrymen (and foreign auxiliaries) to commit horrific crimes.

The origins and singularity of the Holocaust remain deeply controversial. Many scholars see the Holocaust as rooted in German intellectual traditions of racism, nationalism, and antisemitism or the trauma of German defeat in World War I and the later depression. These scholars tend to view the Holocaust as unique based on the high number of victims, the method of industrial murder, the complicity of professional elites, and the fact that it was perpetrated by one of the most "civilized" countries in the world. For such scholars, the Holocaust represents a rupture in European history.

Other scholars, notably Donald Bloxham and Jürgen Zimmerer, see the Holocaust as a logical outcome of European traditions of state building and violence toward minorities, colonialism, and Enlightenment rationality. Zimmerer, for example, argues that colonialism left Europeans versed in a mind-set in which it was both thinkable and doable to eliminate groups of people (as the Germans had done with the Herero in 1904–1907; see Chapter 1). For him, the Holocaust was part of the Enlightenment project to improve the world – in this case, by sweeping away "dirty" or "primitive" peoples. Historians such as Bloxham and Zimmerer argue that the Holocaust was neither unique as a case of genocide nor apart from the general course of European history.

The Holocaust raises profound questions about moral progress. As Jean Améry, a Jewish philosopher and Auschwitz survivor, argued, the worst crime of the Holocaust was that it ruined "trust in the world." Perhaps because the victims were white Europeans, the Holocaust brought home that ordinary citizens could and would disrespect the physical and spiritual selves of others. It proved how easily ordinary people could and would ignore fundamental moral imperatives. While perpetrators ignored the sixth commandment, "Thou shalt not kill," bystanders ignored ethical traditions of resisting injustice or aiding those in need.

Has the world learned from Auschwitz? It would seem not. Genocide has continued – witness Cambodia, Bosnia, Rwanda, and Darfur. Today, Holocaust education emphasizes respect for human rights, toleration of others, and recognition of rescuers. Some educators also highlight the teachings of the Jewish philosopher Emmanuel Lévinas. Lévinas argued that ethics should center on the face of the Other and what it conveys, namely the possibility of suffering and ultimate death. He believed such a focus, which emphasizes the interrelated nature of all human beings, prioritizes one's responsibility to another over the assertion of one's own rights. Only when we all are prepared to be responsible for the humanity of every other person will the danger of genocide subside.

Citations for Quotations

Page   Source

151   "Today I will..." Quoted in Christian Leitz, *Nazi Foreign Policy, 1933–1941: The Road to Global War* (London: Routledge, 2004), 5.

152   "unworthy of life." Quoted in Henry Friedlander, *The Origins of Nazi Genocide: From Euthanasia to the Final Solution* (Chapel Hill: University of North Carolina Press, 1995), 151.

152   "mercy deaths." Quoted in Friedlander, *The Origins of Nazi Genocide*, xxi.

155   "Further crowding..." Quoted in Saul Friedländer, *Nazi Germany and the Jews 1939–1945: The Years of Extermination* (New York: HarperCollins, 2007), 147.

155   "There are epidemics there..." Quoted in Catherine Epstein, *Model Nazi: Arthur Greiser and the Occupation of Western Poland* (Oxford: Oxford University Press, 2010), 169.

156   "The Jews [in Madagascar]..." Quoted in Friedländer, *Nazi Germany and the Jews 1939–1945*, 81.

157   "Express command..." Quoted in Peter Longerich, *Heinrich Himmler* (Oxford: Oxford University Press, 2012), 531.

157   "I decided..." Quoted in Longerich, *Heinrich Himmler*, 539.

157   "mental and nervous strain." Quoted in Sybille Steinbacher, *Auschwitz: A History* (New York: HarperCollins, 2005), 84.

158   "cumulative radicalization." Hans Mommsen, "Cumulative Radicalisation and Progressive Self-Destruction as Structural Determinants of the Nazi Dictatorship," in Ian Kershaw and Moshe Lewin, eds., *Stalinism and Nazism: Dictatorships in Comparison* (Cambridge: Cambridge University Press, 1977), 75–87.

159   "By exterminating..." Quoted in Friedländer, *Nazi Germany and the Jews 1939–1945*, 273.

166   "reversal of hormonal polarity." Quoted in Günter Grau, ed., *Hidden Holocaust? Gay and Lesbian Persecution in Germany 1933–45* (Chicago: Fitzroy Dearborn, 1995), 281.

166   "homocaust." Quoted in Grau, ed., *Hidden Holocaust?*, 5.

167   "Most of you will know..." Quoted in the Nizkor Project, "Himmler's October 4, 1943 Speech in Posen, 'Extermination'," http://www.nizkor.org/hweb/people/h/himmler-heinrich/posen/oct-04-43/ausrottung-transl-nizkor.html (accessed July 25, 2013).

168 "uncompromising generation." From title of Michael Wildt, *An Uncompromising Generation: The Nazi Leadership of the Reich Security Main Office* (Madison: University of Wisconsin Press, 2009).

168 "eliminationist antisemitism." Daniel Jonah Goldhagen, *Hitler's Willing Executioners: Ordinary Germans and the Holocaust* (New York: Knopf, 1996).

169 "Is being alive…" Quoted in Friedländer, *Nazi Germany and the Jews 1939–1945*, 387.

169 "We will not be led…" Quoted in Friedländer, *Nazi Germany and the Jews 1939–1945*, 326.

170 "the everyday life of tyranny." Victor Klemperer, "The Klemperer Diaries," *The New Yorker* (April 27 and May 4, 1998), 134.

171 "the road to Auschwitz…" Ian Kershaw, *Popular Opinion and Political Dissent in the Third Reich: Bavaria 1933–1945* (Oxford: Clarendon Press, 1983), 277.

173 "trust in the world." Jean Améry, *At the Mind's Limits: Contemplations by a Survivor on Auschwitz and its Realities* (Bloomington: Indiana University Press, 1980), 28.

Bibliography

Aly, Götz. *Hitler's Beneficiaries: Plunder, Racial War, and the Nazi Welfare State.* New York: Metropolitan Books, 2006.

Améry, Jean. *At the Mind's Limits: Contemplations by a Survivor on Auschwitz and Its Realities.* Bloomington: Indiana University Press, 1980.

Arendt, Hannah. *Eichmann in Jerusalem: A Report on the Banality of Evil.* New York: Penguin, 1963.

Benz, Wolfgang. *A Concise History of the Third Reich.* Berkeley: University of California Press, 2006.

Bergen, Doris L. *War and Genocide: A Concise History of the Holocaust.* Lanham: Rowman & Littlefield, 2003.

Bloxham, Donald. *The Final Solution: A Genocide.* Oxford: Oxford University Press, 2009.

Browning, Christopher R. *Ordinary Men: Reserve Police Battalion 101 and the Final Solution in Poland.* New York: HarperCollins, 1992.

Browning, Christopher R. *Nazi Policy, Jewish Workers, German Killers.* Cambridge: Cambridge University Press, 2000.

Browning, Christopher R. *The Origins of the Final Solution: The Evolution of Nazi Jewish Policy, September 1939–March 1942.* Lincoln: University of Nebraska Press, 2004.

Caplan, A.L. *When Medicine Went Mad: Bioethics and the Holocaust.* Totowa: Humana, 1992.

Cesarani, David. *Becoming Eichmann: Rethinking the Life, Crimes, and Trial of a "Desk Murderer."* Cambridge, MA: Da Capo Press, 2004.

Coppa, Frank J. *The Life and Pontificate of Pope Pius XII: Between History and Controversy.* Washington, DC: Catholic University of America Press, 2013.

Epstein, Catherine. *Model Nazi: Arthur Greiser and the Occupation of Western Poland.* Oxford: Oxford University Press, 2010.

Friedlander, Henry. *The Origins of Nazi Genocide: From Euthanasia to the Final Solution.* Chapel Hill: University of North Carolina Press, 1995.

Friedländer, Saul. *Nazi Germany and the Jews, 1939–1945: The Years of Extermination.* New York: HarperCollins, 2007.

Gerlach, Christian. "The Wannsee Conference, the Fate of German Jews, and Hitler's Decision in Principle to Exterminate All European Jews." *Journal of Modern History* 70, no. 4 (1998): 759–812.

Goldhagen, Daniel Jonah. *Hitler's Willing Executioners: Ordinary Germans and the Holocaust.* New York: Knopf, 1996.

Grau, Günter, ed. *Hidden Holocaust? Gay and Lesbian Persecution in Germany 1933–45.* Chicago: Fitzroy Dearborn, 1995.

Gruner, Wolf. *Jewish Forced Labor under the Nazis: Economic Needs and Racial Aims, 1938–1944.* Cambridge: Cambridge University Press, 2006.

Hayes, Peter and John K. Roth. *The Oxford Handbook of Holocaust Studies.* Oxford: Oxford University Press, 2010.

Herbert, Ulrich, ed. *National Socialist Extermination Policies: Contemporary German Perspectives and Controversies.* New York: Berghahn Books, 2000.

Herf, Jeffrey. *The Jewish Enemy: Nazi Propaganda during World War II and the Holocaust.* Cambridge, MA: Belknap Press of Harvard University Press, 2006.

Hilberg, Raul. *The Destruction of the European Jews.* New York: Holmes & Meier, 1985.

Johnson, Eric A. and Karl-Heinz Reuband. *What We Knew: Terror, Mass Murder, and Everyday Life in Nazi Germany.* London: John Murray, 2005.

Kassow, Samuel D. *Who Will Write Our History? Rediscovering a Hidden Archive from the Warsaw Ghetto.* New York: Random House, 2007.

Kershaw, Ian. *Popular Opinion and Political Dissent in the Third Reich: Bavaria 1933–1945.* Oxford: Clarendon Press, 1983.

Klemperer, Victor. "The Klemperer Diaries." *The New Yorker,* April 27 and May 4 (1998): 120–135.

Leitz, Christian. *Nazi Foreign Policy, 1933–1941: The Road to Global War.* London: Routledge, 2004.

Levi, Primo. *Survival in Auschwitz: The Nazi Assault on Humanity.* New York: Simon & Schuster, 1993.

Lifton, Robert Jay. *The Nazi Doctors: Medical Killing and the Psychology of Genocide.* New York: Basic Books, 1986.

Longerich, Peter. *The Holocaust.* Oxford: Oxford University Press, 2010.

Longerich, Peter. *Heinrich Himmler.* Oxford: Oxford University Press, 2012.

Lower, Wendy. *Hitler's Furies: German Women in the Nazi Killing Fields.* Boston: Houghton Mifflin, 2013.

Montague, Patrick. *Chełmno and the Holocaust: The History of Hitler's First Death Camp.* London: I.B. Tauris, 2012.

Novick, Peter. *The Holocaust in American Life.* Boston: Houghton Mifflin, 1999.

Phayer, Michael. *The Catholic Church and the Holocaust, 1930–1945.* Bloomington: Indiana University Press, 2000.

Roseman, Mark. *The Villa, The Lake, The Meeting: Wannsee and the Final Solution.* London: Allen Lane, 2002.

Sánchez, José M. *Pius II and the Holocaust: Understanding the Controversy*. Washington, DC: Catholic University of America Press, 2002.

Steinbacher, Sybille. *Auschwitz: A History*. New York: HarperCollins, 2005.

Stoltzfus, Nathan. *Resistance of the Heart: Intermarriage and the Rosenstrasse Protest in Nazi Germany*. New York: W.W. Norton, 1996.

Weiss-Wendt, Anton, ed. *The Nazi Genocide of the Roma: Reassessment and Commemoration*. New York: Berghahn Books, 2013.

Wildt, Michael. *An Uncompromising Generation: The Nazi Leadership of the Reich Security Main Office*. Madison: University of Wisconsin Press, 2009.

Zimmerer, Jürgen. "The Birth of the Ostland out of the Spirit of Colonialism: A Postcolonial Perspective on the Nazi Policy of Conquest and Extermination." In A. Dirk Moses and Dan Stone, eds., *Colonialism and Genocide*. Abingdon: Routledge, 2007, pp. 101–123.

8

Total War, 1942–1945

On February 18, 1943, shortly after a major German military defeat at Stalingrad, Propaganda Minister Joseph Goebbels delivered a rousing speech, broadcast nationwide, to an audience of 14,000 Nazis in the Berlin Sports Palace. Near the end, he engaged the crowd: "Do you want total war? [*Loud cries "Yes!" Loud applause*] Do you want it, if necessary, more total and more radical than we can even imagine it today? [*Loud cries of "Yes!" Applause*]."

In fact, many total-war efforts were already in place. After the failure of the invasion of the Soviet Union, the Nazi regime faced the "winter crisis" of 1941–1942. As the Wehrmacht bogged down in Russia, the Nazis realized that they had a war of attrition on their hands. They now turned to total war, exploiting all economic resources, including all potential manpower, both German and foreign, for the war effort. Military defeat and total war, however, radicalized the Third Reich: military setbacks accelerated exploitation, exploitation led to increased coercion, coercion to more resistance, and resistance to renewed state violence. In the final year of the Nazi regime, this dynamic only intensified.

Misperceptions about the Third Reich's last period abound. There is a common assumption that Hitler's military leadership and/or limited Axis resources brought on defeat. While largely true, these factors do not explain the whole story of German military demise. Concerning the home front, a myth of Gestapo omnipresence persists. This leads some observers to exaggerate resistance, others to underestimate it. At the same time, a variety of topics covered in this chapter may come as a surprise. The Nazi regime relied heavily on forced and slave labor. Most Germans remained loyal to the Third Reich until the day Allied soldiers

Nazi Germany: Confronting the Myths, First Edition. Catherine Epstein.
© 2015 John Wiley & Sons, Ltd. Published 2015 by John Wiley & Sons, Ltd.

marched into their towns. Moreover, by war's end, many Germans saw *themselves* as victims of World War II.

This chapter addresses salient questions about the last years of Hitler's dictatorship. How did global war affect Nazi war efforts? Just how did the regime mobilize Germany's resources? What was the character of resistance? Why, despite many German advantages, did the Allies nonetheless win? And finally, why did Germans continue to stand by Hitler and his regime?

Global War: 1942–1943

Even after military setbacks in the Soviet Union, Germany proved a formidable challenge to the Allies. In spring 1942, the Germans launched an offensive in the Soviet Union, plunging deep into southwestern Russia. In North Africa, General Erwin Rommel, the "Desert Fox," dueled with a series of British commanders. In the Atlantic, German U-Boats sank Allied ships at alarming rates. Everywhere, the Allies were on the defensive. Over the course of 1943, however, the situation reversed. Germany and its Axis allies were now on the defensive.

The eastern front

After the German defeat outside Moscow, Hitler dismissed many of the generals who had run the offensive on Moscow, and made himself commander in chief of operations in Soviet lands. In spring 1942, he began a new campaign in the Soviet Union. Since strapped German forces could manage offensive operations on only one sector of the eastern front, Hitler chose the southern sector. If Germany held both Ukraine and the Caucasus, he believed, it would have the food, fuel, and other raw materials necessary to fight the Allies. Taking the oil-rich Caucasus in southwestern Russia offered not only oil but also the prospect of later German operations in Iran and Iraq. This, in turn, would make the Middle East an Axis stronghold. In late May, the Germans won a major victory in Kharkov en route to the Caucasus. Next, they aimed to secure their right flank. In July, after overcoming staunch Soviet resistance in Sevastopol, the Germans took the whole Crimean Peninsula.

Hitler next decided to capture Stalingrad. There is a myth that the city was a worthless military objective. In fact, taking Stalingrad offered strategic advantages. It would secure the Wehrmacht's left flank in the invasion of the Caucasus. The city was also an important communications hub on the Volga river. If Germans had control of the city, they could sever oil transport lines between the Caucasus and central Russia. Finally, by conquering the city named after Stalin,

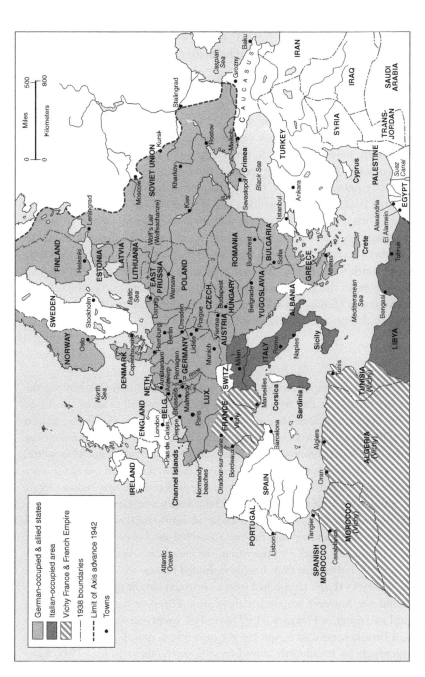

Map 8.1 World War II in Europe and North Africa (1942).

the Führer would win an important propaganda victory. To capture Stalingrad, however, Hitler had to split Army Group South. Army Group A was to drive south to the Caucasus, while Army Group B was to target Stalingrad. By late August, General Friedrich Paulus and his Sixth Army were just nine miles from Stalingrad.

In summer 1942, Soviet defenses were reeling. The Red Army suffered from poor leadership, insufficient training, and inadequate equipment. Moreover, Stalin believed that the Germans intended to take Moscow. Many Red Army units waited in vain for an attack on the Soviet capital that never came. In the next months, however, Soviet fortunes improved. The Red Army mobilized huge manpower reserves. Soviet industry churned out vast quantities of simple but effective military hardware. In July, Stalin proclaimed his famous Order 227, Not a Step Back. Soviet commanders rallied troops to stand their ground.

As the Soviets rebounded, German military weaknesses resurfaced. Hitler and his commanders pursued too many objectives at once. The German armies in the southern sector, for example, were widely separated from each other. One was sent north to Leningrad, another to Stalingrad, and three to different and distant targets in the Caucasus. Advancing German troops outran their supply lines to bases in Ukraine. As fall turned to winter, German troops stalled everywhere – and, most significantly, near Stalingrad.

North Africa

Churchill and Roosevelt recognized that the Soviet Union was bearing the brunt of Hitler's war. But they didn't have the wherewithal to mount a second front in France; not least, they were also fighting a war in the Pacific against Japan. They now decided to focus on North Africa and especially on securing Egypt. This offered numerous military advantages. If successful, the Allies would reopen the Mediterranean, now an Axis sea. This would permit use of the Suez Canal, dramatically reducing the length of shipping routes to the Indian Ocean. By contrast, were Hitler to take Egypt and the Suez Canal, German troops in the Mediterranean could connect with those in southern Russia, or even with Japanese troops advancing from the east. Churchill also believed that it would be easier to eventually attack Germany from the periphery – from the "soft underbelly" of Italy rather than from heavily defended France.

In January 1941, the British had won a campaign against the Italians in Libya. They did not, however, consolidate their gains. This gave Rommel an opening to land in Tripoli in February. The Desert Fox swept eastwards through Libya toward British-controlled Egypt. For the next fifteen months, Rommel and the British fought back and forth across Libya's Western Desert. In June 1942, however, the British suffered a terrible rout when Rommel captured Tobruk and advanced into Egypt.

Roosevelt's response to Tobruk was immediate: he arranged for emergency supplies to be sent to Egypt, including artillery and 400 American tanks. During the summer, a new British commander, Bernard Law Montgomery ("Monty"), rebuilt the British Eighth Army. In August and November 1942, he engaged Rommel in two battles at El Alamein. In the first, he stopped Rommel from further advance into Egypt. In the second, he outwitted the undersupplied Desert Fox and pushed German forces back into Libya and, eventually, Tunisia.

Meanwhile, the Allies hoped to dislodge Axis troops from all of North Africa. In November 1942, just as Monty secured victory at El Alamein, the Allies carried out Operation Torch, the landing of troops in French Morocco and Algeria. In Torch, the Allies received help from North African French commanders who had abandoned Vichy France. After landing, Allied troops pushed eastwards into Tunisia. There, however, they encountered resistance from Rommel. The Desert Fox had new reinforcements, German troops originally stationed in Sicily and Russia.

For a time, Rommel was able to stall the Allies, who suffered from American inexperience and a lack of coordination between British and American commanders. But Rommel had his own difficulties. He did not have sufficient troops and matériel. In addition, Allied intelligence, known as ULTRA, gleaned information from decoded Enigma messages (Enigma was encrypted German code). Montgomery knew of German operations in advance. Despite Rommel's spirited resistance, Allied troops were able to overcome all Axis forces in North Africa in May 1943.

Operation Torch had important consequences for the future shape of World War II. On one hand, because the Germans tied up Allied forces in Tunisia in winter 1942–1943, the Allies could not mount a cross-Channel invasion of France until 1944. On the other, Operation Torch forced Hitler to divert German troops to North Africa, thus hampering German efforts in southern Russia. Torch's success also punctured the myth of German superiority. Some countries, such as Spain, began to tilt toward the Allies. Meanwhile, with North Africa and much of the Mediterranean under their control, the Allies focused on their next objective: Italy.

The Battle of the Atlantic

The Atlantic theater was crucially important. For the Allies, everything depended on shipping men and supplies from the United States to Britain and the Soviet Union. But German submarines, organized in "wolf packs," posed a dreadful threat to shipping operations. Indeed, throughout most of 1942, German U-Boats were winning the Battle of the Atlantic. In February and March, they sank almost a million tons of American war matériel as well as thousands of sailors on downed ships. May and April saw even higher losses.

Churchill later admitted that the Battle of the Atlantic was "the only thing that ever frightened me."

It took the Allies into 1943 to win the Battle of the Atlantic. What made the difference? For one, American shipyards began to produce staggering numbers of ships to replace and then increase lost ships. Better intelligence – drawn from ULTRA, sonar, and high-frequency radio-direction finding – allowed the Allies to detect and then evade or destroy wolf packs. Most important, ships traveled in a convoy system that was continuously strengthened. By 1943, B-24 bombers, navy carriers, and antisubmarine flying boats accompanied the convoys. The Germans gradually began to lose large numbers of submarines – more than 100 in the first five months of 1943. Unlike the Americans, they could not replace them fast enough to halt the influx of men and matériel to Allied strongholds in Europe and North Africa. By summer 1943, the Allies had won the Battle of the Atlantic. Thereafter, they enjoyed relatively unhindered shipping operations.

Stalingrad

Just as Germany was causing havoc for the Allies in the Atlantic and North Africa, it faced a nightmare in Russia: Stalingrad. By September 1942, the German Sixth Army was in the city, battling Soviet troops in street-to-street combat. General Paulus, however, received little reinforcement. After the Luftwaffe sustained heavy losses, for example, it was not replenished – not least, German operations in North Africa drained the Stalingrad theater of additional air support. Meanwhile, Soviet commanders Georgi Zhukov and Aleksandr Vasilevsky sent in just enough support to allow Soviet defenders to hang on inside the city. All fall and winter, however, they built up huge armies outside the city. Soviet troops thus prevented the arrival of additional Wehrmacht armies to Stalingrad. Paulus had only unimpressive Italian and Romanian armies for reinforcement.

In November, Soviet troops pounced on the weak Italian and Romanian flanks, thereby encircling the Sixth Army in a giant pincer movement. Paulus found it impossible to break out of the Stalingrad pocket. With the Luftwaffe unable to fly in new supplies, stranded soldiers subsisted on miniscule rations, dead horses, and, some say, cannibalism. They also battled the merciless cold of a Russian winter. When Paulus sought Hitler's approval for retreat, the Führer refused. Instead, he named Paulus a field marshal, the highest military rank – knowing that no field marshal in German history had ever surrendered. Still, on January 31, 1943, Paulus gave up. By then, the Germans had already lost over 200,000 troops in Stalingrad. Of the 80,000 soldiers who now surrendered, only 5,000 ever returned home. For the Germans, Stalingrad was an unmitigated disaster.

In early 1943, Soviet troops also forced Army Group South to abandon its foothold in the Caucasus. After regrouping that spring, the Germans mounted one last great offensive on the eastern front in July. They hoped to encircle Soviet troops near the Kursk salient while also shortening their lines of defense. But, in the Battle of Kursk, the Soviets triumphed. By every measure – men, tanks, guns, air power, and intelligence – the Germans were outnumbered and outclassed by Soviet forces.

The Kursk defeat occurred just as the Allies landed in Sicily. In late July, in turn, the Italian army deposed Mussolini. Hitler had Mussolini rescued and installed as the leader of a rump northern Italian puppet state. Southern Italy, however, was now in the Allied camp, forcing the Germans to defend positions in Italy. Hitler gave up offensive operations in the Soviet Union so as to rush troops to Italy and the Balkans to secure those areas for Germany. By fall 1943, the Germans thus faced defeat on the eastern front, in North Africa, in the North Atlantic, and in Italy. The same was soon true of the air war, too.

The air war

Although the Germans initially had the advantage in the air war, the Allies eventually came to dominate the skies, a decisive factor in their victory. The Allies prosecuted the air war in lieu of an invasion of France. In February 1942, Arthur Harris, later dubbed "Bomber Harris," took over Bomber Command in Britain. He advocated "strategic" bombing (targeting the enemy state) rather than "tactical" bombing (lending support to land or naval forces). Harris thought that strategic bombing alone might destroy German infrastructure, thereby making it impossible for Germany to continue the war. He also presumed that bombing would weaken morale so that citizens would beg Hitler to end the war.

Neither assumption proved true. Bombing raids were notoriously inaccurate. If bombers flew high or at night to avoid being shot down, they were unable to see their targets. In 1941 only one RAF plane in three struck within five miles of its target. At the same time, if bombs did hit their targets, they rarely caused long-term damage. In an industrial economy like the Third Reich, most bombing damage could be quickly repaired. Rather than demoralizing the population, bombing stiffened resistance – this was as true of Germans as of the British during the London Blitz (see Chapter 6).

The air war posed many challenges. The British decided to fly by night and to target whole cities so that accuracy wouldn't matter. This, however, meant the indiscriminate bombing of German civilians. The Americans flew by day and attempted to target military objectives such as submarine pens, shipyards, and factories. All too often, though, they missed their targets. At the same time, the Luftwaffe mounted tough defenses against the Allied bombing campaign. It downed high numbers of Allied pilots and planes. In spring 1943, for example, the Allies lost 1,000 planes and 7,000 pilots (many of whom became prisoners of war, POWs) in an air campaign against the industrial Ruhr area. During World War II, it was more dangerous to be a pilot flying over Germany than a marine landing on a Pacific island!

Seeking safety in the skies, the Allies desperately tried new tactics. The British dropped thousands of strips of aluminum foil to cloud German radar systems. More important, in early 1944, the Americans began to use P-51 Mustangs, long-range fighters with disposable fuel tanks, to escort their bombers deep into German airspace. The US Army Air Force also took on the Luftwaffe directly. In the five months between February and June 1944 the Luftwaffe lost between one-third and one-half of its fighter aircraft *each month*. While German production of fighter aircraft rose spectacularly in spring 1944, it could not keep pace with Allied production. It was also misplaced: the Germans needed defensive, not offensive, air capabilities. Allied tactics soon reduced the flying life of an average Luftwaffe pilot to just weeks. The Germans could not train new pilots quickly enough.

The morality of the Anglo-American bombing campaign remains controversial. Many critics note that some of the most vicious bombing took place late in the war when, at least in hindsight, it was clear that Germany had lost. Moreover, in their view, the air war was ineffective since German industry quickly recovered from bombing damage. Some, such as Jörg Friedrich, argue that, since the bombing brought little military gain but many deaths to defenseless citizens, strategic bombing was a war crime, akin even to genocide. In late July 1943, for example, the Allies carried out Operation Gomorrah, an attack on Hamburg. More than 3,000 Anglo-American planes dropped 9,000 tons of explosive and incendiary bombs on the port city. The resulting fires created the first man-made firestorm. Tornado-like gusts of fire sucked victims into their vortex. Temperatures in the city reached upwards of 1,000 degrees Fahrenheit. Over 40,000 victims were burned, baked, or asphyxiated from a lack of oxygen. In all, air attacks claimed the lives of more than 500,000 German civilians, the vast majority women, children, or the elderly. Millions of Germans were also left homeless. This terrible toll fed Nazi propaganda about heinous western aggression.

Other observers, including Richard Overy, argue that, while atrocious, the bombing campaign made a difference in a terrible war brought on by Germans. In spring 1943, aerial bombing devastated the Ruhr, making it virtually impossible for Germany to increase armaments output. In February 1944, the Allies carried out "Big Week," destroying 75% of all German aircraft-production facilities. Soon thereafter, bombing shut down Germany's petroleum industry. It also ruined infrastructure in France and Belgium, important for the success of the Allied invasion in Normandy (see below). Most important, the Allies destroyed the Luftwaffe: bombing, together with aerial engagement, decimated the Third Reich's planes and pilots. Germany also had to divert Luftwaffe fighters and deadly weapons such as eighty-eight-millimeter guns to the air war – matériel then unavailable for use on other fronts. Finally, nighttime raids left many

Figure 8.1   Ruins in Hamburg after Operation Gomorrah (July 1943). *Source*: Getty Images.

Germans exhausted and focused on meeting their basic needs, to the detriment of productive work. Even if morally wrong, the bombing campaign *did* make a significant contribution to Allied wartime success.

The Home Front

In response to German military challenges, the Nazi leadership mobilized society for war. Germans now came to experience wartime deprivation. Food rations were cut, and shortages of meat and fat became chronic. Bars and "luxury" stores were shut down. The work week was lengthened to fifty or more hours. Even young people were mobilized for the war effort. The Hitler Youth organized children to forage for mushrooms and medicinal herbs, or to do door-to-door collections of recyclable materials. Teenage girls labored on farms or in munitions factories, or worked as tram conductors and telephone operators. Younger teenage boys served as air-raid wardens, firefighters, and antiaircraft auxiliaries.

The Nazi leadership introduced major changes to the German economy. In February 1942, Hitler tapped the architect Albert Speer as the new minister of armaments and munitions after his predecessor, Fritz Todt, died in a suspicious plane crash. Shortly afterward, Fritz Sauckel was named general plenipotentiary for labor deployment. Sauckel used brutal methods to round up millions of workers in Nazi-occupied Europe. Although very different personalities, Speer and Sauckel together tried to eke out every last bullet and man hour available in the Third Reich.

Speer immediately refocused the German economy on war production. Although many accounts, including those by Speer himself, claimed that the architect was the ultimate technocrat and a courageous opponent of the Schutzstaffel (SS), the opposite was true. In his mobilization of the German economy, Speer proved himself a fanatical Nazi deeply loyal to Hitler and eager to work with SS Chief Heinrich Himmler. Like Hitler, Speer believed in force of will. If pushed to the hilt, he thought, Germany might persevere, somehow, somewhere. He employed ever more draconian methods to push German society to the limit.

Speer closed businesses not essential for the war effort. He insisted on mass-production techniques and simplified production methods. He introduced economies of scale by shuttering small factories. By limiting the number of models in production, he also reduced how many spare parts were necessary for the Wehrmacht. The number of truck models dropped from 151 to 23, and the number of Luftwaffe combat aircraft from 42 to 5. By May 1943, German armaments production had doubled.

Speer's most notable success was a very significant increase in German aircraft production late in the war. Between February and September 1944, production almost tripled to 3,538 aircraft per month. Speer only achieved this figure by channeling resources to aviation and starving other industrial sectors. Moreover, despite this success, the Allies still manufactured more aircraft during these months. Even Speer came up against the natural limits of the German economy. Although the Nazis had conquered much of Europe, they did not capture territories that significantly increased their raw material supplies. The Germans remained short on the coal and steel necessary to produce planes and tanks, and on the oil reserves to fuel those already in use.

Foreign workers

Scholars once believed that the Third Reich used foreign workers because too many middle-class German women refused to (re)enter the workforce (see Chapter 4). In fact, as Adam Tooze has shown, Germany already had a high rate of female employment; large numbers of German women worked on family farms or in small family-owned businesses. Only about 700,000 additional women were available to join the workforce. Hitler, however, did not compel these women to work, even when they were subject to labor conscription. He wanted to retain the support of the German population.

Given the limited potential for recruiting new German workers, the Nazi regime turned to exploiting French and Soviet POWs, as well as Polish and Soviet civilians (known as *Ostarbeiter*, eastern workers). As more and more German men were called up for army service, foreign laborers took their place in farm fields or on factory benches. Eventually, the Nazis forced some seven to eight million foreigners to work in the Third Reich. Late in the war, foreign workers made up more than 20% of Germany's workforce. They comprised more than one-third of all armaments workers.

With so many foreign workers, Germany became a country of camps. Every city and town was home to numerous camps – POW camps, forced-labor camps, and sub-camps of the concentration-camp system. Munich alone hosted at least 120 POW camps, 286 camps or hostels for civilian forced laborers, and seven branch camps of the concentration-camp system. Columns of bedraggled Poles and eastern workers marching to and from their workplaces became an everyday sight in Nazi Germany. Ironically, their presence belied the Nazi claim of forging a pure Aryan nation. The ubiquity of Poles and eastern workers made Germany much more diverse – indeed, multicultural – than had ever before been the case.

Although foreign workers were absolutely essential to the German war effort, the Nazis imposed their racial hierarchy on them. While French POWs enjoyed relatively good labor conditions, the Nazis treated eastern workers miserably. In spring 1942, Soviet POWs and dragooned civilian eastern workers starved and froze to death in makeshift camps. Once, however, Nazi authorities realized their acute labor needs, they made marginal improvements in camp conditions. Still, eastern workers found themselves in terrible straits. They were paid virtually nothing, had few sanitary facilities, and their food and clothing rations were totally inadequate. Moreover, Poles and *Ostarbeiter* were subject to harsh police regulations – not the German legal code – at work and in their barracks.

Nazi authorities were particularly concerned about the supposed racial threat posed by foreign workers. Inevitably, Germans and eastern workers had sexual relations. Not least, many forced laborers were women, and more than half of all female foreign laborers were aged twelve to twenty-two. (The Nazis viewed young women as a more pliant workforce, less likely than their male counterparts to engage in sabotage or other resistance.) The Nazis deployed draconian sanctions against those who violated racial prescripts. They applied the death penalty to male foreign workers convicted of sexual intercourse with German women. They also forced pregnant foreign workers to undergo abortion and/or sterilization. The Germans involved were publicly shamed or, in some cases, imprisoned.

Slave labor

Besides forced laborers, there were also slave laborers in Nazi Germany – the inmates of SS-run concentration camps. In 1942, Himmler expanded the use of concentration-camp labor. Eager to increase SS influence by helping to alleviate the "winter crisis," he charged Oswald Pohl with setting up the SS Business and Administration Main Office (WVHA), which oversaw prison labor. Over the next few years, the concentration-camp inmate population ballooned to over

500,000 individuals. In addition to Jews, Soviet POWs, political opponents, recalcitrant forced laborers, and common criminals were all subject to the new labor regime. In October 1942, for example, Himmler ensured the transfer of 14,351 "dangerous habitual criminals" from regular German prisons to SS concentration camps. SS slaves were imprisoned mostly in Auschwitz, Buchenwald, Dachau, Majdanek, Mauthausen, Sachsenhausen, Stutthof, and sub-camps of these major concentration camps.

Although concentration-camp conditions stabilized over the course of 1943, mortality rates remained very high. Indeed, even if the SS system as a whole shifted toward the exploitation of labor, individual prisoners were still victim to "destruction through labor" (see Chapter 7). Here, too, the SS practiced "selections." The inexhaustible supply of prisoners meant that there were always new slaves to replace those murdered. The productivity of slaves, however, was well below that of German workers; estimates suggest that they were at best 50% and in many cases only 20% as productive as a well-fed German worker.

Speer actively facilitated contacts between industry and the WVHA. Concentration-camp labor came to make up 5% of Germany's industrial work-force. Some slaves built factories for planned SS industries. Others worked on construction projects in Nazi-occupied Europe. Late in the war, "SS Construction Brigades" removed debris and rebuilt rail lines or other vital city infrastructure after Allied bombing raids. The largest number of slave workers, however, some 230,000 individuals, was hired out to private industry. German industrialists had no qualms about exploiting slave labor in their drive for profits, market share, and real estate (which would retain value after war's end). Virtually every major German company – many of them household names today – colluded with the SS in the use of slave labor. German companies such as BMW (aircraft/cars), Daimler-Benz (cars), IG Farben (chemicals), Krupp (steel), Messerschmitt (aircraft), Porsche/Volkswagen (cars), and Siemens (electronics) all made extensive use of slave labor.

The Dora-Mittelbau concentration camp exemplifies links between the SS and industry. This camp became the production site for V-2 rockets, a "miracle weapon" that Hitler hoped would win the war for Germany (see below). In August 1943, the RAF destroyed the V-2 rocket production facility at Peenemünde. The rocket-building team turned to the SS for help. In the next months, the SS oversaw the rebuilding of a new production facility in recently excavated tunnels – once an anthracite mining operation – in the Harz Mountains in Thuringia. Thousands of slave laborers worked in the eerie, gloomy tunnels to construct the new factory. They received little food, slept on site, and rarely saw sunlight or breathed fresh air. Defiant slaves were strung up on rafters to warn those still alive. One prisoner roamed the site just to locate new corpses. Indeed, V-2 rockets proved far more lethal in production than deployment. Estimates suggest that more than 20,000 slave laborers died in the process of building roughly 6,000 V-2 rockets. The rockets themselves, barely ready for use at war's end, killed approximately 8,000 victims.

Coercion

As the war progressed, the Nazis also clamped down on the German population. Insubordinate workers, for example, were sent to "educative work camps," where they temporarily endured concentration-camp-like conditions. The Nazis also put into effect a harsh wartime penal code. Individuals found to "undermine the will to fight" were liable to face the death penalty. So, too, were those guilty of hoarding food supplies or sabotaging armaments production. The Nazis also forbade the listening of foreign radio broadcasts. In the first two years of the war, thousands of individuals were arrested, and small numbers executed, for this offense.

The Gestapo did not have the manpower to identify those engaged in antiwar activity. How, then, did it learn of such "crimes"? As Robert Gellately and others have shown, it relied on voluntary denunciations. Germans thus had every reason to self-censor their speech and actions. Almost three-quarters of known infractions were initially brought to authorities' attention by zealous National Socialist German Workers' Party (NSDAP) members or ordinary citizens. In 1944, for example, two members of the board of directors at Deutsche Bank were executed after peers denounced them for making "defeatist" remarks about Hitler. Not all those who snitched on fellow citizens did so for political reasons. Some sought material gain or emotional revenge – in the latter case, to rid themselves of irritating neighbors, bosses, or even spouses. Even so, the fact that the Nazis depended on voluntary denunciation suggests the regime's deep wellsprings of support. Moreover, contrary to the myth of wide-reaching Gestapo tentacles, the state police was now not proactive but reactive.

During the war years, the judicial system became more draconian. In 1939, 329 individuals had been sentenced to death in the Greater German Reich. That number, however, exploded to 4,457 in 1942 and 5,336 in 1943. The Nazis made more use of extra-judicial courts not subject to constitutional limits. In 1942, Hitler named Roland Freisler, a notorious Nazi jurist, president of the so-called People's Court. Under Freisler, the People's Court carried out vicious show trials of regime opponents. Altogether, it sentenced some 5,200 people to death, more than 2,000 in 1944 alone.

At the same time, the SS held increasing sway in German government and society. This found graphic expression in Himmler's appointment as Reich Minister of the Interior in August 1943. Himmler's authority now stretched over civil servants administering German towns and villages to SS officials guarding death camps. Moreover, the SS's increasing involvement in the economy – from building new SS industries, to aiding the reconstruction of bombed factories, to staffing factory security operations – meant that more and more Germans came into contact with the Nazi coercive apparatus.

Resistance inside Nazi Germany

In the first war years, there was little organized resistance. This, however, changed as the military situation soured. Some Germans, bothered by growing terror at home and brutal practices abroad, came to question the regime. Regime opposition proved a matter of individual conscience rather than group solidarity. Although few in number, resisters were young and old, leftists and conservatives, workers and professionals, students and military officers, foreign forced laborers and wealthy aristocrats. Their actions raise important questions about the failure and the legacy of resistance in Hitler's Germany.

Assassination attempts

Some anti-Nazis believed that, if only Hitler were removed, the Third Reich would crumble. Between 1933 and 1944, there were at least forty-two attempts on Hitler's life. Many potential assassins, acting alone and with very limited access to the Führer, had little chance of success. But, in 1939, Georg Elsner, a cabinet maker with socialist sympathies, tried to kill Hitler during the annual commemoration of the Beer Hall Putsch. In the weeks leading up to the event, Elsner slipped into the Bürgerbräu Beer Hall in Munich and planted an explosive device close to where the Führer always spoke. On the evening of November 8, however, Hitler cut short his speech so as to get back to Berlin for a meeting the next morning. Shortly after he left the hall, the device exploded, killing several individuals. Had Hitler still been speaking – as would normally have been the case – he almost certainly would have died. Elsner was arrested while trying to flee the country. Imprisoned in Dachau, he was executed on Hitler's orders in April 1945. After Elsner's attempt, the SS tightened security around the Führer. Hitler also scaled back his public appearances. It was virtually impossible for anyone without regular access to him to even contemplate assassination.

Resistance on the left

In the early 1940s, leftist resistance groups reemerged, many loosely affiliated with each other. Robert Uhrig, for example, was an underground official of the Communist Party of Germany (KPD) who worked in the Berlin Osram lightbulb factory. He organized factory cells across Berlin that spied for the Soviet Union and engaged in other resistance activities. He also had links to the "Red Orchestra" (*Rote Kapelle*), led by Harro Schulze-Boysen (an attaché in the Air Ministry) and Arvid Harnack (a civil servant in the Reich Economics Ministry). Nazi security forces gave the group its name; it dubbed spies "pianists" and handlers "conductors." The Red Orchestra took part in a range of oppositional actions, including relaying information to *both* American and Soviet authorities.

It was the Soviets, however, who supplied the group with radio equipment that, in turn, proved its downfall. After radio messages were intercepted in late summer 1942, the Gestapo arrested some 130 individuals involved in the Red Orchestra. Eventually, fifty of them, including the leaders, were executed. Uhrig and virtually all other communist resisters were captured and killed, too. While courageous, leftist resistance was too fragmented and isolated to spark an insurrection or otherwise topple the regime.

Disaffected youth

Youth opposition ranged from nonconformist behavior to outright resistance. In Hamburg and other cities, a "Swing Youth" movement emerged among middle-class youths. Swing Youths danced to swing music in clubs and at private parties. They grew their hair long, wore conspicuous makeup, and sported British suits and other western accoutrements.

Was the Swing Youth movement resistance? The youths did not oppose the regime for ethical or political reasons. Rather, they wished to express their individuality and escape the stifling atmosphere of the Hitler Youth. To the Nazis, however, the Swing Youth was a threat: to them, swing music was a Jewish African-American import that encouraged wild and free behavior. Accordingly, the Gestapo stormed dance halls and otherwise broke up swing dance parties. In June 1942, there were mass arrests in Hamburg. Between forty and seventy Swing Youths were sent to the Moringen juvenile concentration camp. There, they endured poor living conditions and forced labor in an ammunitions factory.

Some working-class youths formed oppositional gangs, often known as Edelweiss Pirates. To the Nazis (and later Allied occupation authorities), these youths were juvenile delinquents. Like the Swing Youth, the Pirates rejected the discipline and conformism of the Hitler Youth. Some of their milder behavior included hitch-hiking and organizing their own independent camping trips. Other activities, however, slid into resistance: attacking local Hitler Youth, engaging in sabotage at work, painting anti-Nazi graffiti, and distributing Allied propaganda leaflets. Eventually, some Pirates joined up with gangs of forced laborers and tried to assassinate various Nazi, SS, and police functionaries. One group succeeded in murdering the head of the Cologne Gestapo. Cracking down, the Nazis sent gang members to reform schools, labor camps, and even concentration camps. In Cologne, six were hanged in public in November 1944.

For the Nazis, youth disaffection was frustrating. Young people represented the future of the Third Reich. They had gone through Nazified schools. Most were longtime members of the Hitler Youth. Now they were needed to work in industry and soldier in war. But some young people still refused Nazism. Despite their best efforts, the Nazis had not won over a significant minority of youth.

The White Rose

Unlike the merely disaffected, some young people felt an ethical duty to act against the regime. Hans and Sophie Scholl, students and siblings, spearheaded the "White Rose" group. In their Munich university circles, they found a few like-minded individuals dismayed by Nazi restrictions on personal freedom. Hans and other male students, deployed in the army medic corps, were also horrified by what they saw of the regime's racism, antisemitism, and violence on the eastern front. The White Rose hoped to initiate a mass uprising that would overthrow Hitler and end the war. Hans wrote six leaflets that he and others duplicated and distributed in Munich and beyond. The leaflets pilloried Nazi crimes, condemned the apathy of the population, and urged all Germans to engage in passive resistance.

In February 1943 Hans and Sophie Scholl were caught dispersing leaflets. A university custodian saw them and denounced them to the Gestapo. The siblings were immediately arrested, interrogated, and given a sham trial at a People's Court hearing presided over by Freisler. Condemned to death, they were guillotined hours after conviction. Several close coconspirators were also executed.

Did Hans and Sophie Scholl die in an exercise in futility? They were naive in their belief in the power of leaflets. Their actions, however, became known. Newspapers reported their death sentences. In spring 1943, after a leaflet reached Britain, the Royal Air Force (RAF) dropped hundreds of thousands of copies of it all over Germany. The Scholl example let other regime opponents know they were not alone. The Scholls' influence, however, was most profound in postwar Germany. There, they were turned into the ultimate example of how individuals *should* act in the face of tyranny. Their willingness to stand up and die for what they believed was widely touted in media and schools. Around the millennium, readers of the largest-circulation German woman's magazine, *Brigitte*, voted Sophie Scholl the most important woman of the twentieth century.

The July 20 plot

The best-known case of German resistance to Nazism was the July 20, 1944, plot to kill Hitler. Hundreds of senior government and military officials were involved – precisely those who could stage a successful coup. Not only did they have access to Hitler but also, were they successful in assassinating the Führer, they were in a position to take control of the state and the military. Virtually all, however, were prepared to act only *after* Germany seemed headed for defeat – that is, after Stalingrad. Most had reveled in early Nazi military successes. Some even had blood on their hands; as high-ranking military men and civil servants, they had sanctioned or even carried out crimes against humanity in Nazi-occupied Europe.

The July 20 movement included various overlapping groups that held gener-ally conservative political views. Some hoped for an authoritarian regime akin to Germany before World War I. Others, including Carl Goerdeler (see Chapter 5), wished for a form of democracy that favored conservative social forces. Another group, centered on Helmuth von Moltke and known as the Kreisau Circle, eschewed strong central government and hoped to locate politi-cal authority in smaller units of society. Some of these resisters were loath to give up Germany's military conquests in World War II, particularly in occupied Eastern Europe. Others, though, proposed a European federalism that would reduce the risk of war, thus anticipating the European Union. Many hoped that Christianity would form the basis of social healing and regeneration. The groups' patrician ideals limited their potential mass appeal.

Despite deep political differences, the July 20 conspirators shared a national-istic patriotism. Unlike every other resistance movement in Europe, they opposed their own government, not a regime imposed by an outside conqueror. As conservative nationalists, they faced a stark dilemma. Was resistance treason or ethical imperative? Murdering Hitler would violate the oaths that many had personally sworn to Führer. It would weaken the state and likely bring on Germany's immediate defeat. But Nazism, the conspirators came to believe, was not the "true" Germany. Moreover, the resisters wished to show that Germans had acted on anti-Nazi convictions. As one conspirator, Henning von Tresckow, wrote Claus von Stauffenberg, the central figure in the plot: "The assassination [of Hitler] must be attempted at all costs... What matters now is... to prove to the world and for the records of history that the men of the resistance move-ment dared to take the decisive step. Compared to this objective, nothing else is of consequence." Even if the coup failed, the conspirators believed, its very attempt would provide a powerful legacy for future German generations.

The plotters also had more concrete goals. A successful coup, they hoped, would allow them to leverage better terms for a defeated Germany. They wished to avoid Allied occupation. At the same time, most were deeply anti-Bolshevik. They thus sent feelers to London and Washington, but not to Moscow. To their frustration, however, the western Allies refused to respond to their overtures. The Allies were rightly wary of the conspirators' motives. Moreover, at the Casablanca Conference in January 1943, Churchill and Roosevelt had agreed that Germany must submit to unconditional surrender.

While civilian conspirators endlessly discussed postwar plans, Stauffenberg wished to take action. If Germans were to eliminate Hitler and Nazism on their own, time was of the essence. By summer 1944, the western Allies had already landed at Normandy and were headed toward Germany (see below). After losing an eye, his right hand, and two fingers on his left hand in the North African cam-paign, Stauffenberg was transferred to the War Ministry. There, he linked up with General Friedrich Olbricht, who had prepared Operation Valkyrie, emergency plans for continued governance in the event of massive civil unrest (such as an uprising by foreign forced laborers). Olbricht and others modified those plans to accommodate a military coup following Hitler's assassination. A surprising number of high-ranking military men knew about Valkyrie: Friedrich Fromm, head of the Reserve Army; Admiral Wilhelm Canaris, the head of counterintelligence, and his deputy, Hans Oster; and even Field Marshal Erwin Rommel.

On July 1, 1944, Stauffenberg was made chief of staff to Fromm. He was now permitted to attend Hitler's military conferences. On July 20 he tried to kill Hitler at the Wolf's Lair (Wolfsschanze), Hitler's East Prussian headquarters near Rastenburg. Stauffenberg, however, was not the ideal assassin. As he was preparing his bombs, he was rushed by an orderly demanding his presence at the conference. With just two fingers and a thumb available, Stauffenberg managed to light the fuse on only one of his two bombs. Ushered into the conference, he placed a briefcase with the bomb under a large oak map-table near Hitler. He then excused himself to make a phone call. Shortly afterward, he heard the bomb go off. Assuming Hitler dead, he hurried back to Berlin to set Valkyrie in motion.

But Hitler was alive. A number of factors dissipated the force of the explosion. Only one bomb was used. The military conference took place not in a bunker but in a flimsy wooden barrack with open windows. Someone had moved the briefcase away from Hitler. The massive map-table shielded Hitler from the bomb. While five men were killed, the Führer escaped with burns, shattered eardrums, and other minor injuries. Later that day, he toured Mussolini around the explosion site.

Meanwhile, the conspiracy in Berlin fell apart. Due to poor planning, the plotters did not secure the Propaganda Ministry. Those loyal to Hitler were able to get the message out that the Führer was alive and to ignore all communications from the War Ministry. As events unfolded, virtually every army commander stuck to Hitler. Moreover, once it was known that Hitler had not been killed, some of those in the conspiracy turned on the main plotters. Fromm had Stauffenberg and Olbricht executed on the night of July 20–21. It did him no good, however. In the following weeks and months, neither he nor any known conspirator escaped the Nazi dragnet.

Shocked and angered by the attempt on his life, Hitler demanded revenge. After brutal interrogations, Freisler gave the plotters – close to 200 in all – bogus trials and sentenced most to death. Many, hanged with thin wire, suffered agonizingly slow strangulations. Hitler had the executions filmed for his viewing pleasure. In addition, he had 5,000 individuals, including many older men who had been politically active in the Weimar Republic, imprisoned. Many jailed anti-Nazis were now also executed. The July 20 plot marked an important – and final – turning point in the history of the Third Reich. Hitler used this final wave of terror to rally elites and ordinary Germans to the Nazi total-war effort.

While domestic resistance movements failed to topple Nazism, they proved important both during and after the Third Reich. Their very existence gave heart to others involved in or considering resistance. At the same time, after 1945, past resistance served both to accuse and excuse Germans. The few who prized ethical commitment posed a moral indictment of the many. But the harsh punishments they endured explained and even justified most Germans' refusal to resist Nazism. Moreover, while later celebrations suggested more widespread resistance than was the case, Germans could draw sustenance from the fact that *some* of their own, at least, had resisted the criminal Third Reich.

Ironically, the very failure of resistance, and especially of the July 20 plot, may well have secured Germany's long-term democratic future. After 1945, the Allies did not have to contend with a new Stab-in-the-Back legend (see Chapter 1). They did not have to deal with conservative or other German resistors who could draw political legitimacy from their anti-Nazi activities. Instead, they could impose their vision of a democratic polity on the defeated country. Moreover, the deaths of so many aristocrats in the aftermath of the July 20 plot, coupled with the loss of their social bases of power – their large landed estates in the east were confiscated by incoming Polish and Soviet communist regimes – ended noble influence in Germany. While an enormous personal tragedy for those involved, the failure of resistance likely eased West Germany's transition to democracy.

Partisan Activity

Across occupied Europe, many civilians joined resistance groups in the hope of liberating their countries from Nazi domination. Those who took up arms were outraged by brutal Nazi policies, including ethnic cleansing and starvation tactics. Young people also fled to partisan groupings to escape forced labor in the Reich. Partisans proved more than just an irritant to the Nazi occupiers. They harassed Germans who had had taken over native farms or businesses, thereby thwarting Germanization efforts (see Chapter 6). They assassinated German and collaborationist officials. They hampered German war efforts by destroying railroad tracks and other transportation infrastructure. They hid Jews or helped downed Allied aircraft crews to escape. Perhaps most important, partisans forced the Germans to expend precious manpower on policing occupied areas.

The Nazi response was characteristically brutal. In June 1942, after Czech partisans assassinated Reinhard Heydrich, Himmler's right-hand man, the Nazis rounded up the inhabitants and burned the village of Lidice, where a Nazi official thought that one of the assassins was hiding. Although there was no proven connection between Lidice and the assassins, the SS executed 199 men, deported the women to Ravensbrück, and, after racial screenings, murdered most of the children. Similarly, after the murder of an official in France in 1944, SS troops went to the village of Oradour-sur-Glane, gunned down the men, and burned the women and children alive in a church, 642 villagers in all. In occupied Soviet lands, the Germans were even more draconian. In Belarus, for example, troops burned some *9,000 villages* to counter alleged partisan activity. Roughly one in four Belarusians died during World War II, many in reprisal killings. While these methods deterred resistance, they also embittered local populations. All over Europe, Germans had to battle not only the Allies but also partisan insurgents.

German Defeat

By spring 1944, the Third Reich faced enormous military challenges. In the east, the Red Army advanced, dislodging the Germans from much of Ukraine. In the south, the western Allies slogged through Italy, forcing Hitler to commit manpower there. They also used Italian airfields to bomb areas of Germany previously beyond range. Finally, in the west the Allies prepared a cross-channel invasion of France, Operation Overlord. General Dwight D. Eisenhower, supreme commander of the Allied forces in Europe, led the invasion.

Normandy

Overlord was nothing short of extraordinary. To ensure the surprise necessary for success, the Allies engaged in grand deception; they used double agents to feed the Germans misinformation. Among other ruses, they created fake radio communications between dummy armies that indicated plans to invade Norway and the Pas de Calais area in northern France. The Germans, however, believed the misinformation since it matched their preconceptions: Pas de Calais involved the shortest sea routes from England, and the Germans presumed a harbor invasion. But the Allies had other plans. They intended to land in Normandy, a good distance from Pas de Calais. Moreover, in 1942, an Allied force had launched an unsuccessful attack on the French port of Dieppe. Knowing the dangers of harbor attacks, the Allies decided to land on open beaches – and to bring along their own harbors.

To bolster their chances of success, the Allies had to arrive at dawn so as to benefit from daytime airborne tactical support. They also had to land during low tide so that men could wade ashore. In addition, they had to have a full moon so that advance parachutists could land behind enemy lines. These natural occurrences coincided on June 5–7, 1944. On June 5, however, there was bad weather. Even though the Germans expected an Allied landing, they now presumed it would be postponed. Rommel went home to celebrate his wife's birthday. But Eisenhower knew from aerial reconnaissance that there would be a short spell of good weather on June 6. The Germans, short on planes and fuel, had no such reconnaissance.

Early on June 6, D-Day, some 7,000 ships ferried Allied troops to five Normandy beaches. Once ashore, the men faced menacing steel barriers and land mines that Rommel had placed on the beaches. They also had to scale enormous cliffs. Even though the Germans did not expect the assault, some German defenders were nonetheless on hand. High up on bluffs, the Germans mowed down advancing Allied soldiers; the Allies incurred some 9,000 casualties on D-Day alone. Still, the Allies managed to hold the beachhead and soon consolidated their gains. They towed two "Mulberries," artificial harbors weighing 1.5 million tons, to Normandy. Ships could now dock and unload. By June 11, the Allies had delivered 326,000 men, 54,000 vehicles, and 104,000 tons of matériel to the European mainland.

In comparison with the Allied landing force, the Germans had overwhelming superiority in men, guns, and tanks on D-Day. But they couldn't capitalize on their resources. Due to poor intelligence, they didn't believe that the Allies would land when and where they did. They were slow to respond once the landings occurred. Not least, Hitler was asleep, and his aides, fearful of his wrath, refused to wake him to authorize reinforcements for the Normandy area. The Germans were also convinced that a main invasion force would still come at Pas de Calais. It took them weeks to realize that Normandy *was* the invasion. All the while, they kept forces near Pas de Calais. In addition, Allied bombing destroyed French train tracks and other infrastructure in advance of Overlord. The Germans thus had difficulty moving men and matériel to and around Normandy. Finally, Allied air forces, with an aircraft advantage of seventy to one in northern France, ceaselessly bombarded German defenses.

The long road to Germany

One might expect that, after the successful landing at Normandy, the Allies could quickly have defeated the Germans. Not so. The Allies faced stiff German resistance throughout northern France and, eventually, in Germany. By August, though, they had liberated Paris. They also took Marseilles, an important port in southern France. Still, it took eleven months to secure German defeat – eleven months in which many Jews, including Anne Frank, and other victims of Nazism died. What took so long?

In part, Allied operations were slowed by the competing ambitions of Allied generals. Against Eisenhower's better judgment, Montgomery launched Operation Market Garden in September 1944. Monty hoped to drive across the Rhine River and then push into northern Germany. Due to poor preparation and German resistance, however, Market Garden involved a major setback for the Allies.

Poor logistics proved even more important in halting Allied advances. The Allies faced terrible bottlenecks in their supply system. The Germans skillfully defended port areas, leaving only small or distant harbors available to the Allies. To make use of the Antwerp harbor, for example, the Allies had to dislodge the Germans from the northern bank of the Scheldt estuary. But the Germans held on, and the Allies cleared the estuary only in late November. Thereafter, their supply situation improved immeasurably.

Hitler still thought that Germany could prolong, if not win, the war. Time, he believed, might bring opportunity, perhaps in the form of "miracle weapons" (see below). In his mind, treachery in the Wehrmacht – as shown by the July 20 plot – explained German military reversals. He believed that he could rally the German people to fight against what he deemed biologically inferior invaders. In September 1944 he outlined what he expected: "Every bunker, every block of houses in a German town, every German village, must become a fortification in which the enemy bleeds to death or the occupiers are entombed in man-to-man fighting." In Hitler's fantasies, the Germans would inflict huge casualties on the western Allies, breaking their will to fight. They would recapture Antwerp and drive the Allies into the sea. A U-Boat offensive, based on a new, powerful class of submarines, would halt the arrival of new troops and supplies. With the western Allies stymied, the Wehrmacht would renew its assault on the Red Army.

Based on these notions, Hitler initiated Germany's last offensive in the west, known as the Battle of the Bulge, on December 16. Launched in bad weather to neutralize Allied air superiority, the campaign caught the Allies unawares. The Germans surged forward toward the Ardennes and Antwerp. The Battle of the Bulge proved the bloodiest and costliest battle for US forces during all of World War II. Some 19,000 Americans lost their lives. In a notorious massacre near the Belgian village of Malmédy, the SS gunned down more than eighty American POWs after their surrender. The German campaign, however, petered out in January. The Wehrmacht, exhausted by Allied counterattacks, had insufficient reserves of men and fuel.

Thereafter, despite determined German defense, the western Allies remained on the offensive. After learning that German engineers had failed to blow up a bridge over the Rhine at Remagen, Allied forces hurried across, securing a bridgehead on March 8, 1945. Swarms of Allied troops soon crossed the Rhine and headed into north Germany.

Red Army advances

Meanwhile, the Red Army pushed toward Germany. Grit, determination, and overwhelming force were essential to defeat Nazi Germany. Soviet troops, however, were ready to engage in tough battle. Spurred on by Red Army commanders and Stalin's orders, they were also motivated by a fierce hatred of Nazism (see below). On June 22, 1944, three years to the day after the German invasion, the Red Army launched Operation Bagration. Directed primarily at Army Group Center, Soviet troops pushed through Belarus and eastern Poland. The Wehrmacht incurred over a million casualties, as well as huge losses of tanks and artillery.

Stalin slowed the final assault on Germany so as to ensure Soviet control of Eastern Europe. In August and September 1944, he allowed the Germans to suppress the Polish Home Army's Warsaw Uprising, a brutal operation in which the Nazis leveled the city and killed many insurgents. The ensuing Polish leadership vacuum later helped Stalin impose communism in Poland. Soviet pressure also forced Romania and Bulgaria to sue for peace. Both switched sides and joined in the war against Germany. Finland, too, signed an armistice with the Soviet Union.

By late 1944, Stalin had massed some 3.8 million troops to strike central and northern Germany. His army, the largest in the world, outnumbered the Wehrmacht in every respect: eleven to one in soldiers, seven to one in tanks, and twenty to one in artillery and aircraft. In fall 1944, Soviet forces pushed the Wehrmacht out of Estonia and Latvia and crossed into German territory in East Prussia. In January 1945 they launched their final assault on Berlin. While Hitler attempted a final eastern offensive around Budapest in March, the Wehrmacht was no longer a match for the Red Army. By the end of April, Berlin was encircled, all but the city center in Russian hands.

Why the Allies won

There is a myth that German war efforts were effective, hampered only by a lack of resources and Hitler's leadership. The truth is more complicated. As Richard Overy has convincingly argued, the Allies *did* have superior resources, but not so much and not so many that the Axis could not have prevailed. What really mattered was how each side used the resources it had.

Take equipment. Both the United States and the Soviet Union ramped up military production much faster than expected. They also focused on simple designs and mass production and churned out vast quantities of airplanes, tanks, artillery, and ships. By 1945, American industry had produced an astonishing 86,000 tanks, 297,000 aircraft, and two million army trucks. The Soviet Union manufactured less but effectively streamlined its military hardware. During the entire war, for example, the Soviets deployed just two tanks at once, first the T-34 and KV-1, and later the T-34 and the IS-2. They produced just five aircraft models. This equipment was serviceable, but hardly advanced.

The Wehrmacht, by contrast, privileged technical superiority over serviceable mediocrity. This resulted in highly sophisticated weaponry for relatively specialized tasks. The Germans had numerous models of tanks and aircraft in production, at one time including 425 different aircraft models and variants. All these different models, of course, limited the possibility of mass production. They also resulted in a spare-parts nightmare. In Operation Barbarossa, for example, Army Group Center brought along a million spare parts.

While the Allies mobilized huge economies, the Axis powers failed to do so. Even with Speer's management, the Germans did not optimize their productive capacities. In 1943, the Soviets turned eight million tons of steel into 24,000 tanks and 48,000 heavy guns. Germany, however, turned 30 million tons of steel into just 17,000 tanks and 27,000 heavy artillery pieces. At the same time, Germany's allies, Italy and Japan, had relatively limited industrial capacity. During the war, the Ford Motor Company alone manufactured more military equipment than Italy. Then, too, the Axis powers had fewer natural resources. They controlled only 3% of the world's oil output. Oil, however, is the lifeblood of modern warfare – without it, tanks are stalled, aircraft grounded, and ships docked.

As the military situation grew dire, the Nazis placed great hopes in technological breakthroughs. The navy focused on developing a new class of submarines that would go at fast speeds under water, thereby avoiding detection. Due to Germany's urgent wartime needs, development was cut short and the U-Boats were built and launched without sufficient testing. In the end, design shortcomings meant that these submarines failed to sink even a single Allied ship. Yet their construction ate up enormous steel and man-power resources that could have been devoted to simple, yet more effective, weaponry.

The same was true of "miracle" weapons. German science had the potential to develop atomic weapons, but Hitler deemed nuclear physics a "Jewish" science and did not prioritize an atomic weapons program. Rockets, however, were another matter. During the war, German engineers developed pilotless flying bombs (V-1) and liquid-fueled rockets (ballistic missiles, V-2), nicknamed "retribution" weapons (*Vergeltungswaffen*). The V-weapons were launched against London and Antwerp in 1944 and 1945. They were, however, too few and inaccurate to change the war's course.

The V-2 rockets were the weapons of the future. Indeed, after the war, Wernher von Braun, the rocket scientist responsible for the V-2 program, was brought to America to build the United States' missile program. Ironically, just as Germany was developing sophisticated weaponry for the future, its armed forces underwent a process of demodernization. In 1941, the Germans had 2,500 aircraft in use on the eastern front, but in 1944 just 1,700. While developing 1950s weaponry, Germany thus failed to win a war that drew largely on the technology of the 1930s: tanks, airplanes, and ships.

Besides disadvantages in resources, a number of other factors contributed to German defeat. Hitler was unlucky in his allies. Neither Japan not Italy could supply Germany in the way that the United States could aid Britain and the Soviet Union. Moreover, the Axis powers engaged in little partnership. The Germans repeatedly bailed out Italian troops from various misadventures about which there was no prior consultation. In addition, Japan and Germany essentially fought two separate wars, one in Europe, the other in the Pacific. With virtually no coordination, they did not benefit from cooperation in areas where this might have been possible – such as intelligence operations or the sharing of technology.

Hitler's military leadership also undermined Germany's war efforts. Stalin, Roosevelt, and Churchill were all deeply involved in military affairs. But they left day-to-day operations to experts, to generals trained and experienced in warfare. Not Hitler. He often ignored domestic matters (see Chapter 3), but he micromanaged the military. This helped to secure German victories in Poland and France, but it clearly hurt in Russia and, later, northern France. Not trusting his generals, Hitler intervened in the smallest details of operations. Blaming him, though, absolves German generals of any responsibility. They, too, were at fault. Rommel and other generals, for example, emphasized tactics over logistics. They abjectly deferred to Hitler's wishes. Even in the face of imminent defeat, they refused to challenge the Führer.

Hitler's leadership proved detrimental in other ways, too. His racial views led him to underestimate American, British, and Soviet potential. His disdain for Eastern Europeans turned potential allies into partisan enemies. His style of rule fragmented the Nazi state. He refused to create a high-level body to coordinate Germany's total-war efforts. The commanders of the army, air force, and navy all competed for his attention. The existence of duplicate agencies also encouraged rivalry, not partnership. Military intelligence, the Abwehr, for example, vied against the SS's security branch, the Sicherheitsdienst (SD) (see Chapter 3). The two agencies spent much time spying on each other – one explanation, perhaps, for Germany's poor intelligence operations. Finally, the most influential Nazis (besides Hitler) in the waning days of the regime – Martin Bormann, Goebbels, Himmler, and Speer – were all at war with each other. Each tried to enhance his own authority at the expense of the others.

Death throes of Nazism

The suppression of the July 20 plot reenergized Hitler and the Nazi leadership. As early as July 25, the Führer made Goebbels plenipotentiary for total war. Goebbels cut government and other services so as to mobilize manpower reserves for the Wehrmacht. By year's end, his efforts had resulted in an extra million men in arms. In an attempt to stiffen German resistance to Allied invaders,

Goebbels also circulated misleading reports about Germany's situation and largely true reports of Soviet atrocities (see below). Meanwhile, Hitler named Himmler commander of the Reserve Army, the locus of the July 20 plot. Himmler's ideological fervor thus penetrated further into Germany's armed services. Speer, too, managed to sustain extraordinary armaments production, even in the face of aerial bombardment. His organizational genius ensured rapid repairs of damaged railway tracks and bridges. His efforts alone are said to have prolonged the war by several months, if not a year or more.

Now more than ever, Hitler privileged ideological zeal. The Third Reich saw "partification," the tight vise of the NSDAP on all aspects of government and society. The renewed emphasis on party activism accompanied Bormann's ascendancy late in the war. Hitler's personal secretary, Bormann controlled all access to the Führer. He also directed the party bureaucracy, which oversaw eight million NSDAP members. Eager to assert his authority, he made the *Gauleiters* – provincial party bosses – Reich defense commissars and charged them with mobilizing the last defenses of the regime. Beginning in October 1944, local party officials organized the Volkssturm (People's Storm), a citizen militia made up of all males aged sixteen to sixty not otherwise in arms. In April 1945, some also organized the Werewolf, zealous Nazi partisans who were to launch an underground movement against the Allies. Werewolf members did assassinate some "defeatists." Mostly, though, they fueled Nazi fantasies of resurgence while also serving as convenient bogeymen who justified harsh Allied occupation measures.

During the last period of war, Germany faced chaos. On February 3, the Allies dropped 2,000 tons of bombs on Berlin, claiming the lives of 5,000 civilians. On the night of February 13–14, they destroyed the baroque city of Dresden, killing some 22,000–25,000 individuals. Although Dresden was an industrial center and communications hub, observers ever since have questioned this savage attack so late in the war. The bombing campaign worsened the housing crisis, exacerbated by a flood of refugees arriving from the east (see below).

Until the last months of the war, Hitler sought public backing by protecting Germans from the worst privations. German rations were actually the highest of any European belligerent. Now, however, that and much else changed. Germans faced food shortages as well as cuts in electricity, coal, and gas supplies. In many urban areas, water was available only from pumps in the streets. Schools closed and hospitals strained to provide services. The railway system was only partially functioning, the postal service close to collapse. The regime's inability to ward off destruction and provide for the population led to a loss of faith in the party and even in Hitler himself.

Still, to the bitter end, most Germans stood against the Allied invaders. This was true even though some 450,000 Wehrmacht soldiers were killed in January

1945 alone, more than either American or British losses during the *entire* global conflict. Indeed, more than a quarter of all German military deaths in World War II took place in 1945, after Germany had, by all rational measures, lost the war. Why the continued defense of Hitler's Germany? Arguments that emphasize Allied insistence on unconditional surrender put misplaced blame on the Allies. Other factors were more salient. By then, many patriotic Germans were fighting to save their country, Germany, rather than for Nazism. Nazi coercion also unnerved the population: "defeatists" received death sentences. Fear of Bolshevism also proved a potent motivator. Widespread knowledge of Nazi crimes left some Germans worried about Allied retribution. Most important, Hitler rejected any surrender. Accordingly, military leaders, chastened by the repression following the July 20 plot, refused to halt the fighting. Hitler's continued hold over his top military and civil servants ensured Germany's ongoing defense.

As befitted his apocalyptic worldview, if not victory, Hitler willed Germany's total defeat. There was to be no armistice as in 1918, no possibility of a renewed stab in the back by internal "enemies." Total destruction, Hitler believed, would inspire future generations of Germans seeking redemption in the epic, world-historical racial struggle. He thus allowed the terrible carnage to continue, even though absolutely nothing was to be gained – and much to be lost – from utterly ruined cities and monstrous death tolls.

Germans as "victims"

In the last months of war, Germans reaped the violence that they had sowed. Soviet soldiers, bent on revenge, committed brazen atrocities against German civilians. They had borne the brunt of anti-Nazi warfare, including some 12 million dead soldiers. They had endured years of wartime deprivation and suffered familial and other losses at home. They knew the extent of German crimes – in late July 1944, they were the first to liberate a death camp, Majdanek. As one Red Army soldier noted, "We hate Germany and the Germans very much… the Germans deserve these atrocities that they unleashed… One need only think of Majdanek and the theory of supermen [*Übermenschen*] to understand why our soldiers are happily doing this."

Marching westwards, Soviet troops terrorized German civilians. In winter 1944–1945, some five million Germans were fleeing Eastern Europe in advance of the Red Army. Soviet troops overtook many refugee columns, menacing panicked Germans. On January 30, the Soviets also torpedoed the *Wilhelm Gustloff*, a former Strength through Joy ship ferrying refugees across the Baltic to the Reich. Some 9,000 civilians drowned in the worst maritime disaster in history. In the exodus from the east, several hundred thousand German civilians lost their lives.

Reports of marauding Soviet troops inside the Third Reich are shocking. Soviet soldiers savagely murdered German men, women, and children. They tortured them, slicing off body parts and stringing victims up on barn rafters. They also engaged in mass rapes. Soldiers do not rape out of pent-up sexual lust. They rape to mark domination of the enemy, to impress on the defeated their abject loss. As many as 1.4 million women in eastern Germany and one in two women in Berlin were raped, many repeatedly. Mass rape, Anglo American bombing, and flight from the east formed a narrative of suffering that allowed Germans to think that *they* were the true victims of World War II.

All the while, though, the Nazis continued *their* atrocities. In January and February 1945, the SS emptied concentration camps in the east. They were eager to hide Nazi crimes, to further exploit camp labor, and to use prisoners as pawns in potential Allied negotiations. SS officials thus forced inmates on icy "death marches." When starving prisoners could walk no further, they were shot. Inside the Reich, the SS compelled prisoners on similar treks. Some 200,000–250,000 near-survivors perished on these death marches. At the same time, Nazi authorities continued the outright execution of prisoners, sometimes just hours before the arrival of Allied troops. Among other grisly discoveries, Allied soldiers often found heaps of fresh corpses in newly liberated jails and camps.

Figure 8.2 A British soldier uses a bulldozer to move piles of bodies (Bergen–Belsen, April 1945). *Source*: akg images.

Hitler's death

In late April 1945, Soviet troops closed in on central Berlin. Hitler, holed up in an underground bunker on the Chancellory grounds, wished to evade imprisonment and a show trial. He now readied his suicide. Late on the night of April 28–29, he married Eva Braun, rewarding her for long years as his patient mistress. His entourage celebrated the eerie marriage with champagne and cake.

That same night, Hitler dictated his last will and political testament. In his testament, he railed against the Jews, insisting that they had brought on the war and all its ensuing destruction. He justified their murder, claiming that the "real criminal" – read Jewry – was "to atone for this guilt." To his dying day, Hitler harbored a fanatical antisemitism that blamed Jews for the ills of the earth.

In a sign of the suspicious mistrust that surrounded the top Nazi leadership, Hitler expelled two loyal aides, Hermann Göring and Himmler, from the NSDAP. Bormann had wrongly convinced Hitler that Göring, head of the failed Luftwaffe and Hitler's designated successor, wished to usurp his power. The Führer's trust in Himmler was shattered when he learned that the SS chief had offered German surrender to the western Allies. (Himmler thought the western Allies would want to work with him against the Soviet Union.) Hitler now designated three men as his successors: Grand-Admiral Karl Dönitz as Reich president, Goebbels as Reich chancellor, and Bormann as head of the NSDAP.

On the afternoon of April 30, believing that all was lost, Hitler and Eva Braun retired to his study. There, Hitler shot himself in the head while Braun took poison. As per prior orders, their bodies were quickly taken outside and burned. Soviet authorities undertook an exhaustive search for Hitler's body but could identify only a lower jaw bone and a dental bridge.

Along with Hitler, other fanatical Nazis soon committed suicide. On May 1, Goebbels and his wife Magda not only took poison themselves but poisoned their six children, too. Bormann took poison to avoid capture in the center of Berlin on May 2 (this was long disputed, explaining why he stood trial *in absentia* at Nuremberg). On May 23, after Himmler identified himself to British captors, he bit into a cyanide capsule and died minutes later.

After Hitler's death, Grand-Admiral Dönitz took charge of the German government. On May 1, it was announced that Hitler had fallen "at the head of the heroic defenders of the Reich capital." Dönitz held out for as long as possible to give German troops time to make their way to Anglo-American troops rather than surrender to vengeful Soviet units. Just a week later, though, he ordered Germany's capitulation. On May 8, 1945, World War II in Europe ended, the Third Reich defeated.

Citations for Quotations

Page	Source

179 "Do you want total war? ..." Quoted in Richard J. Evans, *The Third Reich at War* (New York: Penguin, 2009), 424.

182 "Not a step back." Quoted in Thomas W. Zeiler, *Annihilation: A Global History of World War II* (Oxford: Oxford University Press, 2012), 197.

184 "the only thing that ever frightened me." Quoted in History Learning Site, http://www.historylearningsite.co.uk/atlantic.htm (accessed May 21, 2013).

191 "undermine the will to fight." Quoted in Robert Gellately, *Backing Hitler: Consent and Coercion in Nazi Germany* (Oxford: Oxford University Press, 2001), 183.

195 "The assassination [of Hitler] must be..." Quoted in Klemens von Klemperer, *German Resistance against Hitler: The Search for Allies Abroad, 1938–1945* (Oxford: Clarendon Press, 1992), 384.

200 "Every bunker, ..." Quoted in Ian Kershaw, *The End: The Defiance and Destruction of Hitler's Germany, 1944–45* (New York: Penguin, 2011), 69–70.

205 "We hate Germany..." Quoted in Stephen G. Fritz, *Ostkrieg: Hitler's War of Extermination in the East* (Lexington: University Press of Kentucky, 2011), 450–451.

207 "real criminal" and "to atone for this guilt." Quoted in Jeremy Noakes, ed., *Nazism 1919–1945. Volume IV: The German Home Front in World War II: A Documentary Reader* (Exeter: University of Exeter Press, 1998), 669.

207 "at the head..." Quoted in Kershaw, *The End*, 346.

Bibliography

Allen, Michael Thad. *The Business of Genocide: The SS, Slave Labor, and the Concentration Camps*. Chapel Hill: University of North Carolina Press, 2002.

Bessel, Richard. *Germany 1945: From War to Peace*. New York: HarperCollins, 2009.

Blatman, Daniel. *The Death Marches: The Final Phase of Nazi Genocide*. Cambridge, MA: Belknap Press of Harvard University Press, 2011.

Evans, Richard J. *The Third Reich at War*. New York: Penguin, 2009.

Friedrich, Jörg. *The Fire: The Bombing of Germany, 1940–1945*. New York: Columbia University Press, 2006.

Fritz, Stephen G. *Ostkrieg: Hitler's War of Extermination in the East*. Lexington: University Press of Kentucky, 2011.

Gellately, Robert. *Backing Hitler: Consent and Coercion in Nazi Germany*. Oxford: Oxford University Press, 2001.

Hamerow, Theodore S. *On the Road to the Wolf's Lair: German Resistance to Hitler*. Cambridge, MA: Belknap Press of Harvard University Press, 1997.

Herbert, Ulrich. *Hitler's Foreign Workers: Enforced Foreign Labor in Germany under the Third Reich*. Cambridge: Cambridge University Press, 1997.

Hoffmann, Peter. *German Resistance to Hitler*. Cambridge, MA: Harvard University Press, 1988.

Kershaw, Ian. *The End: The Defiance and Destruction of Hitler's Germany, 1944–45*. New York: Penguin, 2011.

Majer, Diemut. *"Non-Germans" under the Third Reich: The Nazi Judicial and Administrative System in Germany and Occupied Eastern Europe, with Special Regard to Occupied Poland, 1939–1945*. Baltimore: Johns Hopkins University Press, 2003.

Moorhouse, Roger. *Killing Hitler: The Plots, the Assassins, and the Dictator Who Cheated Death*. New York: Bantam Books, 2006.

Noakes, Jeremy, ed. *Nazism 1919–1945. Volume IV: The German Home Front in World War II: A Documentary Reader*. Exeter: University of Exeter Press, 1998.

Overy, Richard. *Why the Allies Won*. New York: W.W. Norton, 1995.

Overy, Richard. *The Bombing War: Europe 1939–1945*. London: Allen Lane, 2013.

Scholl, Inge. *The White Rose: Munich 1942–1943*. Middletown, CT: Wesleyan University Press, 1983.

Tooze, Adam. *The Wages of Destruction: The Making and Breaking of the Nazi Economy*. New York: Penguin, 2006.

Trevor-Roper, H.R. *The Last Days of Hitler*. New York: Macmillan, 1947.

von Klemperer, Klemens. *German Resistance against Hitler: The Search for Allies Abroad, 1938–1945*. Oxford: Clarendon Press, 1992.

von Plato, Alexander, Almut Leh, and Christoph Thonfeld, eds. *Hitler's Slaves: Life Stories of Forced Labourers in Nazi-Occupied Europe*. New York: Berghahn Books, 2010.

Weinberg, Gerhard L. *A World at Arms: A Global History of World War II*. New Edition. Cambridge: Cambridge University Press, 2005.

Yelton, David K. *Hitler's Volkssturm: The Nazi Militia and the Fall of Germany, 1944–1945*. Lawrence: University Press of Kansas, 2002.

Zeiler, Thomas W. *Annihilation: A Global History of World War II*. Oxford: Oxford University Press, 2012.

Epilogue

In May 1945, Germany suffered total defeat; the country lay in physical ruins. Many Germans suffered from spiritual exhaustion, often traumatized by their recent experiences of Nazi persecution, soldiering in the Wehrmacht, or aerial bombing, rape, and expulsion. Few Germans contemplated any sort of Nazi resurgence. The once formidable regime quickly crumbled.

The Third Reich bequeathed many geopolitical, judicial, and moral legacies, some quite surprising. World War II remade the global order in ways that might have encouraged Germans to seek vengeance. Germany not only lost its eastern areas to Poland but also was itself divided into two, East and West Germany. The two Germanys, however, posed little threat to world peace. While East Germany became a Soviet-style dictatorship, West Germany became a liberal, democratic country. At the same time, while the most prominent Nazis were put on trial, many perpetrators evaded justice. The process of confronting Nazi atrocities nonetheless advanced international judicial standards and human rights.

Geopolitical Legacies

Expulsion

At war's end, the Allies sanctioned the largest population transfer in human history: the removal of ethnic Germans from Eastern Europe. Czechoslovakia, Hungary, Poland, Romania, and Yugoslavia expelled some 12–14 million ethnic Germans from their midst. In part, the expulsion was motivated by revenge: this

Nazi Germany: Confronting the Myths, First Edition. Catherine Epstein.
© 2015 John Wiley & Sons, Ltd. Published 2015 by John Wiley & Sons, Ltd.

was payback for all that Germans had wrought in Nazi-occupied Eastern Europe. Although the Allies called for the transfer to occur in an "orderly and humane manner," expulsion proved a violent affair. Estimates suggest that at least 500,000 Germans died during this process.

The expulsions established facts on the ground intended to secure postwar territorial changes. In 1945, the Soviet Union moved its borders westwards to those agreed upon in the secret protocol of the 1939 Nazi–Soviet Non-Aggression Pact. In turn, Poland was compensated for territories lost to the Soviet Union with eastern German lands. Germany thus lost significant territory to Poland, including East Prussia and Lower Silesia. The expulsion of ethnic Germans also undermined any future claims that Germany might make to eastern areas (such as when Hitler stirred up German minority feeling in the Sudetenland in 1938–1939; see Chapter 5). Finally, the removal of ethnic Germans from Eastern Europe – following the Nazi murder of Jews – was an important element in the "unmixing" of Eastern Europe into today's largely homogenous nation-states.

The division of Germany

Besides losing territory in the east, a shrunken Germany suffered forty-five years of division. Prior to German surrender, the Allies had agreed to set up an occupation government for all of Germany. For practical reasons, however, they also divided Germany into American, British, and Soviet occupation zones and the capital, Berlin, into similar sectors. Britain and the United States soon agreed to carve out a French occupation zone and sector from their respective areas. Although the Allies agreed on basic aims for postwar Germany – democracy, demilitarization, and de-Nazification – their understanding of these terms diverged. Allied disagreements led to a growing gulf between the western and Soviet zones of Germany. By 1949, these divisions had led to the creation of the Federal Republic of Germany (West Germany) and the German Democratic Republic (East Germany). The western Allies imposed democracy on West Germany; the Soviets foisted communist dictatorship on East Germany.

With more than forty years of communist oppression, East Germans paid a high price for Nazism. During the peaceful 1989 revolution, however, East German dissidents were joined by ever larger crowds against the communist regime. In an attempt to placate demonstrators, the communist leadership, by then either inept or sclerotic (or both), issued new travel regulations that inadvertently opened the Berlin Wall. Coincidentally, the Wall fell on November 9 – the anniversary of the German Revolution in 1918, the Beer Hall Putsch in 1923, and Kristallnacht in 1938. In the months following the 1989 revolution, the Allied powers, who had retained residual rights concerning Germany as a whole, gave their consent to German unification. Unification and various other

1990 agreements marked the final peace settlement concerning Germany and World War II.

In 1958, six European countries, including West Germany and France, established the European Economic Community, the precursor to today's European Union. A major impetus for European unity was the belief that integrating West Germany into a community of states would prevent future European wars. Over the years, this has proven true. While Germany today is the powerhouse of the twenty-eight-member European Union, its dominance is tempered by the country's commitment to democracy and social justice in Europe. It is all but unthinkable that Germany would launch a war against another member of the European Union.

Global consequences

The geopolitical consequences of Nazism were hardly confined to German lands or the European continent. Hitler's unleashing of World War II remade the world order. Given the failure of the League of Nations to restrain Hitler and prevent world war, Roosevelt and others were eager to establish a more robust international body. The United Nations was founded in San Francisco in spring 1945.

Victory in World War II rescued western-style democracy, a political system under siege during the interwar years. Triumph in World War II, however, also strengthened the Soviet system, giving communism a new lease on life. The revival of both democracy and communism led to the Cold War, an American–Soviet rivalry that dominated postwar global developments. In the decades after 1945, the United States and the Soviet Union fought proxy wars for influence in Africa, Asia, and Latin America.

World War II also ushered in the era of decolonization, arguably the most enduring global consequence of Hitler's war. After the western Allies fought Nazism in the name of freedom and self-determination, native populations and some western governments came to believe that it was hypocritical for European powers to uphold their colonial empires. Britain and France nonetheless fought bitter wars in Kenya and Algeria to retain their colonies. By the early 1960s, however, liberation movements had pushed the European powers out of virtually all of their erstwhile colonies. The dismantling of Europe's empires fundamentally altered the balance of power in world affairs: Europe's global importance dramatically receded.

Nazism also had a profound impact on the Middle East. After the Holocaust, western powers were more sympathetic to the founding of a Jewish state in Palestine: Israel. At the same time, scholars have recently posited links between Nazi Germany, Arab nationalism, and Islamic fundamentalism. During World War II, as Jeffery Herf has shown, the Nazis widely circulated antisemitic and antiwestern propaganda throughout North Africa and the Middle East. Ever since, Arab nationalists and Islamic fundamentalists have drawn on this reservoir of ideas – as well as other wellsprings of hatred – to articulate their hostility toward Jews and western modernity. There are thus indirect links between Nazism and ongoing conflicts in the Middle East, as well as Nazism and the events of September 11, 2001 (when al-Qaeda, an Islamic fundamentalist group, launched a series of terrorist attacks on the United States).

Imperfect Justice

Nuremberg

As early as the Moscow Declaration of November 1943, the Allies had vowed to prosecute Nazi criminality. Still, when Allied soldiers liberated concentration and death camps, they were shocked at the true depravity of the Third Reich. Hitler, Himmler, and Goebbels were dead, but the Allies soon arrested and indicted other top Nazis, including Hermann Göring and Albert Speer. From November 1945 to October 1946, the International Military Tribunal – organized and staffed by American, British, French, and Soviet officials – held proceedings against twenty-four high-ranking Nazis in the city of Nuremberg. The trial resulted in a first inventory of Nazi crimes. Although the murder of Jews was included among many other Nazi crimes, the proceedings did not focus exclusively on what we now call the Holocaust. There were four main counts to the indictment. All of the accused were charged with the first count, conspiracy (to commit at least one of the group of crimes listed in the additional counts). The other counts included crimes against peace, war crimes, and crimes against humanity.

Many Germans viewed the Nuremberg trial as "victor's justice." Certainly, the defendants were at a legal disadvantage. They had limited resources, the rules of the court were biased against them, and they were subject to *ex post facto* law. But they were able to mount a defense, and their individual cases were heard. Göring and Martin Bormann (*in absentia*), along with ten others, were sentenced to death by hanging. Speer received a prison sentence of twenty years, and six others received sentences ranging from ten years to life. Three defendants were acquitted. The varied sentences suggest that the Allies aimed to follow the rule of law, not the dictate of vengeance. As US Supreme Court Justice and Nuremberg prosecutor Robert H. Jackson declared in his opening statement at the trial, "We must never forget that the record on which we judge these defendants today is the record on which history will judge us tomorrow."

Nuremberg advanced international legal and moral standards. It is perhaps best remembered for the popularization of the term "crimes against humanity" – crimes in which unprotected civilians are murdered, enslaved, and/or deported based on their racial, ethnic, political, or religious identities. For the first time in history, Nuremberg subjected political leaders and military commanders to international court proceedings for sanctioning heinous crimes against civilians. Nuremberg was also the precursor for court actions based on the notion that state sovereignty would *not* protect heads of state and others from international prosecution. Still, it took over fifty years to establish an international, independent, and permanent criminal court. The international community agreed to the legal basis for an International Criminal Court in 1998, and it began work in 2002.

After the main Nuremberg trial, US authorities held twelve subsequent Nuremberg trials in American military courts between 1946 and 1949. These proceedings tried various groups of Nazi perpetrators, including industrialists, high-ranking civil servants, and those involved with the mobile killing squads (*Einsatzgruppen*) that carried out the Holocaust. The first of these was the Doctors' Trial. It brought widespread attention to Nazi medical experiments on human subjects. At the time, however, there were no established guidelines on human medical experimentation. The verdict in the case addressed this issue, and the judges' words on the matter became known as the Nuremberg Code. Among other guidelines, the Nuremberg Code states that "the voluntary consent of the human subject is absolutely essential" and "the experiment should be so conducted as to avoid all unnecessary physical and mental suffering and injury."

Escaping justice

While the Allies tried some high-ranking Nazi criminals, many perpetrators escaped justice. For a long time, there was an ODESSA myth, according to which former Schutzstaffel (SS) men had forged an all-powerful network, ODESSA, to provide each other aid. Although ODESSA had an active presence in the fantasies of some, no one has ever been able to prove its existence. Instead, other organizations – their identities more shocking – *did* aid Nazi perpetrators: the Vatican, the International Red Cross, and the US government.

Italy became the focal point of the "ratline," escape routes for Nazi perpetrators out of Europe, often to Latin America. In the immediate postwar chaos, the International Red Cross in Italy issued identity papers to many refugees, including Nazi perpetrators who claimed to be displaced persons. An agency linked to the Vatican, the Pontificia Commissione di Assistenza, also provided aid and papers; the recipients were believed to be Catholics fleeing communist Eastern Europe. Adolf Eichmann escaped with the help of the Red Cross *and* the Pontificia Commissione di Assistenza to Argentina (before his eventual kidnapping, trial, and 1962 execution in Israel). Along with Eichmann, at least 180 compromised Nazis entered Argentina. Josef Mengele escaped via Italy to Brazil, where he died in a 1979 swimming accident. American officials also smuggled

SS officers through the "ratline," believing that these operatives would make useful intelligence agents in the emerging Cold War.

Many "ordinary" killers – those who did guard duty at camps or who manned SS mobile killing squads – also evaded justice. After 1949, the western Allies turned over the prosecution of Nazi war criminals to West Germany. The pace of prosecution slowed. Although there were some trials, notably the Frankfurt Auschwitz Trial in 1963–1965, relatively few killers were ever brought to justice. While state prosecutors launched numerous investigations, it proved difficult to obtain guilty verdicts. Court authorities often insisted that there was insufficient evidence linking a particular individual to a specific crime. They were suspicious of witness testimony: with the passage of time, memories dulled, faces aged. Who could be certain that a particular individual had really committed a specific crime? Although a judicial failure, the criminal investigations produced reams of evidence that have served as a boon to historical study. Indeed, criminal investigations have likely served history better than justice.

Countless German professionals complicit in Nazi crimes were also never brought to justice. In 1949, West Germany passed an amnesty law for fellow travelers and minor perpetrators. Soon thereafter, it allowed the social reintegration of some 30,000 civil servants and professional soldiers. University professors who had done research supporting Nazi aims, doctors who had carried out euthanasia, urban planners who had redesigned the east into a German redoubt – all helped to rebuild West Germany after 1945. Ironically, though, this may have strengthened German democracy. The longtime postwar West German chancellor, Konrad Adenauer, firmly believed that former Nazis should be integrated into rather than alienated from the new democratic order. As onetime Nazis lived the benefits of democracy, many came to appreciate a form of government they had once disdained. Although morally dubious, the integration of former Nazis into West German society had its advantages.

As a self-proclaimed "antifascist" state, communist East Germany claimed that it punished all Nazi criminals in its midst. Moreover, many Nazi criminals, it asserted, evaded justice by fleeing to "fascist" West Germany (East Germany insisted that fascism was inexorably linked with capitalism and that West Germany was a "fascist" state). In the first postwar years, officials in what would become East Germany *did* carry out extensive anti-Nazi proceedings. Up until the end of 1950, East German courts convicted some 8,000 Nazi perpetrators. Twenty-three individuals received death sentences and thirty-five life sentences. Most, however, received much shorter jail terms. Moreover, by 1956 East German authorities had amnestied all but the most serious Nazi offenders. Thereafter, they pursued few cases against Nazi perpetrators. Acknowledging the presence of such individuals would have belied East Germany's self-image as an "antifascist" state. Recent research suggests that many professionals complicit in Nazi crimes were also integrated into East German society. Erstwhile Nazis helped to rebuild both Germanys.

Advancing Human Rights

Even though many Nazi perpetrators escaped justice, knowledge of Nazi crimes helped to advance human rights. In 1948, the United Nations approved the Universal Declaration of Human Rights. Its preamble acknowledged "disregard and contempt for human rights have resulted in barbarous acts which have outraged the conscience of mankind." Article 1 declared, "All human beings are born free and equal in dignity and rights. They are endowed with reason and conscience and should act towards one another in a spirit of brotherhood." The Universal Declaration aimed to ban heinous practices such as slavery. With no enforcement mechanism, however, it voiced a set of moral aspirations rather than realities. Still, the Universal Declaration set an international standard for action on human rights that remains apposite today.

In 1948, the United Nations also approved the Convention on the Prevention and Punishment of the Crime of Genocide. Raphael Lemkin, a lawyer and Polish Jew who lost family members in the Holocaust, worked tirelessly to achieve this Convention. The Convention defined the term "genocide" and required states to intervene to try to stop an ongoing genocide. The United States, however, ratified the Convention only in 1988. Even today, countries are reluctant to label mass murder "genocide" since that would compel them to act. Genocide has thus continued, most notably in Cambodia in 1975–1978, Bosnia in 1992–1995, and Rwanda in 1994. Despite worldwide hopes of "never again," the Convention has not prevented genocide.

In the wake of World War II, there were some 250,000 Jewish displaced persons in (Allied-)occupied western Germany. The presence of these displaced persons, along with anticommunist displaced persons fleeing Eastern Europe, caused a sea change in the treatment of refugees. Both the United Nations Relief and Rehabilitation Administration and International Refugee Organization coordinated multilateral governmental responses to the refugee problem, once the preserve of private relief agencies. In 1951, the United Nations approved the Refugee Convention. It defined a refugee as someone unwilling to return to his or her country of origin "owing to well-founded fear of being persecuted for reasons of race, religion, nationality, [or] membership of a particular social group or political opinion." The Refugee Convention outlined protections for stateless persons that citizens generally enjoy. Amended by a 1967 protocol to address new waves of displacement, the convention remains in effect. In addition, Germany today has a liberal asylum law. It extends the right to asylum to all those who are "politically persecuted" in their native countries – a direct response to its Nazi past.

Memory and Restitution

The Holocaust looms large in our moral imagination. That was not always so. After 1945, Jews were seen as one of many groups of Nazi victims. The Nazi regime, it was thought, had carried out an assault on humanity; there was little sense that it had singularly targeted Jews. During the first postwar decades, Jews did little to alter this notion. They were reluctant to focus on their victimhood. As they built the state of Israel or assimilated into mainstream American life, they wanted to foster strong, active Jewish identities.

From the 1960s onward, however, Holocaust consciousness became much more pronounced. For one, the term "Holocaust" became synonymous with the Nazi murder of the Jews; before that, the term was not used much in that connection. At the same time, the Holocaust became *the Holocaust*: the standard against which all evil is measured. This had multiple causes. Over time, public awareness of the Holocaust grew. *The Diary of Anne Frank* was first published in English in 1952. The Eichmann Trial, the focus of worldwide attention, was held in Jerusalem in 1961. American Jewish leaders, wishing to muster support for the state of Israel, increasingly invoked Nazi criminality toward Jews. As American society became much more focused on race and ethnicity, the status of victim also became prized. Jews effectively argued that their people had endured extraordinary suffering. In the 1990s, a host of Holocaust museums, including the United States Holocaust Memorial Museum, opened. Today, Holocaust education is used to inculcate the virtues of tolerance and standing up to tyranny; it is also often employed to teach antibullying strategies.

As early as the first postwar years, the state of Israel and Jewish organizations pressed Germany for monetary compensation. Understandably, the German confrontation with the Nazi past was a vexed process. East Germany insisted that, since it was a communist state, it bore no responsibility for Nazi crimes; it refused to pay any compensation to victims of Nazism. West Germany took a different stance. Since 1952, West Germany and now united Germany has paid some $60 billion in restitution to the state of Israel and individual Jewish victims. Belatedly, West Germany also addressed the claims of non-Jewish victims. In 1980, the West German parliament approved onetime payments in the amount of 5,000 DM (approximately $2,500) to victims of the compulsory sterilization program. In 2000, the united German government, in conjunction with German businesses, set up a $5 billion fund to address compensation demands from forced and slave laborers, mostly non-Jews in Eastern Europe. This fund also supported restitution to the Roma and Sinti (Gypsies) and victims of medical experimentation. No amount of material restitution, however, will ever rectify Nazi injustice.

While compensation was sometimes slow in coming, (West) Germany has proved a model of how countries may confront their troubled histories. Although many West Germans initially thought of themselves as victims of World War II, their attitudes changed during the postwar era. Most came to recognize that their country – and often they themselves – had committed terrible crimes and/ or silently watched as these unfolded. Today, the sheer mass of Holocaust and other memorials and museums in united Germany is truly extraordinary. The process of erecting these memorials, however, has been controversial. Who should be remembered? What is the best form of commemoration? One prominent scholar of memory, James Young, argues that the best memorial to the Holocaust is, in fact, ongoing controversies about its commemoration. The longer and deeper the discussion, the more intense the engagement with Germany's shameful past.

Right-wing Germans such as the historian Michael Stürmer question whether it is time for Germany to stop its preoccupation with the Nazi past. Is the focus on the Third Reich, they wonder, compromising efforts to inculcate pride and patriotism in young Germans? At what point should a country no longer be held hostage to the past? When is enough enough? These are legitimate questions. Today, however, the Holocaust is the measuring rod against which all evil is judged. Until another monstrous crime plays a similar role in the world's moral imagination, Germany will have no alternative but to confront its past.

Toward the future

West Germany "won the peace." In the postwar decades, West Germans enjoyed a remarkable economic boom. Since democracy finally delivered material goods, many West Germans came to be strong advocates of liberal democracy. This is not to say, though, that Germany today is free of racism or xenophobia. In the past half-century, (West) Germany – like much of Western Europe – became a multicultural society with significant minority populations. This, in turn, spawned some extremist groups, including the right-wing National Democratic Party. Whenever racist incidents occur in Germany, commentators inevitably opine that racism lurks just beneath the veneer of German civility. But today, even conservative German politicians condemn racism and insist that it must be addressed. Their reactions underscore how much Germany has evolved from the Third Reich.

There is no redemption in the story of Nazism. Although a response to the ills of modernity, Nazism proved that totalizing impulses destroy rather than recreate traditional worlds. Animated by notions of racial purity and German dominance, Hitler hoped to remake the European continent, and perhaps the globe. In the process, he sowed incomparable tragedy. Nazism left a world full of death and devastation: 55 million dead and continents awash in ruin. It is true that the aftermath has proven more salutary than might have been expected – seventy-five years of relative peace in Europe (except for the Balkans), democracy across much of the continent, and a greater appreciation of human rights. But the death tolls were too high, the material losses too devastating, and Nazi indignities to fellow man too great to find solace in these developments.

Ultimately, though, while we condemn Nazism, its history forces us to examine ourselves. What choices would we make in a tyrannical regime? Would we simply watch as our neighbors are deported? Would we join in killing actions? The study of Nazism, I believe, reinforces the importance of critical inquiry and individual responsibility. We must each confront injustice, whether as members of our communities or as citizens of the world. We must each prevent the emergence of Nazi-like regimes, however quixotic the goal may be. We must each be vigilant in raising awareness about racism and genocide. Together, we must insist on "never again."

Citations for Quotations

Page	Source

212   "orderly and humane manner." "Excerpts from the Report on the Potsdam Conference (Potsdam Agreement) (August 2, 1945)," The German Historical Institute, http://germanhistorydocs.ghi-dc.org/docpage.cfm?docpage_id=2985 (accessed January 15, 2014).

214   "We must never forget…" Quoted in Michael R. Marrus, *The Nuremberg War Crimes Trial, 1945–46: A Documentary History* (Boston: Bedford Books, 1997), 81.

215   "the voluntary consent…" The United States Holocaust Memorial Museum, www.ushmm.org/information/exhibitions/online-features/special-focus/doctors-trial/nuremberg-code (accessed January 12, 2014).

217   "disregard and contempt…" and "All human beings…" Quoted in Lynn Hunt, *Inventing Human Rights: A History* (New York: W.W. Norton, 2007), 223–224.

217   "owing to well-founded fear…" The United Nations High Commissioner for Refugees, www.unhcr.org/3b66c2aa10.html (accessed January 12, 2014).

Bibliography

Cohen, Gerard Daniel. *In War's Wake: Europe's Displaced Persons in the Postwar Order.* Oxford: Oxford University Press, 2012.

Douglas, R.M. *Orderly and Humane: The Expulsion of the Germans after the Second World War.* New Haven: Yale University Press, 2012.

Herf, Jeffery. *Nazi Propaganda for the Arab World*. New Haven: Yale University Press, 2009.

Hunt, Lynn. *Inventing Human Rights: A History*. New York: W.W. Norton, 2007.

Marrus, Michael R. *The Nuremberg War Crimes Trial, 1945–46: A Documentary History*. Boston: Bedford Books, 1997.

Niven, Bill. *Facing the Nazi Past: United Germany and the Legacy of the Third Reich*. London: Routledge, 2002.

Steinacher, Gerald. *Nazis on the Run: How Hitler's Henchmen Fled Justice*. Oxford: Oxford University Press, 2011.

Young, James E. *The Texture of Memory: Holocaust Memorials and Meaning*. New Haven: Yale University Press, 1993.

Abbreviations and Glossary

Axis	Germany, Italy, and Japan, along with other countries that fought against the western Allies in World War II
BDM	Bund Deutscher Mädel, or League of German Girls
Blitzkrieg	lightning war
DAF	Deutsche Arbeitsfront, or German Labor Front
DAP	German Workers' Party (precursor to the NSDAP)
DDP	German Democratic Party
Deutsches Frauenwerk	German Women's Enterprise
DNVP	German National People's Party
Einsatzgruppen	SS mobile killing squads
Führer	leader
Gauleiter	regional Nazi leader
Gestapo	Geheimes Staatspolizei, or Secret State Police
Gleichschaltung	coordination
KdF	Kraft durch Freude, or Strength through Joy
KPD	Communist Party of Germany
Kristallnacht	"Night of Broken Glass," pogrom on November 9, 1938
Lebensborn	well of life
Lebensraum	living space
Luftwaffe	air force (German)

Nazi Germany: Confronting the Myths, First Edition. Catherine Epstein.
© 2015 John Wiley & Sons, Ltd. Published 2015 by John Wiley & Sons, Ltd.

Mischlinge	"mixed bloods," individuals who had two Jewish grandparents
NSDAP	National Socialist German Workers' Party
NS-Frauenschaft	National Socialist Womanhood
Panzer	tank
PO	Political Organization
POW	prisoner of war
RAF	Royal Air Force (British)
Reich	empire
Reichstag	parliament
Reichswehr	German military 1919–1935
RSHA	Reich Security Main Office
SA	Sturmabteilung, or storm troopers
SD	Sicherheitsdient, or security service
Sipo	Sicherheitspolizei, or Security Police
SPD	Social Democratic Party
SS	Schutzstaffel, or Protection Squad, elite of Nazi storm troopers
Stahlhelm	Steel Helmet (veterans' association)
T4	*Aktion* T4, Nazi euthanasia program
Volk	(German) people
Völkisch	pertaining to the (German) people (adjective)
Volksgemeinschaft	national community
Wehrmacht	German military 1935–1945
WVHA	SS Business and Administration Main Office
ZOB	Jewish Combat Organization

Timeline

1871
January 18   German unification; establishment of German Empire
1889
April 20   Adolf Hitler born
1914
June 28   Archduke Franz Ferdinand of Austria assassinated in
                   Sarajevo; World War I ensues
1918
November 9   Revolution in Germany
November 11   Armistice ends World War I
1919
January 5   German Workers' Party (DAP) founded
June 28   Treaty of Versailles signed
July 31   Weimar Constitution adopted
September 12   Hitler joins the DAP
1920
February 24   DAP renamed National Socialist German Workers' Party
                   (NSDAP)
1923
January 11   French occupation of the Ruhr
June–November   The Great Inflation in Germany
November 8–9   Beer Hall Putsch
November 15   Introduction of new currency

Nazi Germany: Confronting the Myths, First Edition. Catherine Epstein.
© 2015 John Wiley & Sons, Ltd. Published 2015 by John Wiley & Sons, Ltd.

1924

April 1   Hitler sentenced to five years in prison (with parole eligibility) for high treason

December 20   Hitler released from prison

1925

July   Publication of *Mein Kampf*

1928

May 20   NSDAP wins 2.6% of vote in national elections

1929

October 4   Wall Street Crash begins

1930

March 30   Heinrich Brüning named chancellor

July 16   Brüning uses Article 48 to impose budget

September 14   NSDAP wins 18.3% of vote in national elections

1932

April 10   President Paul von Hindenburg reelected president in run-off against Hitler

May 30   Franz von Papen named chancellor

July 20   Papen removes SPD prime minister and declares martial law in Prussia

July 31   NSDAP wins 37.4% of vote in national elections

August 13   Hitler refuses position of vice-chancellor

November 6   NSDAP wins 33.1% of vote in national elections

December 2   Kurt von Schleicher named chancellor

1933

January 30   Hitler appointed chancellor

February 27   Reichstag fire

February 28   Reichstag Fire Decree suspends basic civil liberties

March 5   NSDAP wins 43.9% of vote in national elections

March 20   First concentration camp, Dachau, opened

March 23   Enabling Act gives Hitler full dictatorial powers

April 1   Boycott of Jewish businesses

April 7   Law for the Restoration of the Professional Civil Service

May 2   Destruction of independent labor unions

May 10   Burning of "un-German" books

July 14   NSDAP declared only legal party; Sterilization Law announced

July 20   Concordat between Germany and Vatican

October 14   Germany withdraws from League of Nations

1934

January 26	Non-Aggression Pact with Poland
June 30	"Night of the Long Knives," also known as the Röhm Affair
August 2	President Hindenburg dies; Hitler assumes presidential functions

1935

January 13	Inhabitants of Saar region vote to rejoin Germany
March 10	Existence of Luftwaffe (air force) announced
March 16	Hitler announces universal conscription
June 18	Anglo–German Naval Agreement
September 15	Nuremberg Race Laws proclaimed

1936

March 7	Reoccupation of Rhineland
August 1	Summer Olympic Games open in Berlin
October 18	Hermann Göring named head of Four-Year Plan

1937

November 5	Hitler holds military conference documented in Hossbach Memorandum

1938

February 4	Hitler assumes direct control of military
March 13	Annexation of Austria (*Anschluss*)
September 29	Munich Agreement; Czechoslovakia cedes Sudetenland to Germany
November 9	Kristallnacht ("Night of Broken Glass")

1939

March 15	Occupation of Czech lands; establishment of Protectorate of Bohemia and Moravia
May 22	Pact of Steel between Italy and Germany
August 23	Nazi–Soviet Non-Aggression Pact
September 1	German invasion of Poland; Hitler authorizes secret euthanasia program (T4)
September 3	Britain and France declare war on Germany
October 26	Annexation of western Polish provinces, including Warthegau

1940

April 9	German attack on Denmark and Norway
May 1	First ghetto opened in Nazi-occupied Poland, the Litzmannstadt (Łódź) ghetto
May 10	German attack on France
September 7	Germany launches Blitz on London and other British cities

1941

April 6	German invasion of Yugoslavia and Greece
June 22	German invasion of Soviet Union
September 19	Jews forced to wear Yellow Star in Germany
September 29–30	Massacre of 33,771 Jews at Babi Yar, outside Kiev
December 7	Japanese attack on Pearl Harbor
December 8	Gassings of Jews in mobile gas vans at Chełmno
December 11	Hitler declares war on United States

1942

January 20	Wannsee Conference
June 21	Germans take Tobruk
July 22	Start of deportation of Jews from Warsaw Ghetto to Treblinka
November 4	Allied victory at second battle at El Alamein
November 8	Operation Torch, Allied invasion of North Africa

1943

January 15	Casablanca Conference; Roosevelt and Churchill declare policy of "unconditional surrender"
January 31	Field Marshal Friedrich Paulus surrenders at Stalingrad
February 18	Goebbels' Total War speech; Hans and Sophie Scholl, leaders of the White Rose, arrested
April 19	Warsaw Ghetto Uprising begins
July 10	Allies land in Sicily
July 13	German defeat in the Battle of Kursk
July 25	Mussolini deposed
July 28	Operation Gomorrah aerial attack on Hamburg

1944

June 6	D-Day, Allied invasion of Normandy
July 20	Assassination attempt on Hitler
July 23	Red Army liberates Majdanek
August 1	Polish Home Army starts Warsaw Uprising
December 16	Battle of the Bulge begins

1945

January 27	Liberation of Auschwitz
February 13–14	Allies bomb Dresden
March 8	Allies cross the Rhine at Remagen
April 30	Hitler commits suicide
May 8	Germany surrenders

Index

References to illustrations are in italics, e.g. *16*.

Nazi Germany: Confronting the Myths, First Edition. Catherine Epstein.
© 2015 John Wiley & Sons, Ltd. Published 2015 by John Wiley & Sons, Ltd.

Printed and bound by CPI Group (UK) Ltd, Croydon, CR0 4YY

25/03/2025

14647327-0002